Guide to the Code of Ethics for Nurses
with Interpretive Statements

Development, Interpretation, and Application

Second Edition

by **Marsha D. M. Fowler,**
PhD, MDiv, MS, RN, FAAN

American Nurses Association
Silver Spring, Maryland 2015

The American Nurses Association is the premier organization representing the interests of the nation's 3.6 million registered nurses. ANA advances the nursing profession by fostering high standards of nursing practice, promoting a safe and ethical work environment, bolstering the health and wellness of nurses, and advocating on health care issues that affect nurses and the public. ANA is at the forefront of improving the quality of health care for all.

American Nurses Association
8515 Georgia Avenue, Suite 400
Silver Spring, MD 20910-3492
1-800-274-4ANA
http://www.Nursingworld.org

Cataloging-in-Publication Data on file with the Library of Congress

ISBN-13: 978-1-55810-603-1   SAN: 851-3481   01/2017R

First printing: March 2015. Second printing: March 2015. Third printing: January 2017.

Dedication

To my family
Donald, Katherine,
Robert, Allison,
Ætley, Laura
Raven, Tucker, Wolfgang, Hero

Y Gwir yn erbyn y Byd, A oes Heddwch?
Calon wrth Galon, A oes Heddwch?
Gwaedd uwch Adwaedd, A oes Heddwch?

The Truth against the World: is there Peace?
Heart to Heart, is there Peace?
Shout above resounding Shout, is there Peace?"

Gorsedd Beirdd Ynys Prydain
Liturgy of the Bardic Ceremony of the
Unsheathing of the Grand Sword

Contents

Acknowledgments

No book is the work of one person. Even single-author works owe a debt of gratitude to all those who went before them, as well as those who helped along the way. This book is indebted to the nurses who, from the inception of modern nursing to the present, have devoted themselves both to nursing and to its ethical tradition and have sought to build that tradition. Florence Nightingale, Isabel Robb, Charlotte Aikens, Charlotte Talley, Sara Parsons, Rose Helené Vaughn, Patricia Goodall, and Lystra Gretter are some of the names that any student of nursing ethics history will come to know. It is upon the remarkable foundation that their work laid that nursing ethics continues to develop.

In the present there are many colleagues whose commitment to nursing ethics is enduring, rigorous, scholarly, and always ultimately directed toward the recipients of nursing care, while also with a heart for nurses themselves. A number of persons are deserving of special acknowledgement in the preparation of this work. In particular, Col. Martha Turner, PhD, RN-BC, USAF NC (Ret.) who read and critiqued the manuscript with great knowledge, insight, and wisdom, and who responded to all my annoying late night queries with alacrity. I also acknowledge the invaluable assistance of Denise Gehring, MS (LIS), MA who used her magical librarian skill to scour the globe for obscure articles that were needed to support the research for this volume. I firmly believe, and have written elsewhere, that a good librarian is the right arm of a researcher. There have been many over the years who have been faithful nursing colleagues and friends of *inflorescent dignity* (see Chapter 1) who also possessed just the right balance of humor, imagination, curiosity, scholarship, and eccentricity: Anne Davis, Verena Tschudin, Patricia Benner, Marilyn Flood, Sonya Grypma, Marianne Hattar, Barb Pesut, Sheryl Reimer-Kirkham, Rick Sawatzky, and Beth Johnston Taylor. Co-conspirators though they may have been over the years, the blame for any "dodgy bits" in this manuscript belong solely to me and not to them. Thanks also to Eric Wurzbacher, editor extraordinaire at ANA, who was intrepid in his efforts to bring this work ever so rapidly to print.

Finally, to my dear family, friends, personal trainer, dogs, hens, bicycle, and garden, which were sorely neglected during this process, I apologize and promise to mend my ways.

Marsha Fowler
Thanksgiving Day 2014

Author's Preface.
Review & Renewal: The Half-Life of a Code

A code of nursing ethics cannot be static, neither can it be unstable. It must be enduring and rooted in the core of nursing identity, but must also be responsive to the growth, development, and context of practice. Thus, approximately every decade a profession's code of ethics must be reviewed for datedness, fit with practice, and inclusion of emerging concerns and directions. However, the central importance of this code of ethics requires that its periodic revision be undertaken with great care and with attention to the voices from all of nursing's specialties and settings. Thus the 2001 ANA *Code of Ethics for Nurses with Interpretive Statements* (the Code) underwent a four-year process of revision that led to the renewed *Code of Ethics for Nurses with Interpretive Statements*, 2015. The process began in 2010 and concluded in August 2014 after which it was approved by the Ethics Advisory Board and the Board of Directors of the ANA for formal adoption.

From October 2010 to March 2011, the Ethics Advisory Board (EAB) reviewed the 2001 Code, recommended that it undergo a review process, and submitted this request to both the ANA President and CEO. The request was approved. A workgroup to review the Code was formed with the following charge:

> You will not edit the Code provisions or Interpretive Statements but will seek input by preparing a request for public comment to determine need for clarification, change, or addition. Recommendations will be to a) allow current Code of Ethics for Nurses to stand or b) form a committee to draft edits based on comments and review.[1]

The Code Review Workgroup reviewed the Code itself and, via NursingWorld (NursingWorld.org), conducted an online public survey of nurses and interested persons who also reviewed the Code and suggested revisions. The Workgroup analyzed approximately 2,800 suggestions for revision that were made on the survey and via other communications. The Code Review Workgroup then recommended to the EAB that the Code be revised and that the EAB communicate this recommendation to the ANA President and CEO.

The recommendation and request were received and subsequently a 15-member steering committee for the revision of the Code was formed with the following charge:

> To complete a revision of the Code of Ethics for Nurses based upon the recommendations of the Code of Ethics Review Workgroup recommendations to retain what is possible of the 2001 Code, make changes to the content of interpretive statements to improve organization, streamline the wording, expand to be inclusive of new/ current concepts, and update the vocabulary.[2]

The steering committee met monthly by conference call between September 2013 and April 2014 to draft a revision that incorporated public comment. That draft was posted for public comment between May and June 2014. Approximately 1,500 comments and suggestions were received on the draft. In a meeting in Silver Spring, Maryland, the steering committee evaluated the suggestions and prepared a final draft for submission to the EAB for their vote of approval and with a recommendation that it be sent on to the Board of Directors for approval. The EAB received the final draft and approved it in October 2014. It was then forwarded to the ANA Board of Directors who approved it for adoption on November 12, 2014.

In 1950, the *Code for Professional Nurses* referred only to the provisions of that Code. At that time there were no interpretive statements, although a series of articles on the Code was subsequently published in the *American Journal of Nursing*. The 1960 Code consisted of 17 provisions that were accompanied by interpretive statements that were explanatory in nature. With reference to the 1950, 1960, and 1968 Codes, the title *Code for Professional Nurses* applied *only* to the provisions themselves. The 1976 revision of the Code was a turning point in two major ways. First, the number of provisions was significantly reduced. Second, the interpretive statements took on new force as they shifted from explanatory to interpretive, and the nature of the language changed from permissive to mandatory. From 1985 onward (2001, 2015), the interpretive statements become the definitive interpretation of the provisions with the force of standards. Thus, today, the *Code of Ethics for Nurses with Interpretive Statements*, including both provisions and interpretive statements, forms the non-negotiable moral standard for the profession.

The *Code of Ethics for Nurses with Interpretive Statements* is remarkable in its breadth and compass. It retains nursing's historical and ethical values, obligations, ideals, and commitments, while extending them into the ever-growing art, science, and practice of nursing in 2015. As a foundational ethical standard of practice, the Code should also be a source of "pride of profession."

Marsha D.M. Fowler, PhD, MDiv, MS, RN, FAAN
Professor of Ethics
Senior Fellow, Institute for Faith Integration
Azusa Pacific University, Azusa, CA
Assistant Pastor, New Hope Presbyterian Church, Pasadena, CA
Member, ANA Committee on Ethics, 1985–87; Chairwoman, 1987–89
Member, project team for the evaluation of the 1985 *Code for Nurses with Interpretive Statements*, for revision, 1995
Member, Task Force for the Revision of the 1985 *Code for Nurses with Interpretive Statements*, 1996–2001
Member, ANA 2001 *Code of Ethics for Nurses with Interpretive Statements* Revision Workgroup, 2012–2013
Historian and Code Scholar, co-lead writer, ANA Steering Committee for the Revision of the 2001 *Code of Ethics for Nurses with Interpretive Statements*, 2013–2014

Preface 2015.
Nursing's 2015 Code of Ethics

A code of ethics stands as a central and necessary mark of a profession. It functions as a general guide for the profession's members and as a social contract with the public that it serves. The group that would eventually become the American Nurses Association first discussed a code of ethics in 1896. When ANA's nursing code of ethics was first developed, it was used as a model by nursing organizations elsewhere in the world, so it had considerable influence both in this country and internationally. As American nursing education and practice advanced over the years, and we developed a deeper understanding and appreciation of ourselves as professionals, the ANA Code has been updated on several occasions to reflect these changes. However, the core value of service to others has remained consistent throughout. This second edition of the *Guide to the Code of Ethics for Nurses* provides material foundational to understanding the 2015 Code, its development, interpretation, and application.

One major change that can be found in the Code is the re-conceptualization of the patient. Formerly limited to an individual person usually in the hospital, now the concept of the patient includes individuals, their families, and the communities in which they reside. Another change of great significance reminds us that nurses owe the same duties to self as to others. Such duties include the promotion of personal health, safety, and well-being; preservation of wholeness of character and personal integrity, maintenance of competence, and continuation of professional, and personal growth. Just as the health system and professional organizations need to attend to the rights of patients, they also must support nurses and help them to take the actions necessary to fulfill these duties.

You will need to read this *Guide to the Code*; it will assist you to carefully and repeatedly reflect on the nine provisions for what they mean in your daily life as a nurse. Ethics and ethical codes are not just nice ideas that some distant committee dreamed up. Rather, they are what give voice to who we as professional nurses are at our very core. This Guide reflects upon the fundamental values and ideals of nurses as individuals and as members of a profession as found in the current *Code of Ethics with Interpretive Statements* (the Code).

When the ANA House of Delegates first unanimously accepted the *Code for Professional Nurses* in 1950, years of consideration had been given to the development of this code, consideration that continues to this day. The ANA modified the Code in 1956, 1960, 1968, 1976, 1985, 2001, and again in 2015 so that it could continue to guide nurses in increasingly more complex roles, functions, and settings. The Guide explains how these revisions reflect not only the changing roles and functions of nurses and their relationships with colleagues, but also, and more importantly, the commitment of professional nursing across the decades to maintaining one of its most important and vital documents that continues to inform nurses, other health professionals, and the general public of nursing's central values.

This edition of the Guide includes explanations of a variety of ethical methods such as principles, ethics of care, virtue ethics. It gives historical and contextual development of each provision and provides extensive citations including links to key national and international documents. Additionally, this edition has developed foundational concepts such as human dignity, compassion, social justice, care, and human rights. Included also is an extensive discussion of social ethics, social justice, and nursing. This demonstrates the reciprocating interrelationships among nursing, ethics, and social forces. And finally, the Guide addresses the 2015 Code's expanded focus on global nursing that has become more necessary in our interconnected world.

We in the nursing profession can be proud of our values and this Code that reflects them. These values underpin the new revision of the *Code of Ethics for Nurses with Interpretive Statements*. This Guide will assist you to interpret and use that Code wisely.

And finally, join me in thanking the latest ANA task force for its excellent work in revising our Code.

Anne J. Davis, PhD, DS, MS, RN, FAAN
American Academy of Nursing Living Legend, 2012
Professor Emerita, University of California, San Francisco
Professor Emerita, Nagano College of Nursing, Japan

Former Chair, ANA Ethics Committee

Preface 2008.
The Initiating Edition of
Guide to the Code

A code of ethics stands as a central and necessary mark of a profession. It functions as a general guide for the profession's members and as a social contract with the public whom it serves. The group that would eventually become the American Nurses Association first discussed a code of ethics in 1896. When the ANA nursing code of ethics was first developed, it was used as a model by nursing organizations elsewhere in the world, so it had considerable influence both in this country and internationally. As American nursing education and practice advanced over the years since then, and we developed a deeper understanding and appreciation of ourselves as professionals, the Code has been updated on several occasions to reflect these changes. However, the core value of service to others has remained consistent throughout. One major change that can be found is the re-conceptualization of the patient. Formerly limited to an individual person usually in the hospital, now the concept of the patient includes individuals, their family, and the community in which they reside. Another change of great significance, detailed in the fifth provision of the Code, reminds us that nurses owe the same duties to self as to others. Such duties include professional growth, maintenance of competence, preservation of wholeness of character, and personal integrity. Just as the health system and professional organizations need to attend to the rights of patients, they also must support nurses and help them take the actions necessary to fulfill these duties.

You will need to read this Code carefully and repeatedly to reflect on these nine provisions for what they mean in your daily life as a nurse. Ethics and ethical codes are not just nice ideas that some distant committee dreamed up. Rather, they are what give voice to who we as professional nurses are at our very core. This Code reflects our fundamental values and ideals as individual nurses and as a member of a professional group.

When the ANA House of Delegates first unanimously accepted the *Code for Professional Nurses* in 1950, years of consideration had been given to the development of this code, consideration that continues to this day. The ANA modified the Code in 1956, 1960, 1968, 1976, 1985, and 2001 so that it could continue to guide nurses in increasingly more complex roles and functions. These revisions reflect not only the changing roles and functions of nurses and their relationships with colleagues, but also and more importantly, the commitment of professional nursing to maintaining one of its most important and vital documents that continues to inform nurses, other health professionals, and the general public of nursing's central values. These values underpin this Code. Read it often and use it wisely.

And finally, join me in thanking the latest ANA task force for their excellent work in revising our Code.

Anne J. Davis PhD, RN, DSc (hon)
Professor Emerita, University of California, San Francisco
Professor, Nagano College of Nursing, Japan
Former Chair, ANA Ethics Committee

Foreword

Dr. Marsha Fowler has given both society and nursing a *tour de force* in this new second edition of the *Guide to the Code of Ethics for Nurses* (the Guide). This book is far more enlightening and transformative than its title "Guide" reveals. More than a mere guide, this book provides a breath-taking synthesis of the evolving identity and mission of nursing as a Civic Profession.[i] As a nurse and nurse ethicist, I read with awe and appreciation of the breadth, scope, and wisdom of the 2015 Guide to the newly adopted 2015 ANA *Code of Ethics for Nurses with Interpretive Statements* (the Code). I am gripped and inspired as I read this work's responses to the sweeping societal changes in health care and to the nursing profession's changes in identity and functions in the rapidly changing healthcare delivery systems.

Dr. Marsha Fowler respectfully seeks to understand our past ethical stances, and to encourage us to embrace past wisdom and aspirations as we gain new knowledge and responsibilities in our evolving role as Civic Professionals. By Civic Professionalism, I refer to the nursing profession's civic (citizen) responsibility to contribute to a good society by taking seriously the obligations, skills, and virtues required to protect the rights of patients and clients, while seeking to limit risks and vulnerabilities of whole persons and entitled citizens.

This Guide makes evident the necessity of the new changes in our 2015 Code in order to improve the health of society and to improve healthcare delivery. Nurse readers are called to fully embrace the essential contributions of nurses and the nursing profession to create a better and healthier society as activist nurses, clinicians, scholars, and policy makers. The difficult challenges of ethical formation and comportment of nurses is taken up with insight, honesty, and intelligence. The 2015 Code embraces the ethical demands of respecting the wholeness of the person dwelling in a family and community. Health is emphasized as a universal right rather than as a commodity to be bought and sold in the marketplace with little concern for equitable distribution, quality, and access to health care. This stance is evident in the new Code's 2015 statement of nursing's duties and aspirations as a profession:

> Nursing encompasses the protection, promotion, and restoration of health and well-being, the prevention of illness and injury; and the alleviation of suffering, in the care of individuals, families, groups, communities, and populations. All of this is reflected, in part, in nursing's persisting commitment both to the welfare of the sick, injured, and vulnerable in society and to social justice. Nurses act to change those aspects of social structures that detract from health and well-being.[ii]

The challenge of developing a nursing code of ethics that embraces the nursing profession's concern with health promotion, illness prevention and care in all stages of injury and illness, and social justice is presented as nursing's current, future, and past missions. The broad goals to increase distribution of healthcare resources and make access to health care more equitable is presented as an essential and challenging civic professional goal for all nurses. In every page I see advancement of understanding of nursing's civic professionalism, to address health promotion, illness prevention, and care needs of the society as good professional citizens. Refreshingly absent are commercial and self-interested concerns of professionals. Yet, the nurse is viewed as a person of worth and integrity, one who deserves the same attentiveness to well-being, integrity, and identity as a whole person, as those whom nurses serve. When focusing on the needs of the patient, the nurse is to be self-regarding, not self-aggrandizing or diminishing, while placing the needs and ends of practice above self-interests or personal advantage.

Professional nurses confront those who are vulnerable due to illness and/or lack of knowledge or understanding of their plight. Nurses, as good citizens, must ensure that they skillfully and ethically relate to patients as whole persons who deserve advocacy and assurance that the nurse has the patient's concerns and best outcomes front and center. The Guide, in illuminating Provision 5 of the new Code, follows Kant's Moral Imperative to "act so that you treat humanity, *whether in your own person* or in that of another, always as an end and never as a means."[iii] Persons are considered ends in themselves as rights- and dignity-bearing whole persons. Nurses who consider all persons as ends in themselves avoid manipulation, disrespectful uses of power, coercion, or usurping their own or others' ends. In this articulation of the ethics of respect for the dignity and worth of self and others, this work seeks to prevent potential pathologies of helping in nursing practice and self-neglect among nurses, themselves.

This Guide vigilantly addresses past excesses and omissions in the *Code of Ethics for Nurses with Interpretive Statements*. Virtues and ethics of obligation are taken up with a reinforcing view of the necessity of both. In Provision 5, the Guide states:

> …both a virtue and a duty-based approach to ethics are essential. If duties are to have any power and if virtues are to have any direction, both must be operative. The problem of a duty-based ethics is that obligations are empty if the person does not possess the moral character to meet those obligations. The problem of a virtue-based ethics is that it runs the risk of abuse through unwarranted intrusion into the private life of the individual, an intrusion that was amply evident in early nursing schools, even into the 1960s.

The Guide, in emphasizing both virtue-based ethics related to formation and ethical comportment *and* the obligations associated with the responsibilities of nurses, clearly describes professional nursing as a way of being as well as a way of skillfully and knowledgeably acting in the practice thereof. The practice itself is viewed as having notions of *good* internal to it.

A stronger emphasis on social ethics is evident in the 2015 Code and this Guide. As stated in Chapter 9 of the Guide:

> Social ethics is fundamentally about the application of ethics to large, even global, social problems and issues with an emphasis on the sociopolitical conditions and structures that foster injustice. Social ethics may be defined as the domain of ethics that deals with "issues of social order—the good, right, and ought in the organization of human communities and the shaping of social policies. Hence the subject matter of social ethics is moral rightness and goodness in the shaping of human society."[iv] Social ethics engages in social criticism, applying a range of ethical and critical theories that can frame the discussion and move toward policies that will help to redress unjust conditions such as the social determinants of illness, poverty, hunger, illiteracy, and so forth.

Nurses are in a unique position in the healthcare system, in that they are the professionals who spend the most direct time with patients. Nursing insights on how to improve nursing and healthcare policy and delivery are sorely needed. The Guide emphasizes three functions of social ethics: a) reform of the profession so that it is self-improving and continues to live up to its ethical and moral values and aspirations; b) meaningful ethical discourse that encourages and calls the practice community to live up to its own moral vision; and c) social activism and reform that improves health promotion, illness prevention, care of the suffering, and equitable distribution, safety, and quality of health care.

Dr. Fowler brilliantly traces the history of the profession's moral and ethical understanding, and broadens that understanding to match the current depth and breadth of nursing practice at the beginning of 2015. I believe that both the 2015 Code and this intelligent and inspiring Guide should be a must-read for all nurses. Every student entering nursing deserves to read the brilliant synthesis of the development and evolution of the self-understanding and societal understanding of nursing practice illustrated and articulated in this, the current guide to the 2015 *Code of Ethics for Nurses with Interpretive Statements*. I predict that readers will come away from reading this book invigorated and inspired to continue to earn the high trust that public polls continue to place in the nursing profession and nurses themselves.

Patricia Benner, PhD, RN, FAAN
Professor Emeritus, University of California San Francisco School of Nursing
American Academy of Nursing Living Legend, 2011

ENDNOTES

[i] Sullivan, W. *Work and Integrity: The Crisis and Promise of Professionalism in America, 2nd Edition*, (San Francisco: Jossey-Bass, 1905.)

[ii] Kant, Immanuel. *Groundwork of the Metaphysics of Morals*. Mary J. Gregor, ed. Cambridge, England: (Cambridge University Press, 1998.)

[iii] American Nurses Association, *Code of Ethics for Nurses with Interpretive Statements* (Silver Spring, MD: ANA, 2015), vii.

[iv] Winter, Gibson. *Elements for a Social Ethics*. (New York: Macmillan, 1966), 215.

Introduction.
Provisions, Decisions, and Cases: Getting to What is Right and Good

This book, *Guide to the Code of Ethics with Interpretive Statements: Development, Interpretation, and Application*, is intended to set the Code within its developmental context, provide resources that further the readers' understanding of the Code, identify pivotal documents that have and continue to inform nursing ethics, and to guide nurses in the application of the Code. An attempt has been made to provide all the information needed for a basic understanding of the Code, which includes both the provisions and interpretive statements. Each section of the interpretive statements is discussed in detail. Additional information, beyond the basics, is also provided in order to nurture curiosity and to provide a rich foundation that can challenge the reader to achieve a greater depth of understanding. Most of all, this material will foster a pride of profession of which nursing is eminently worthy.

The book consists of nine chapters, each corresponding to a provision of the Code. The introduction to each provision is intended to go beyond a mere notation of how previous Codes stated the provision. Instead, each provision is set within its developmental context by showing how it originated historically, and how and why it changed over the decades. The changes to each provision are also set within their social context in an attempt to demonstrate how society has influenced change in nursing and its codes, how nursing's own growth, interests, and ideals have interacted with society, and how both come together to influence the provisions of the Code. In some instances, the introduction also develops key concepts (e.g., compassion, human dignity) in the specific provision. The introductory material of each chapter is especially relevant when examining issues and trends in nursing or nursing and society and nursing history. The discussions under each interpretive statement are focused on how the provision should be interpreted and how it is to be applied in practice.

For each chapter, an attempt has been made to include ample citations for pivotal documents so that those who wish to go more deeply into their study of specific issues will have an easy point of access. These citations include documents of historical importance, documents that are internationally binding or advisory, national regulatory documents, and nursing research articles that are of great significance or have had a great impact on nursing ethics. Where these documents are available in full text online, website links are included in the endnotes. The American Nurses Association has a wealth of information available online and these webpages have also been cited in the endnotes.

A number of the chapters have illustrative cases. These cases are intended for group discussion and personal reflection and are designed to provide an opportunity to explore the particular concepts or issues related to the specific provision. The cases are based on real situations but all identifying features have been substantially altered or removed entirely to preserve the anonymity of the individuals and institutions involved.

Conceptual models or theories in nursing govern the categories, concepts, and vocabulary of practice. Likewise, ethical theories and models of ethical decision-making govern the categories, concepts, and vocabulary of data and analysis of ethical issues in clinical practice. It is therefore difficult to specify the particular questions that should be asked of a specific case, as the nature of the ethical decision-making method used will determine how those questions are formulated. One model might ask "Is the patient autonomous?" while another might ask "Has care been received?" However, to facilitate discussion, a series of questions is given below. These questions may or may not reflect the reader's preferred ethical decision-making model.

The Nursing Process, Models of Ethical Decision-Making, and Using the Cases

There are a number of approaches that can be used to analyze ethical issues and cases in professional practice. It is useful to become familiar with and develop expertise in one approach, but at the same time, knowledge of varied approaches expands one's repertoire for addressing ethical issues. Three commonly used approaches are discussed below. These descriptions are extremely brief. Space and the purpose of this book do not permit a full analysis or evaluation of ethical decision-making models. For a more substantive discussion of each method identified below, and the controversies over models of decision-making, please refer to the original works as cited in the endnotes.

Using the Nursing Process in Clinical-Ethical Situations and Case Discussion

It is possible to reflect upon clinical–ethical situations by using the nursing process to frame a specific ethical theory.[3,4,5] The nursing process is not itself an ethical theory. It provides an organizing template expected in all nursing practice in accordance with the standards of practice and legal–regulatory requirements. Thus, nurses are expected to use the nursing process even when the clinical matter at hand is ethical in nature. In clinical ethics, the following steps of the nursing process remain the same but the content of the steps of the nursing process is modified to accommodate the preferred ethical theory used to guide data collection and ethical analysis.

> Assessment/Data collection: What is happening? What sort of a problem is it: ethical, moral, practical, relational? Who are the people involved? Once an issue is identified as an ethical issue, collect the morally relevant data including both facts (e.g., about the patient's medical or health status, pain, suffering, treatments, uncertainties) and values (e.g., patient and family values, beliefs, preferences, concerns, disagreements). Data collection should also include the concerns, values, opinions, and preferences of relevant others, such as the healthcare team, other health professionals, and perhaps the patient's community of reference. The specific data that must be collected will depend upon the ethical theory or approach that one chooses.

> Assessment/Analysis: Analyze the factual and values data that has been collected using an ethic of care, virtue theory, principles of biomedical ethics, or another ethical theory.

> Diagnosis. Make a clinical judgment about the care context, ethos, and issues including points of agreement or tension, conflicts of obligations, or conflicts of values. The diagnosis should reflect the fuller patient context including the patient herself or himself, relational network, community of reference, healthcare team, consultants, institutional circumstances or constraints. More than one moral issue may surface.

> Outcomes/Planning. Ask "What would happen if…?" This is where the different approaches to ethics can be looked at and tried out. Based on the assessment and diagnosis, and in collaboration with the patient (and other health professionals as indicated), identify a range of approaches, or the best available approach when the possibilities are less than optimal. Some plans will include patient, family, and institutional interventions.

> Implementation. What is the fitting answer? Ensure that it is the fitting answer, that is, one that is suitable and appropriate. A fitting answer

should also be right, but not all right answers are appropriate or fitting in a particular context. What is the outcome people can live with? Implement the plan in collaboration with the patient, family, and other health professionals.

Evaluation. What has happened? What can be learned from this situation? Both the patient's status and the effectiveness of the nursing care must be continuously evaluated, and the care plan modified as needed.

Sample Models of Ethical Decision-Making in Clinical Practice

These four models discussed below demonstrate different but widely accepted approaches to ethical analysis and decision-making in a range of professional practice roles and settings.

Jonsen's "Four Boxes"

Jonsen, Siegler, and Winslade have developed a useful means of evaluating moral dilemmas in clinical medical practice. Their approach has four domains or topics, often referred to as "the four boxes" because they are commonly arranged on a grid. The four domains are: medical indications, patient references, quality of life, and contextual features. This approach is heavily influenced by ethical principlism, that is, the use of the principles articulated by Beauchamp and Childress in their work *Principles of Biomedical Ethics*.[6] These principles are also articulated in *The Belmont Report* that governs the protection of human subjects in biomedical and behavioral research.[7] Jonsen, Siegler, and Winslade explain the four topics:

> Our four topics or boxes provide a similar pattern for collecting, sorting, and ordering the facts of a clinical ethical problem. Each topic or "box" is filled with the actual facts of the clinical case that are relevant to the identification of the ethical problem, and the contents of all four are viewed together for a comprehensive picture of the ethical dimensions of the case.
> *Medical indications refer to the diagnostic and therapeutic interventions that are being used to evaluate and treat the medical problem in the case. Patient preferences state the express choices of the patient about their treatment, or the decisions of those who are authorized to speak for the patient when the patient is incapable of doing so. Quality of life describes features of the patient's life prior to and following treatment, insofar as these features are pertinent to medical decisions. Contextual features identify the familial, social, institutional, financial, and legal settings within which the particular case takes place, insofar as they influence medical decisions.*[8] [italics original]

Summary of the Four Boxes[9]

Medical Indications

Principles of Nonmaleficence and Beneficence

Data examples: diagnosis, treatment, prognosis, acuity, chronicity, reversibility, terminality, goals of treatment, treatments that are not indicated, probability of success, benefit to the patient

Patient References

Principle of Respect for Autonomy

Data examples: patient informedness, comprehension, voluntariness, free consent, mental capacity, legal status, advance directive and/or prior expressed preferences, surrogate, cooperation

Quality of Life

Principles of Nonmaleficence, Beneficence, and Respect for Autonomy

Data examples: patient prospects of returning to normal life, deficits that might be predicted, what the patient desires in terms of quality of life, whether quality of life can be improved, under what conditions should treatment be stopped

Contextual Features

Principles of Justice and Fairness

Data examples: risks of professional or institutional conflicts of interest, vested interests, financial factors, institutional/social scarcity of resources, potential legal issues, public safety issues

Note that because the four boxes approach relies upon principles of ethics for data collection and analysis, many of the questions asked in ethical principlism will also be asked in this model as well.

Ethical Principlism

Ethical principlism is currently the dominant approach to ethical decision-making in clinical and research practice. Beauchamp and Childress discuss four bioethical principles in their landmark book *Principles of Biomedical Ethics.* These principles (respect for autonomy, nonmaleficence, beneficence, and justice) are held to be abstract, universal, value-neutral ethical principles that are used as tools to analyze moral dilemmas and issues and to specify ethical obligations. In practice, the first three principles are the "bedside" principles while justice is more often used at the societal or macro-level. Beauchamp and Childress maintain that these "pivotal moral principles...function as an analytical framework of general norms derived from the common morality that form a suitable starting point for biomedical ethics. These principles are general guidelines for the formulation of more specific rules."[10] These principles and their subsidiary rules give rise to specific points of analysis. For example, the principle of respect for autonomy and its rule of informedness and voluntariness give rise to the following questions (not an exhaustive list):

- Is the patient autonomous?
- Is the patient's autonomy stable or fluctuating?
- Has autonomy been assessed on a renewing basis?
- Is the patient legally autonomous?
- Has the patient been informed?
- Has the patient waived informedness?
- Has the patient been given adequate, complete, and truthful information relevant to their situation?
- Does the patient have the capacity to understand the information?
- Has the patient understood the information?
- Does the patient have internal or external constraints to voluntariness?
- Can any constraints be ameliorated?
- Has the patient been unduly influenced?
- Has the patient given free consent?
- Has the consent fluctuated?

These questions, and those related to the other principles, form the basis of data collection for ethical decision-making. Each of the four principles and their subsidiary rules give rise to a set of questions that can be used to guide data collection and analysis in order to arrive at a specification of duty. The principles do not specify precisely how that duty will be met (e.g., whether the patient is given information by the physician or by the nurse), as there may be more than one way to meet that duty.

An Ethic of Care

While Jonsen, Siegler, and Winslade's four boxes model overlaps with Beauchamp and Childress's ethical principlism, an ethic of care approach is often seen to overlap with virtue ethics. Gastmans maintains that care is a virtue, but that an ethic of care is not virtue ethics.[11] In an ethic of care, "caring always takes place within the framework of a relationship where the caregiver and the care receiver are reciprocally involved…the caregiver and care receiver give care together…. Care can only be considered 'completed' if the care offered is affirmed."[12] Care is set within the larger framework of societal expectations, institutional facilitators or hindrances, health professionals, relatives, the patient; all of these together constitute the healthcare team. Tronto identifies four phases of caring, each having a related moral element. The four phases are: caring about, taking care of, care giving, and care receiving. The four moral elements of an ethic of care are: attentiveness, responsibility, competence, and responsiveness.[13] Each of these phases and moral elements must be present for care to be demonstrated.

Four phases of caring	Four moral elements
Caring about	Attentiveness
Taking care of	Responsibility
Care giving	Competence
Care receiving	Responsiveness

In the first phase, the nurse must be attentive to needs within relationships, including all of the relationships surrounding the patient—nurse, family, health professions, institution, and societal expectations for care. The nurse must "pay attention to all relevant clinical factors involved, such as the patients' expectations, pains, fears, etc., as well as the professional and personal experiences of the caregivers."[14] These include questions of vulnerability, dignity, and meaningfulness. Patient wishes are focused within the relational identity of the patient and family, not in isolation. All their different viewpoints must be interpreted. Taking care of requires taking responsibility for each of the needs that have been observed, not as a set of principles of obligation, but as a situated ethics. An ethic of care emphasizes responsibility *to* people, not responsibility *for* another person. In care giving, the nurse acts upon those responsibilities, exercising the requisite knowledge, skill, and wisdom, that is, competence. In the care receiving phase, the patient or family affirms that care has been received. Only by virtue of this patient acknowledgement does it become clear that care has taken place. Without patient responsiveness there is no measure by which nurses can know that they and the patient shared in the identification and care of the same need.

A Brief Note on the Decision-Making Controversy

One of the main controversies in nursing over ethical decision-making models is the disagreement between advocates of an ethic of care and those who advocate ethical principlism. An ethic of care is understood by its proponents to address several issues that render ethical principlism less satisfactory for ethical decision-making in nursing. These theorists note that there are several difficulties with the principle-based ethics that dominates bioethical discourse, particularly in the form of Beauchamp and Childress's four principles and the "universal ethical principles" of Kohlberg (see Chapter 2). First, the principles themselves are mid-range and do not have a theory of ethics behind them that binds them together and makes them cohere. There is no common agreement on foundational principles as opposed to secondary principles, and some disagreement on which principles are morally relevant. Second, when principles conflict there is no theory or standard that guides arbitrating the conflict. Third, these abstract principles are described as universal, and value-neutral, but there is argument that the principles are rooted in the cultural values from which they arose. Callahan notes the strengths of principlism: "Taken in its own terms, principlism has two key virtues: it reflects the liberal, individualist culture from which it emerged, and is thus culture congenial; and it is relatively simple in its conceptualisation and application, and thus particularly attractive to clinical decision making."[15]

Thus, the very strength of principlism is at the same time its critique. Callahan sees two important failings of principlism: "For me, however, two problems have stood in the way of any enthusiastic embrace: its individualistic bias, and its capacity to block substantive ethical inquiry."[16] Another critique of ethical principlism is that it decontextualizes clinical decision-making and by doing so fails to take account of the morally relevant attributes of the case. An ethic of care is focused on clinical practice, especially on the relational context of care. This includes but is not limited to the nurse–patient relationship. It extends to all parties involved, plus the surrounding institutional environment and societal expectations for the nature of care.

Critics of an ethic of care argue that it is unclear whether care is an obligation, a virtue, or an end that is sought. They also argue that aspects of an ethic of care are vague and that decision-making must also utilize principles.

The reader is directed to the literature on models of decision-making to examine a fuller range of models, as well as exploring the controversies that exist over method.

Suggested Questions for Case Discussions

Is this an ethical or moral issue? The following questions are provided to facilitate classroom discussion or personal reflection upon the cases in each of the chapters. As noted above, these questions may or may not reflect the reader's preferred ethical decision-making model.

- What are the values, virtues, or obligations at stake in this case?
- What values, virtues, or obligations should be affirmed and why?
- How would you assess this situation morally?
- What are the clinical and medical dimensions of this situation?
- What are the patient's needs or desires?
- What are the needs or desires of others involved?
- What relationships are affected in this situation?
- What institutional factors affect this situation?
- What principles or rules are in conflict?
- What values are in conflict?
- What elements of the Code pertain?
- How might the Code inform your analysis or decision?
- If you were that nurse, how would you reason, ethically, about this?
- What arguments would you make for your position?
- What do you believe to be the strongest argument?
- In your ethical analysis, what would be acceptable options for action?
- What would not be acceptable options?
- What choice of action might promote the most good while causing the least harm?
- What actions might best affirm the relationships that exist?
- How might that be done?
- What are the ethical responsibilities of each of those involved?

Concluding Remarks

The ANA *Code of Ethics for Nurses with Interpretive Statements* continues to be the foundational moral document of American nursing. It encompasses the profession's values, obligations, ethical standards, aspirations, and ideals. The Code is also responsive to new issues or concerns that arise. New issues are neither morally disruptive nor morally innovative, nor beyond the compass of the Code. Because it is an expression of the values of the profession, the Code is capable of being extended to address new, unexpected issues. The Code is intended to guide nurses now and for the near future as they respond to the present and changing health and nursing needs of patients and populations. Through this 2015 revision and the revisions in the future, the Code is and will always be an enduring statement of the ethical core of nursing.

ENDNOTES

[1] Internal communiqué, American Nurses Association.

[2] Ibid.

[3] Albert Jonsen, Mark Siegler and William Winslade, *Clinical Ethics: A Practical Approach to Ethical Decisions in Clinical Medicine*

[4] Verena Tschudin, *Ethics in Nursing: The Caring Relationship* (3rd ed.) (Edinburgh: Butterworth Heinemann, 2003).

[5] Verena Tschudin, Personal communication with author, December 4, 2014.

[6] Tom Beauchamp and James Childress, *Principles of Biomedical Ethics* (7th ed.) (NY: Oxford University Press, 2013).

[7] National Commission for the Protection of Human Subjects of Biomedical and Behavioral Research of the U.S. Department of Health and Human Services, *The Belmont Report: Ethical Principles and Guidelines for the Protection of Human Subjects of Research* (Washington, D.C.: DHHS/USGPO, 1979), http://www.hhs.gov/ohrp/humansubjects/guidance/belmont.html

[8] Jonsen, Siegler, and Winslade, *Clinical Ethics*, 3.

[9] Ibid., 8–9.

[10] Beauchamp and Childress, *Principles of Biomedical Ethics*, 13.

[11] Chris Gastmans, "A Fundamental Approach to Nursing," *Nursing Ethics* 9, no. 5 (2002): 494–507.

[12] Chris Gastmans, "The Care Perspective in Healthcare Ethics," in *The Teaching of Nursing Ethics: Content and Methods*, eds. Anne Davis, Louise de Raeve, and Verena Tschudin (London: Elsevier, 2006), 137, 146–48.

[13] Joan Tronto, *Moral Boundaries: A Political Argument for an Ethic of Care* (New York: Routledge, 1993), 126–34.

[14] Gastmans, "The Care Perspective," 141.

[15] D. Callahan, "Principlism and Communitarianism," *Journal of Medical Ethics* 29 (2003): 288.

[16] Ibid.

Provision 1

The nurse practices with compassion and respect for the inherent dignity, worth, and unique attributes of every person.

Provision 1. Affirming Health through Relationships of Dignity and Respect

Introduction

There is, perhaps, no better place to begin a discussion of ethics in nursing than with attention to the momentous concepts of *compassion* and *human dignity*. Because of their magnitude and central importance to nursing, it warrants dwelling a moment on these concepts of compassion, suffering, and human dignity. That compassion responds to suffering is to be expected, as the word itself joins together the Latin *com-* (meaning together with) and *pati* (meaning to suffer), thus "to suffer with" another.[1] Sharing the same root, the *patient*, also from the Latin *pati*—meaning to suffer or to endure affliction is the subject of compassion.[2] This relationship between compassion and suffering has been a topic of intense reflection for millennia in both religious and philosophical literature.

Hinduism, in its urreligious (oldest, primeval, or proto) form, is thought to have its origins around 2,600 BCE and is sometimes referred to as "the oldest religion."[3] It has no single founder and is an amalgamation of numerous indigenous religions of the Indian subcontinent. It coalesces into a "Hindu synthesis," that is, a more unified form, around the beginning of the Common Era.[4,5] Hinduism would seem an odd place to start a discussion of *compassion* in modern nursing, yet 4,600 years of human observation and reflection can provide some astute insights of relevance to nursing.

Hinduism has not one but several words that translate into English as the single word *compassion*. Each has a subtle shade of meaning. The three most common words are *daya* (Hindi: दया), *karuna* (करुणा), and *anukampa* (अनुकम्पा).
[6] *Daya* is the first among the eight essential qualities of the soul that must be developed. It means "the desire of one's bosom to mitigate the sorrow and

difficulties of others by putting forth any amount of efforts." It is also defined as "…to treat a stranger, a relative, a friend or foe as one's own self," as someone who is as susceptible to suffering as I am. *Karuna* is "…born of grief on account of loss or difficulties of [persons] near and dear." *Anukampa* means "to experience mild and gentle movement in the heart following the observance of pain and suffering in the other person."[7]

It is evident from these definitions that they are based on critical reflection and address a number of pivotal underlying questions that are deeply relevant to nursing ethics. These questions include:

Is compassion a virtue? If so, what kind of virtue? Is it innate or learned? Can compassion be taught? Is compassion the same as sympathy or pity? Does compassion involve empathy or mercy? Is compassion a response? What is the function of compassion? Is compassion nothing more than a feeling? Is compassion a cognitive decision? Does compassion require tangible action? Who or what is the object of compassion? Who or what is worthy of my compassion? Is compassion toward one's self or a loved on the same as compassion toward a foe? Need a person merit compassion? How does compassion relate to my own potential or real suffering? Is the one who expresses compassion in a superior position? Are there degrees of compassion? If there are degrees of compassion, on what are those degrees based? Are there constitutive elements in a compassionate response? Why be compassionate? Must I show compassion toward myself?

Within the sacred Hindu texts one finds discourses that grapple with these questions and provide profound answers.

Buddhism also addresses compassion. The Buddha lived sometime between the 6th and 4th centuries BCE. The words of the Buddha were originally passed via oral tradition, then recorded in the *Path of Purification* (*Visuddhimagga*) and other works. The Buddha's understanding of compassion was as follows:

> When there is suffering in others it causes (*karoti*) good people's hearts to be moved (*kampana*), thus it is compassion (*karuóá*). Or alternatively, it combats (*kióáti*) others' suffering, attacks and demolishes it, thus it is compassion. Or alternatively, it is scattered (*kiriyati*) upon those who suffer, it is extended to them by pervasion, thus it is compassion (*karuóá*).[8]

Restated in more modern language: "Compassion is that which makes the heart of the good move at the pain of others. It crushes and destroys the pain of others; thus, it is called compassion. It is called compassion because it shelters and embraces the distressed."[9]

In Buddhist thought, compassion is a virtue. Compassion rises above respect, sympathy, and pity. In compassion we identify with the other and try to understand from her or his point of view. Buddhist scholar William Irwin writes:

> Compassion and kindness are virtues that direct us away from ourselves and our craving.... We owe it to ourselves to treat other people with something greater than respect, namely compassion... Compassion involves both the recognition that others are suffering and the fellow-feeling that the recognition brings.... I do not feel sorry for them or have pity for them; I have compassion for them, recognizing their state of being as my own.... Compassion thus involves an ethics of intention. While the carelessness and foolishness of certain actions makes them blameworthy even with good intentions, it is charitable, kind, and appropriate for us to consider others' intentions. Looking to others with their intentions in mind helps me to cultivate compassion... And on a daily basis, empathic listening requires compassionate intentionalist interpretation. The goal is not to understand the other person as suits me; or from my point of view; or to find some piece of common ground. The goal is to understand the other from his point of view, as he intends and hopes to be understood.[10]

Note that the questions that underlie Hindu perspectives on compassion are shared in the Buddhist considerations—and those of other religions as well.

Religious discourse on compassion goes beyond the definitional and theoretical to encompass actual "interventions." Take, for example, the man named Job in the Jewish *Tanakh* (Bible). The Book of Job dates between the 7th and 4th centuries BCE, with the 6th century as the probable date.[11] Job, a righteous man experienced calamity. His children were killed when a wind caused their house to fall in, his sheep and servants were killed in a fire storm, his camels stolen, and Job himself became covered with "loathsome sores... from the sole of his foot to the crown of his head."[12] In addition, he had a nagging wife and friends with a knack for saying exactly the wrong thing. But his friends did get one thing right: they showed compassion.

> Now when Job's three friends heard of all these troubles that had come upon him, each of them set out from his home... They met together to go and console and comfort him. When they saw him from a distance, they did not recognize him, and they raised their voices and wept aloud; they tore their robes and threw dust in the air upon their heads. They sat with him on the ground for seven days and seven nights, and no one spoke a word to him, for they saw that his suffering was very great.[13]

In their compassion, Job's friends engage in *presence*, a key means of expressing compassion. Presence receives considerable discussion in theological literature, and is a concept and intervention fundamental to nursing and one that nurse scholars have recently begun to explore. However, the Jewish literature also offers insight into hearing another's *lament*. It is in expressing, fully expressing, one's lament—and having that lament heard by another rather than stifled that compassion meets and mitigates suffering. There are, in this ancient literature, specific literary forms or templates for the expression of individual and collective lament. These forms guarantee the full expression of lament and prompt the person to end on a note of hope that they can draw from within.[14]

These are but three examples. Extensive discussions of compassion are found in all major and most smaller religious traditions. There are also discussions of compassion in the philosophical literature.

Aristotle (384–322 BCE) held that there are five essential social virtues (sing. *arête*; pl. *aretai*): courage, compassion, self-love, friendship, and forgiveness. He sees virtues as larger than moral virtues alone. For Aristotle, *moral virtues* are aimed at *fine* and *right* action. He taught that virtues, as moral aspects of character, can be learned, cultivated, and strengthened. The goal of moral education is to control unruly desires and habits so that desires might be rightly ordered and that virtues might be cultivated. (See Chapter 5 for additional discussion of virtues.) Aristotle distinguished compassion from pity. Pity is condescending and not welcome by its recipient. Compassion, on the other hand, sees the suffering of the other as if it were one's own suffering. It is possible to have an excess of compassion—softheartedness—as well as a deficiency of compassion as cold-heartedness or callousness. Aristotle ascribes distinctive content to each virtue, including actions, motives, and capacities.[15]

Aristotle argues that compassion is a painful emotion in response to another person's suffering or misfortune.[16] There are three constitutive elements for compassion: (a) the person's misfortune or suffering must be of significance, that is, not trivial, (b) the person has no role in causing her or his suffering, i.e., it is undeserved, and (c) an awareness that I, and those whom I love, share in the vulnerabilities and weaknesses of this person and are likewise susceptible to suffering. Martha Nussbaum takes issue with Aristotle's third condition and maintains that:

> in order for compassion to be present, the person must consider the suffering of another as a significant part of his or her own scheme of goals and ends. She must take that person's ill as affecting her own flourishing. In effect, she must make herself vulnerable in the person of another. It is that *eudaimonistic* judgment, not the judgment of similar possibilities, that seems to be a necessary constituent of compassion.[17]

Eudaimon, often translated as happiness, welfare or even well-being, is more accurately understood as a concept of *human flourishing*. What Nussbaum is saying is that we all have a concept of what *human flourishing* looks like and we make a *eudaimonistic* judgment about persons who are suffering—that they are or are not flourishing—consistent with our understanding of the goals and ends we would seek for our own flourishing. She agrees with Aristotle that we all share in the human condition of susceptibility to suffering, and thus share in a sense of common human community. Where she disagrees with him is that she believes that is it not a judgment of similar possibility of suffering that drives compassion, but rather a judgment about what it takes for me or that person to flourish.

Aristotle is hardly alone in his concern for compassion. Other philosophers have argued about compassion, including the Stoics, Seneca, Schopenhauer, Hume, Hutcheson, Nietzsche, and Kant.

Nurses tend to skim the religious or philosophical literature in their investigations of compassion. Van der Cingel is an exception; she explores selected philosophical works, including those of Aristotle, Schopenhauer, and Nietzsche (largely through Nussbaum's work). She writes that:

> Compassion is an answer to suffering despite the fact that suffering will not disappear by it. Serious suffering can happen to everyone because to suffer is part of human existence. Still, suffering is not always easy to recognize because the meaning of what is lost differs from person to person. In order to recognize the meaning of a loss it is necessary to set aside one's own perspective. This is troublesome when the relevant perspective is remote from one's own experience and ideas.... Imagination and reflection...help to develop susceptibility for the other person's perspective.... Compassion is also defined by the specific thought that suffering is terrible.... Further, compassion is unconditionally valid for everyone suffering.... There is a choice to be made in showing or not showing compassion. To acknowledge suffering by showing compassion means to acknowledge the loss of something valuable, to deny this means adding suffering to suffering that already exists. Therefore, compassion is the morally right thing to express.[18]

In the empirical portion of her study (with older persons with chronic diseases), she identifies seven dimensions of compassion: attentiveness, active listening, naming of suffering, involvement, helping, being present, and understanding.[19] While not identical to the discussions of compassion in the philosophical literature, her findings corroborate a number of the elements that they raise.

Only a few, including van der Cingel, have drawn rigorously upon the rich religious sources on compassion that are available.[20] Those resources continue to develop through theological discourse, and also through such vehicles as the Parliament of the World's Religions and the *Charter for Compassion.* In these venues, compassion becomes a social and political force, much like the context of an *ethic of care* (see Chapter 2) that extends beyond the dyadic nurse–patient relationship. *Compassion* becomes a social force to address suffering globally by addressing the social determinants of suffering. The text of the *Charter for Compassion* says, in part:

> The principle of compassion lies at the heart of all religious, ethical and spiritual traditions, calling us always to treat all others as we wish to be treated ourselves. Compassion impels us to work tirelessly to alleviate the suffering of our fellow creatures, to dethrone ourselves from the centre of our world and put another there, and to honour the inviolable sanctity of every single human being, treating everybody, without exception, with absolute justice, equity and respect. It is also necessary in both public and private life to refrain consistently and empathically from inflicting pain. To act or speak violently out of spite, chauvinism, or self-interest, to impoverish, exploit or deny basic rights to anybody, and to incite hatred by denigrating others—even our enemies—is a denial of our common humanity. We acknowledge that we have failed to live compassionately and that some have even increased the sum of human misery in the name of religion.[21]

Note that the *Charter for Compassion* encompasses many of the facets of compassion addressed by the religious and philosophical traditions noted above, speaking to many of the concerns that nursing shares. The extension of compassion into the larger social and political realm can also be found in these same traditions.

Considering how important compassion is to nursing, it does not appear in the codes to the degree that it should. The successive revisions of the Code err on the side of scientifically skilled nursing, and to some degree have neglected the *art of nursing* for the science of nursing. This is, in part, a reflection of nursing's aspirations to be regarded as scientific and as a profession. To some degree, compassion, comfort, and care were assumed and subsumed under rights and patient protection language. In addition, the codes were rightly influenced by shock and outrage at the Nazi experiments exposed after WWII, the disclosures by both Beecher and Pappworth of morally reprobate medical experiments in the United States and UK, the multiple international documents incorporating human rights and self-determination, as well as the rise of bioethics in the mid-1960s emphasizing respect for autonomy. (See Chapter 7 for additional discussion.) These influences lead to a resolute affirmation of rights, self-determination, respect for autonomy, and the like in the successive iterations of the Code. This content displaces the interpersonal art of nursing concerns that remain at the heart of nursing care and are encompassed in part in the developing *ethic of care*. (See Chapter 3). Though *compassion* is not mentioned specifically, the *Tentative Code* (1940) does state that the nurse is a "bearer of comfort," "a source of strength and comfort," and that "honesty, understanding, gentleness, and patience should characterize all of the acts of the nurse. A sense of the fitness of things is particularly important."[22] Compassion appears in the 2001 revision of the Code: "Provision 1. The nurse, in all professional relationships, practices with compassion and respect for the inherent dignity, worth and uniqueness of every individual, unrestricted by considerations of social or economic status, personal attributes, or the nature of health problems."[23]

The 2015 revision of the Code retains the concern for compassion and continues to assert it in the actual provision itself: "Provision 1: The nurse practices with compassion and respect for the inherent dignity, worth, and unique attributes of every person."[24]

Compassion is inextricably linked to valuing the *other*, whether the *other* is another human being, other sentient life, or the environment. This valuing calls for a response of respect in the case of human life, and more specifically those lives that come into contact with nurses, respect for human dignity.

1.1 Respect for Human Dignity

Human dignity first appears in the 1960 *Code for Professional Nurses*, and in every successive revision thereafter. This is, again, reflective of the international concern for the protection of human dignity. There are some subtle shifts in language as the "dignity of man" (1968 Code) subsequently becomes "human dignity." The concern for human dignity shifts from the second to the first provision after 1960. Through 1985, the emphasis is on affirming and preserving human dignity in patient care. From the 2001 revision forward, the Code emphasizes affirming and preserving the human dignity of all those with whom nurses have contact, in all nursing roles and settings. This would include the preservation of the human dignity of patients, clients, participants in research, nursing students, co-workers, other health professionals, and colleagues—in short, everyone, including ourselves!

The requirement to respect, affirm, protect, and preserve human dignity still does not explain or define the concept of *human dignity*. When the concept of human dignity was introduced through the 1948 UN *Universal Declaration of Human Rights* no attempt was made to define human dignity.[25] Düwell notes that when human dignity was introduced, it was intended to serve as a moral reference point and that:

> Most people believed that they knew what human dignity was about: a consensus within the humanistic tradition, a secularized version of the Judeo-Christian concept of Imago Dei [humankind made in the image of God], an overlap between the ethical doctrines of important thinkers like Kant and Confucius, the normative core of the natural law tradition, a moral-political statement against the atrocities of the Nazi régime, etc....it thus appeared superfluous to strive for a theoretical explanation and justification of the concept.[26]

Sulmasy identifies three different uses of *dignity* in moral discourse: *attributed, intrinsic,* and *inflorescent.*[27] *Attributed dignity* refers to worthiness conferred upon a person based on one's social standing, reputation, or civic office; it is based on *merit* in a social or public sense. *Intrinsic dignity,* based in Immanuel Kant's formulation, is:

> that worth or value that people have simply because they are human, not by virtue of any social standing, ability to evoke admiration, or any particular set of talents, skills, or powers. Intrinsic dignity is the value that human beings have simply by virtue of the fact that they are human beings. Thus we say that racism is an offense against human dignity. Used this way, dignity designates a value not conferred or created by human choices, individual or collective, but is prior to human attribution. Kant's notion of dignity is intrinsic.[28]

This is the sense in which this Code and all prior codes use the term *dignity. Inflorescent* is an odd term, as it refers to a flower coming into bloom. *Inflorescent dignity,* for Sulmasy, refers to the person who is coming into the "full bloom" of virtuous humanity:

> to individuals who are flourishing as human beings—living lives that are consistent with and expressive of the intrinsic dignity of the human. Thus, dignity is sometimes used to refer to a state of virtue—a state of affairs in which a human being habitually acts in ways that expresses the intrinsic value of the human. We say, for instance, that so-and-so faced a particularly trying situation with dignity.[29]

Inflorescent dignity is seen in the caring, compassionate, skilled nurse who brings genuine comfort to the anxious patient; in the researcher who diligently and rigorously pursues a line of inquiry with integrity, skill, perseverance, and a best effort; and in the nursing educator who seeks to advance the knowledge of both the strongest and weakest students with rigor, compassion, wisdom, and devotion to their learning. We can also see inflorescent dignity in the legend of Florence Nightingale, the attributed founder of modern nursing.

Düwell identifies five models of the term dignity that correlate with Sulmasy's three forms. Düwell's particular concern is to identify that form of dignity that will undergird human rights. Of the five models—rank, virtue and duty, dignity and religious status, the cosmological status of the human being, and respect for the dignity of the individual human being—he identifies respect for the dignity of the individual human being as best suited to the task of undergirding human rights, with direct links to the moral and political dimensions of life:[30]

> the specific idea can be distinguished that each single human individual would have dignity. In this line, human dignity should be seen as an expression that signifies a status which other human beings and political institutions have to respect. This respect can be interpreted primarily in a sense of moral obligations or – as happened in the twentieth century – in the sense of individual rights that can be legally enforced. And since this respect is of immanent importance from a moral point of view, it can be seen as a reason to understand the entire legal and political state and international order as based on the respect for the dignity and rights of each individual human being. This concept of 'human dignity'…is universal; it signifies a status that cannot be lost, and thus may provide a foundation of rights.[31]

This perspective on human dignity is that which is found in the nursing ethical literature: that human dignity has three distinct features: it is *inherent* (i.e., it is essential and permanent as it inheres, or "sticks" and is "fixed"), *intrinsic* (i.e., it is "situated within"; "inner," and naturally belonging), and *inviolable* (i.e., it may not be violated).[32]

However, Macklin has maintained that bioethics has no need for the concept of human dignity, that "dignity is a useless concept in medical ethics and can be eliminated without any loss of content."[33,34] While she uses the principles of *respect for per*sons and *respect for autonomy* interchangeably, she argues that the principle of respect for persons or respect for autonomy will suffice without the concept of human dignity. Nursing, and particularly an *ethic of care* (see Chapter 2), would challenge Macklin on this point and would agree with Schulman, who notes that:

> in locating human dignity entirely in rational autonomy, Kant was forced to deny any moral significance to other aspects of our humanity, including our family life, our loves, loyalties, and other emotions, as well as our way of coming into the world and all other merely biological facts about the human organism. His exclusive focus on rational autonomy leaves Kant with a rather narrow and constricted account of our moral life.[35]

In its embrace of the concept of human dignity, nursing would maintain that respect for autonomy does not exhaust the full meaning of human dignity, that human dignity is an essential moral concept and ground for respect, protection, human rights, and caring.

1.2 Relationships with Patients

Nurses must not, must never, behave prejudicially. In one way or another, this has been a part of all nursing codes, unadopted and adopted. However, reflective of what might be called ever-dawning social awareness, the list of potential sources for prejudice has been an ever-growing list. What began as a proscription against prejudice on the basis of race, creed, and nationality eventually expanded to include religious beliefs, color, status, country, ethnic identification, beliefs, living conditions, customs, attitudes, economic status, culture, life stage, socioeconomic status, personal attributes, nature of the health problem, age, sex, personality, background; political, educational, economic, developmental, personality, role and sexual differences; value systems, religious or spiritual beliefs, lifestyle, social support system, sexual orientation or gender expression, and primary language. There is really no end to the attributes that could be added to the list. The following list demonstrates how the concerns have enlarged across successive revisions of the Code.

1940   "Section 4. A truly professional nurse with broad social vision will have a sympathetic understanding of different creeds, nationalities, and races and in any case you will not permit her personal attitude toward these various groups to interfere with her function as a nurse."

Section 1. The nurse has a basic concern for people as human beings, confidence in the fundamental power of personality for good, respect for religious beliefs of others, and a philosophy which will sustain and inspire others as well as herself. Failure to possess these qualities means inability to live up to the responsibilities and to make the most of her opportunities.[36]

1950   "Provision 4. Religious beliefs of the patient must be respected."[37]

1960   "Provision 2. The nurse provides services based on human need, with respect for human dignity, unrestricted by considerations of nationality, race, creed, color or status."[38]

1968   "Provision 1. The nurse provides services first with respect for the dignity of man, unrestricted by considerations of nationality, race, creed, color, or status."[39]

1976   "Provision 1. The nurse provides services with respect for human dignity and the uniqueness of the client unrestricted by considerations of social economic status, personal attributes, the nature of health problems."

Interpretive Statement 1.3. Age, sex, race color, personality, or other personal attributes, as well as individual differences in background, customs, attitudes, and beliefs influence nursing practice only insofar as they represent factors the nurse must understand, consider and respect in tailoring care to personal needs and in maintaining the individual value systems and life-styles should be included in the planning of health care for each client.[40]

1985   "Provision 1. The nurse provides services with respect for human dignity and the uniqueness of the client, unrestricted by considerations of social or economic status, personal attributes, or the nature of health problems."

Interpretive Statement: 1.2. The need for health care is universal, transcending all national, ethnic, racial, religious, cultural, political, educational, economic, developmental, personality, role and sexual differences. Nursing care is delivered without prejudicial behavior.[41]

2001   "Provision 1. The nurse, in all professional relationships, practices with compassion and respect for the inherent dignity, worth and uniqueness of every individual, unrestricted by considerations of social or economic status, personal attributes, or the nature of health problems."

"Interpretive Statement 1.2 The need for health care is universal, transcending all individual differences."[42]

2015   "Provision 1. The nurse practices with compassion and respect for the inherent dignity, worth, and unique attributes of every person."

Interpretive Statement 1.2: Relationships with Patients. Nurses establish relationships of trust and provide nursing services according to need, setting aside any bias or prejudice. Factors such as culture, value systems, religious or spiritual beliefs, lifestyle, social support system, sexual orientation or gender expression, and primary language are to be considered when planning individual, family and population-centered care. Such considerations must promote health and wellness, address problems, and respect patients' or clients' decisions. Respect for patient decisions does not require that the nurse agree with or support all patient choices. When patient choices are risky or self-destructive, nurses have an obligation to address the behavior and to offer opportunities and resources to modify the behavior or to eradicate the risk.[43]

In an attempt to constrain infinitely expansible lists in the Code, the committee working to revise the 1985 Code made the decision to write using categories where possible. The committee to revise the 2001 Code consciously sought to do the same.

It is important to take specific note of the dates of these provisions. They are evidence that in many instances nursing was significantly ahead of society in its demand for respect for persons regardless of their personal attributes. In particular, nursing's ethical concern and actions on behalf of and for persons of color was decades ahead of the civil rights movement. The directives are resolute and crystal clear: patient personal attributes, circumstances, or life choices are never grounds for prejudice and may be used *only* to individualize care in accord with patient needs. Nurses are expected to have a "broad social vision," that is a tolerance, or better, to be welcoming of human differences, and to affirm human dignity whatever those differences. Prejudice is never acceptable and where present must be set aside.

What is *prejudice*? It is a harmful or damaging opinion of another person or a class of persons that is rooted in bias, preference, preconception, antagonism, or unreasoned dislike.[44] *Discrimination* is different in that it differentiates between and among persons on the basis of relevant differences (e.g., age-based drinking, driving, voting, and marriage requirements) and should not be confused with prejudice which is a form of *unjust discrimination*. Prejudice can occur at individual or societal (structural) levels, and include processes of *othering* (regarding another person or group as alien, as different from the norm),[45] marginalization, silencing their voice, essentializing, racializing, classing, subordinating, and more.[46] These processes are challenged by a wide range of feminist, postcolonial, and critical theories.

Patient care decisions are rightly affected by all of those attributes listed above, not to be used prejudicially, but in order to provide care that is individualized based on those attributes. In relationships with patients, nurses respect patient decisions, but:

> respect for patient decisions does not require that the nurse agree with or support all patient choices. When patient choices are risky or self-destructive, nurses have an obligation to address the behavior and to offer opportunities and resources to modify the behavior or to eradicate the risk.[47]

The focus of this brief interpretative statement is upon patient attributes and factors that could potentially provoke a nurse's prejudice(s) and negatively influence nursing care. The second provision includes a section on the primacy of the patient's interests and speaks further to the nurse–patient relationship. (An ethic of care is discussed under Interpretive Statement 2.1.)

1.3 The Nature of Health

The nurse's responsibility regarding health has expanded over the last 150 years. Initially the focus was upon the health of the patient and those about the patient and the health of the public. It is important to note that from the start of modern nursing in the United States in the 1870s, nurses were directed toward both the health of the patient and the health of the public. Eventually, in 2001, this obligation came to encompass the promotion and access to health nationally, internationally, and globally, as well as the development of health policy and health diplomacy, and the ablation of health disparities worldwide. The progression of these obligations can be seen in provisions of each of the successive codes. Selected examples include the following:

1926   "the mutuality of aim of medicine and nursing; the aims, to cure and prevent disease and promote positive health," and "the health of the public...building positive health in the community."[48]

1940   Her role as a bearer of comfort and health to the sick, the injured, and the feeble, dates from the early days of Christianity, but in the modern conception of nursing the prevention of disease and the promotion of health are at least as important...as the care and treatment of the sick. Indeed, these functions cannot be separated although they are undoubtedly represented in different proportions in the different fields of nursing. Moreover, the nurse is essentially a teacher and an agent of health in whatever field she may be working.

"she will welcome and utilize opportunities to offer suggestions and help for the health protection of the individual, the family, and the community."[49]

1976 and 1985 "Provision 11: The nurse collaborates with members of the health professions and other citizens in promoting community and national efforts to meet the health needs of the public."[50,51]

2001   "Provision 8: The nurse collaborates with other health professionals and the public in promoting community, national, and international efforts to meet health needs."[52]

2015   "Provision 8: The nurse collaborates with other health professionals and the public to protect human rights, promote health diplomacy, and reduce health disparities."[53]

In the late 1960s, the Code still emphasizes both the health of the patient and the public (at times identified as "citizens"), but by 1976 it comes to include national health needs. The transition point in the expansion of the understanding of influences upon health is in the 2001 Code. Provision 8.1 becomes a major expansion of nursing's scope of concern for health:

> The nursing profession is committed to promoting the health, welfare, and safety of all people. The nurse has a responsibility to be award of not only health needs of individual patients but also of broader health concerns such as world hunger, environmental pollution, lack of access to health care, violation of human rights, and inequitable distribution of nursing and healthcare resources. [54]

Through 1985, the word *citizens* is used—nurses were to collaborate with other health professions and citizens to promote health. With an increased public awareness of the health needs of non-citizen immigrants, especially those persons who immigrated without documents, the term citizens is dropped from the Code.

Between 1985 and 2001, global interactions escalated through technological means and the globe began to shrink. The current Ebola crisis in 2014 made US residents acutely aware of global health and the danger of contagion and pandemic. The health of the public must move from citizens to all residents of the nation, and from an insular regional or national concern to global concern.

Nursing, in part through its historic concern for public health and the social determinants of illness, has increased its civic engagement and civic professionalism decade by decade. This is reflected in the 2001 Code in its concern for nursing organizations:

> to speak collectively for nurses in shaping and reshaping health care within our nation, specifically in areas of healthcare policy and legislation…. In these activities health is understood as being broader than delivery and reimbursement systems, but extending to health-related sociocultural issues such as violation of human rights, homelessness, hunger, violence and the stigma of illness.[55]

Civic engagement refers to taking the values and ideals of nursing into political life. While technical professionalism focuses on the acquisition, mastery, and implementation of the technical knowledge and skills of nursing in the delivery of patient care, civic professionalism sets nursing and nursing care within the broader moral and political context that shapes health and health care. (See also Chapter 2 on an ethic of care that sets care within the broader social, moral, and political context.) Boyte and Fretz write of the task of civic engagement as engendering "civic professionals who will renew a robust sense of the public purposes of their work and will develop and sustain a far more public culture for collaborative, visible, open work."[56] Nursing has never lost the "robust sense of public purpose of [its] work." However, the 2015 Code amplifies that role in several ways, calling nurses to engagement that serves the common good, seeks social justice, raises international health diplomacy to parity with economic and other concerns, leads collaborative efforts for health policy and legislation that positively impacts health, protects human rights, and address the structural, social, and institutional inequalities and disparities that are damaging to health and well-being.[57] While every nurse is called upon to contribute, no one nurse can meet this obligation alone. Civic engagement through civic professionalism requires collaborative and united efforts among nurses and with other health professions, activists, and organizations.

1.4 The Right to Self-Determination

The right to self-determination does not appear in the Code until 1968, at which point it refers to the patient's right to self-determination as a participant in research. From 1976 forward, with the rise of the field of bioethics, however, the patient's right to self-determination receives considerable emphasis in the first provision and interpretive statements, from the 1976 to 2015 Codes.[58,59,60]

While the content of these provisions is essentially the same, they become more precise over the years. In addition, unlike the 1976 provision and inferentially in the 1985 provision, the 2001 Code explicitly roots self-determination in human dignity, as does the 2015 Code.

The bioethical principle that generates the duty to respect patient self-determination is the principle of respect for autonomy. It is one of the four principles commonly used in bioethics discussions and on institutional ethics committees: respect for autonomy, nonmaleficence, beneficence (sometimes combined with nonmaleficence), and justice. Principles are used to specify our moral duties and aid in ethical analysis and decision-making. The principle of respect for autonomy specifies that we have an ethical duty to respect the autonomous decisions of others. The principle is best explicated in the work of Beauchamp and Childress, *Principles of Biomedical Ethics*,[61] and more briefly in *The Belmont Report.*[62] Both works largely follow Kant's interpretation of autonomy and the need to respect it.

In Kant, autonomy is *rational self-legislation* (self-rule), which describes persons who make rational choices free of non-rational internal constraints or influences (such as habit, compulsion, depression, mental illness, inebriation) and also free of non-rational external constraints (such as duress, fraud, coercion, undue influence). Autonomous choices are intentional, rational, and free. The autonomous person acts freely in accord with her or his own values and a self-chosen plan. At times one may rationally choose to not to affirm one's own values, and it remains an autonomous decision nonetheless.

For example, a person may refuse medical treatment necessary to sustain life because of the financial burden it would impose. In the context of ethics, even children can make autonomous choices (though the law does not necessarily honor those choices). Autonomy may also fluctuate, as in a person with Alzheimer's disease who has good days and bad days. In addition, persons who are generally autonomous may not always be autonomous. An acute knee injury involving a degree of severe pain may render the athlete non-autonomous. Assessments of autonomy need to be made in the moment.

The *principle of respect for autonomy* specifies our duty to respect the autonomous choices of others. It is important to note that the principle is not a principle of autonomy. It is the principle of *respect for autonomy*. There is no principle of autonomy; *autonomy* by itself is not a principle. Often when it is listed as a principle, look carefully and you will see "respect for" in the nearby text. Recall that principles specify duties. If autonomy itself were a principle, it would mean that each of us has a duty to act autonomously. We are not, however, obligated to act autonomously. Many of life's choices are made non-autonomously, whether by habit, compulsion, coercion, or simply without rational consideration. We do things we would rather not because we have been asked by a friend; we choose on the basis of taste, color, preference, or habit; we go into 'auto-pilot mode' when tired; we succumb to peer pressure and "go with the flow" when we would rather not; we eat the whole batch of snickerdoodle cookies before we realize that the plate is empty. Where healthcare decisions are required, however, we want patients to make free, intentional, autonomous decisions, and we are called upon to respect them.

For patient decisions to be autonomous, two conditions must be met. Patients need adequate and accurate information and their decisions need to be *voluntary*. In clinical practice these two conditions are actualized through the process of informed consent. *Informedness* requires that the patient or research participant have all the materially relevant information necessary to make a decision in accord with her or his values, situation, and context. *Voluntariness* specifies the need to be free of controlling influences, whether internal or external.

The emphasis upon respect for autonomy, informed consent, and voluntariness emerged, in large part, as a response to the Nazi medical atrocities of WWII. These came to light in 1947, at the trial of 27 Nazi physicians.[63] In the aftermath of the discoveries of the horrific, often lethal, experiments that were conducted on non-consenting human prisoners, a number of international documents were ratified that enshrined the legal and moral requirement to protect persons who might become research participants by requiring consent.[64] These documents include The *Nuremberg Code*,[65] the 1949 World Medical Association (WMA) *Declaration of Geneva*,[66] and the

WMA *Declaration of Helsinki – Ethical Principles for Medical Research Involving Human Subjects,*[67] and later documents such as *The Belmont Report* noted above. It is important to note that nurses were complicit in the medical killings in Nazi Germany, both in euthanizing persons and in the conduct of medical experimentation on unwilling prisoners.[68,69,70,71]

Because valid informed consent requires voluntariness, in situations where the person is nonvoluntary and thereby unable to make a decision by reason of her or his situation (e.g., in a coma, too young, too ill, inebriated, etc.), decisions are to be made in the *best interests* of the patient and may be made by a *surrogate* decision-maker. Interpretive Statement 1.4 includes legal surrogates in the informed consent process. A *surrogate* is someone who acts on behalf of another when that person cannot act on his or her own behalf. Surrogates are needed for persons whose condition or status does not allow them to participate, such as a person who is unconscious, an infant, or a person with severe intellectual compromise. A surrogate might be appointed by a court or might be designated by a patient through an advance directive. The duty of a surrogate is to make the decision on behalf of the person or patient that they themselves would have made if they were able to do so, or if the person's wishes could not be ascertained, to make the decision in the best interests of the person or patient.

At times, a court may appoint a surrogate, in which case the surrogate may or may not know the patient. In the situation of a formerly autonomous patient whose surrogate knows the patient, the *substituted judgment* standard is used. That means that the surrogate stands in for the patient and makes a decision that the patient would have made were he or she able to do so. That is, the surrogate should base the decision on the known views, values, and desires of the patient. Where the surrogate does not know what the patient would have wanted, and those wishes cannot be known through other means (e.g., they were put in writing), or where the patient was never autonomous, then the surrogate must make the decision that is in the best interests of the patient. In neither case does the surrogate make the decision based on the surrogate's own preferences and desires. Beauchamp and Childress note that "the best interests standard protects an incompetent person's welfare interests by requiring surrogates to assess the risks and probable benefits of various treatments and alternatives to treatment. It is therefore inescapably a quality-of-life criterion."[72]

Autonomous decisions do not have to be made solely by the individual patient alone. Autonomous decisions may be made by a patient with family members, or the patient within her or his community of reference. This may reflect a cultural pattern or may simply reflect a patient's preferences and commitments.

At times, an overweening commitment to respecting patient autonomy has lead health professionals to refuse to advise patients. This goes too far. Respect for patient autonomy does not mean that health professionals may not offer a professional opinion or advice. It does mean that such advice should be offered truthfully and noncoercively. In the 2015 Code, nursing bases its commitment to respect for autonomy in human dignity. Nurses offer information and advice to patients in ways that exercise compassion, affirm patient dignity, and recognize the uniqueness of the patient as a person.

1.5 Relationships with Colleagues and Others

The content of this interpretive statement introduces several themes to be repeated throughout the 2015 revision. Some would argue the content more properly belongs under Provision 6, and in fact some of the concepts of this section are elaborated under Provision 6. However, this brief section on relationships with colleagues is placed here to emphasize that this provision—"The nurse practices with compassion and respect for the inherent dignity, worth, and unique attributes of every person"—is meant to be applied everyone, not only to patients. Some of the themes are ethical environment, caring relationships, fair treatment, and conflict resolution. This interpretive statement also introduces the explicit intent of the Code to include all nurses, in all roles and all settings. It also recognizes the excellent contributions of others who work alongside nurses to achieve safe, effective, quality outcomes everywhere they work.

Lateral violence or *bullying* (or *mobbing*) in the workplace is denounced by the following quote: "[T]he nurse creates an ethical environment, a culture of civility and kindness, treating colleagues, coworkers, employees, students, and others with dignity and respect. This standard of conduct includes an affirmative duty to act to prevent harm."[73] This includes all nursing relationships with colleagues, administrators, educators, researchers—in short—,with everyone. That nurses have an affirmative duty is clearly articulated. This duty goes beyond not participating in harassment or intimidation; nurses must be proactive; they must to act to prevent harm. The hallmarks of these relationships are respect, caring, fairness, transparency, integrity, civility, kindness, dignity, respect, and collaboration. This is a relational environment in which all might thrive and flourish.

Cases

The cases in each of the chapters are intended to provide the opportunity to reflect upon the content of the specific provision and interpretive statements. The cases may be used for group discussion or for personal reflection. A list of suggested questions for consideration of the cases is provided in the introduction to the book.

Case 1

Jean Thatcher is a 47-year-old single white attorney with multiple sclerosis. She is frequently admitted to the transitional care facility for complications related to her multiple sclerosis. Since she quickly exhausts the patience and best efforts of the staff, she is rotated among several units, all of whom know her well and her inpatient stays on their unit are anticipated with fear and trepidation. The staff's best efforts to educate her about appropriate self-care and preventive practices have fallen on deaf ears. She refuses to cooperate when her support is elicited for bathing, position changes, and the like. Her one visitor, her mother, believes that the staff discriminates against her and complains frequently to administration. Both the patient and her mother frequently threaten to sue the hospital for neglect and discrimination. Jean admits that she is refusing to eat or help with bathing and positioning. She says she has "had enough" and wants to give up. Most of the staff have already given up and ask why they should try to help Jean when she has been clear about not wanting their help. Today, one nurse was overheard saying, "I'm not going to sprain my back trying to get her to move when she refuses to cooperate. It's on her if her skin breaks down." The nurse manager calls a meeting to explore how the team might more effectively and compassionately respond to the challenges of caring for Ms Thatcher.

Case 2

Ms Rogers staggers into the emergency room at 2:00 a.m. complaining of abdominal pain. Well-known to the ER staff, she is a homeless Gulf War Veteran, retired US Army Sergeant, and has a history of alcoholism and PTSD. There are too few homeless shelters for women and those few are currently full. She does not go to the VA hospital to receive care as it is 22 miles away and she has no transportation. The night is cold and there is freezing rain. The resident called to examine Ms Rogers does not "work-up" the complaint of belly pain, instead saying that, once again, Ms Rogers only wants a warm bed for the night, a bath, and something to eat.

Case 3

Victoria Oliver is the dean of a small nursing school, respected for the excellence of its programs. The school is successful and has a welcoming and collegial environment and because of this, low faculty turnover. However, health problems have brought about the resignation of one of the pediatric nursing faculty. Multiple candidates have applied but two have risen to the top. Both are highly qualified with excellent backgrounds in teaching, research, publications, and professional engagement. Candidate #1 has slightly more experience. The faculty search committee has come to a draw and has recommended both candidates to the dean, who must now choose one of them. Candidate #1 is from a well-known and prestigious university, and Candidate #2 is from a small, well-regarded school similar in size to the Dean's school. Prior to interviewing the candidates, it is brought to Dean Oliver's attention that Candidate #1 has posted to her social media page that her father has macular degeneration. In addition, that candidate has also posted information that displays an extreme political bent. The faculty member who brought this information to the Dean's attention is a friend of Candidate #2.

ENDNOTES

All URLs were current when accessed on January 9, 2015.

[1] *Oxford English Dictionary Online*, "Compassion," http://0www.oed.com.patris.apu.edu/view/Entry/37475?isAdvanced=false&result=1&rskey=bl0Sx2&

[2] Oxford English Dictionary Online, "Patient," http://0www.oed.com.patris.apu.edu/view/Entry/138820?result=1&rskey=fhetaF&

[3] Joseph Kitigawa (ed.), *The Religious Traditions of Asia: Religion, History, and Culture* (New York: Routledge, 2013).

[4] Alf Hiltebeitel, "Hinduism," in *The Religious Traditions of Asia: Religion, History, and Culture*, ed. Joseph Kitigawa (New York: Routledge, 2013), 120–121.

[5] BC (Before Christ) and AD (Anno Domini; In the Year of Our Lord) is a system of dating that uses the life of Jesus of Nazareth as the referent. It is customary in academic circles to use the designation BCE (Before the Common Era) and CE (in the Common Era) in place of BC and AD. The year designations otherwise remain the same.

[6] *SpokenSanskrit*, "Compassion," http://spokensanskrit.de/index.php?tinput=compassion&direction=ES&script=HK&link=yes&beginning=0

[7] Kutumba Sastry, "Compassion: Etymology, Rituals, Anecdotes from the Hindu Tradition," in *Compassion in the World's Religions: Envisioning Human Solidarity*, eds. Anindita Balslev and Dirk Evers (Münster, Germany: Lit Verlag, 2010), 43–44.

[8] Bhikkhu –Ñāóamoli, trans., *Bhadantácariya Buddhaghosa's Visuddhimagga*, 3rd online edition. Translated from the Pali by Bhikkhu –Ñāóamoli, 2011, 311.

[9] Chinese Buddhist Encyclopedia, "Karuṇā," http://www.chinabuddhismencyclopedia.com/en/index.php?title=Karuṇā

[10] William Irwin, "Liberation through Compassion and Kindness: the Buddhist Eightfold Path as Philosophy of Life," *Journal of Philosophy of Life* 3, no. 1 (January 2013): 69–70.

[11] Robert Kugler and Patrick Hartin, *An Introduction to the Bible* (Grand Rapids, MI: WB Eerdmans, 2009), 193.

[12] Bruce Metzger and Roland Murphy (eds.), *The New Oxford Annotated Bible with Apocryphal/Deuterocanonical Books: New Revised Standard Version* (NY: Oxford University Press, 1994), 6260T.

[13] Ibid.

[14] Marsha Fowler, "Come; Give Me a Taste of Shalom," in *Nursing and Health Care Ethics: A Legacy and a Vision*, eds. W. Pinch and A. Haddad (Silver Spring, MD: ANA Publishing, 2008), 269–81.

[15] Aristotle, *Nichomachean Ethics*, Book III, trans. Martin Ostwald (Indianapolis, IN: Bobbs-Merrill, 1962), 33–51.

[16] Aristotle. *Rhetoric* (Book 1), trans. W. Rhys Roberts (Mineola, NY: Dover Publications, 2004) Chapter 7, section 1385b.

[17] Martha C. Nussbaum, *Upheavals of Thought: The Intelligence of Emotions* (Cambridge, UK: Cambridge University Press, 2001), 319.

[18] Margreet van der Cingel, "Compassion and Professional Care: Exploring the Domain," *Nursing Philosophy* 10, no. 2 (April 2009): 134–35.

[19] Margreet van der Cingel, "Compassion: The Missing Link in Quality of Care," *Nurse Education Today* 34, no. 9 (September 2014): 1255.

[20] See for example: Collette Straughair, "Exploring compassion: Implications for contemporary nursing, P. 1," *British Journal of Nursing* 21, no. 3 (February 2012): 160–64.

21 The full text of the *Charter for Compassion* is available at this webpage: http://charterforcompassion.org/charter

22 American Nurses Association, "A Tentative Code," *American Journal of Nursing* 40, no. 9 (1940): 977–80.

23 American Nurses Association, *Code of Ethics for Nurses with Interpretive Statements* (Silver Spring, MD: ANA, 2001), 11.

24 American Nurses Association, *Code of Ethics for Nurses with Interpretive Statements* (Silver Spring, MD: ANA, 2015), 1.

25 United Nations, *Universal Declaration of Human Rights* (General Assembly, 1948), http://www.un.org/en/documents/udhr/

26 Marcus Düwell, "Human Dignity: Concepts, Discussions, Philosophical Perspectives," in *The Cambridge Handbook of Human Dignity: Interdisciplinary Perspectives*, eds. Marcus Düwell, Jens Braarvig, Roger Brownsword, and Dietmar Mieth (Cambridge, UK: Cambridge University Press, 2014), 23.

27 Daniel Sulmasy, "Dignity and Bioethics: History, Theory, and Selected Applications," in President's Council on Bioethics, *Human Dignity and Bioethics* (Washington, DC: USGPO, March 2008), 493.

28 Ibid.

29 Ibid.

30 Düwell, "Human Dignity," 25–27.

31 Ibid., 27.

32 *Oxford English Dictionary Online*, "Inviolable," http://0-www.oed.com.patris.apu.edu/view/Entry/99105?redirectedFrom=inviolable&

33 Ruth Macklin, "Dignity is a Useless Concept," *British Medical Journal* 327, no. 7429 (December 2003): 1419–20.

34 Ruth Macklin, "Reflections on the Human Dignity Symposium: Is Dignity a Useless Concept?" *Journal of Palliative Care* 20, no. 3 (Autumn 2004): 121–26.

35 Adam Schulman, "Bioethics and the Question of Human Dignity," in President's Council on Bioethics, *Human Dignity and Bioethics* (Washington, DC: USGPO, March 2008), 11.

36 ANA, Tentative Code, 978.

37 American Nurses Association, *A Code for Professional Nurses* (NY: ANA, 1950).

38 American Nurses Association, *Interpretation of the Statements of the Code for Professional Nurses* (New York: ANA, 1960), 6.

39 ANA. *A Code for Professional Nurses.* (New York: ANA, 1968), 3.

40 ANA, *Code of Ethics for Nurses with Interpretive Statements* (Kansas City, MO: ANA, 1976), 4.

41 ANA, *Code of Ethics for Nurses with Interpretive Statements* (Kansas City, MO: ANA, 1985), 3.

42 ANA, *Code of Ethics for Nurses with Interpretive Statements*(2001).

43 ANA, *Code of Ethics for Nurses with Interpretive Statements*(2015), 1.

44 *Oxford English Dictionary Online.* "Prejudice," http://0-www.oed.com.patris.apu.edu/view/Entry/150162?rskey=IfkR4q&result=1#eid

45 Edward W. Saïd, *Orientalism* (25th Anniversary Edition) (New York: Pantheon Books, 1978).

46 Sheryl Reimer-Kirkham and Joan Anderson, "Postcolonial Nursing Scholarship: From Epistemology to Method," *Advances in Nursing Science* 25, no. 1 (2002): 1–17.

47 ANA, *Code of Ethics for Nurses with Interpretive Statements* (2015), 1.

48 American Nurses Association, "A Suggested Code," *American Journal of Nursing* 26, no. 8 (August 1926): 599–601.

[49] ANA, "Tentative Code."

[50] ANA, *Code of Ethics for Nurses with Interpretive Statements*(1976), 19.

[51] ANA, *Code of Ethics for Nurses with Interpretive Statements*(1985), 16.

[52] ANA, *Code of Ethics for Nurses with Interpretive Statements*(2001), 29.

[53] ANA, *Code of Ethics for Nurses with Interpretive Statements*(2015), 31.

[54] ANA, *Code of Ethics for Nurses with Interpretive Statements*(2001), 28–29.

[55] Ibid., 31.

[56] Harry Boyte and Eric Fretz, "Civic Professionalism," *Journal of Higher Education Outreach and Engagement* 14, no. 2 (2010): 69.

[57] ANA, *Code of Ethics for Nurses with Interpretive Statements*(2015), 32.

[58] ANA, *Code of Ethics for Nurses with Interpretive Statements*(1976), 4.

[59] ANA, *Code of Ethics for Nurses with Interpretive Statements*(1985), 2.

[60] ANA, *Code of Ethics for Nurses with Interpretive Statements*(2001), 12–13.

[61] Tom Beauchamp and James Childress, *Principles of Biomedical Ethics* (7th ed.) (New York: Oxford University Press, 2013).

[62] The National Commission for the Protection of Human Subjects of Biomedical and Behavioral Research of the U.S. Department of Health and Human Services, *The Belmont Report: Ethical Principles and Guidelines for the Protection of Human Subjects of Research* (Washington, D.C.: DHHS/USGPO, 1979) , available at http://www.hhs.gov/ohrp/humansubjects/guidance/belmont.html

[63] George J. Annas and Michael A. Grodin, *The Nazi Doctors and the Nuremberg Code* (New York: Oxford University Press, 1992).

[64] Robert Jay Lifton, *The Nazi Doctors: Medical Killing and the Psychology of Genocide* (New York: Basic Books, 1986).

[65] "The Nuremberg Code," Department of Health and Human Services, http://www.hhs.gov/ohrp/archive/nurcode.html

[66] World Medical Association, *Declaration of Geneva*(1949), available at http://www.wma.net/en/30publications/10policies/g1/

[67] World Medical Association, *Declaration of Helsinki – Ethical Principles for Medical Research Involving Human Subjects* (Helsinki, Finland: General Assembly, 1964), http://www.wma.net/en/30publications/10policies/b3/

[68] Thomas Froth, "Nurses, medical records and the killing of sick persons before, during, and after the Nazi regime in Germany," *Nursing Inquiry* 20, no. 2 (2013): 92–100. See also: Thomas Froth, "Understanding 'Caring' through Biopolitics: The Case of Nurses under the Nazi Regime," *Nursing Philosophy* 14, no. 4 (2013): 284–94.

[69] Susan Benedict, Arthur Caplan, and Traute Lafrenz Page, "Duty and 'Euthanasia': The Nurses of Meseritz-Obrawalde," *Nursing Ethics* 14, no. 6 (2007): 781–94.

[70] Andrew McKie, "'The Demolition of a Man': Lessons from Holocaust Literature for the Teaching of Nursing Ethics," *Nursing Ethics* 11, no. 2 (2004): 138–49.

[71] Mary Lagerwey, "Nursing Ethics at Hadamar," *Qualitative Health Research* 9, no. 6 (November 1999): 759–72.

[72] Beauchamp and Childress, *Principles of Biomedical Ethics*, 228–29.

[73] ANA, *Code of Ethics for Nurses with Interpretive Statements*(2015), 4.

Provision 2

The nurse's primary commitment is to the patient, whether an individual, family, group, community, or population.

Provision 2. The Patient as Nursing's Foundational Commitment

Introduction

Even though this commitment is present in the nursing literature from the earliest days, it first appears as a provision in the 2001 Code. This provision addresses the question "What is the nature of the relationship that the nurse has with a patient?" It is a relationship that is both complicated and simple. It is complicated in that frequently the nurse is an employee and there is an employer expectation of loyalty. But the nurse is also caring for a patient, and the nurse–patient relationship, the primary relationship, is also one that creates loyalty. This creates a situation of dual or competing loyalties for the nurse. Competing loyalties arise when the nurse has allegiances or commitments, with attendant obligations, to separate entities that may come into conflict with one another. Competing loyalties occur in a wide variety of situations: the nurse involved in clinical care on a research unit, or serving in a hurricane when their own family might be in danger, or called upon to give care to an enemy combatant, assigned to force feed prisoners, or asked to place an intravenous line for the lethal injection of a criminal. All persons hold multiple, potentially conflicting, loyalties. Ronald Corwin, who examines the role conflict that arises when professional nursing values and ideals come into conflict with bureaucratic (employer) values, maintains that nurses must have some loyalty to patients, some loyalty to the employer, and some loyalty to the profession, and that it is the relative weight and priority accorded to each of those loyalties that is the ground for potential conflict.[1] (See Provision 6 on moral distress.)

Loyalty has been under-researched by nursing. Much of the research that has been done relates loyalty, without defining it, to employer and nurse satisfaction, employee retention, or to nurses remaining in nursing. What loyalty is, as a concept, is not explored. It is necessary to turn to the philosophical literature for a conceptual analysis of loyalty, particularly its relationship to ethics. Oldenquist maintains that loyalties are "self-dependent normative judgments," that is:

> When I have a loyalty toward something I have somehow come to view it as mine…I am disposed to feel pride when it prospers, shame when it declines, and anger or indignation when it is harmed. In general, people care about the objects of their loyalties, and they acknowledge obligations that they would not acknowledge were it not for their loyalties. Unlike the object of self-interest, an object of loyalty can be shared or "owned" by a number of people. In this case I (and others) can speak of *our* family, community, country, etc. and not just of *my* family.[2]

So loyalty arises because this is *my* school of nursing, *my* hospital, *my* community, *my* profession—and it is also *our* school, *our* hospital, *our* community, and *our* profession, as a shared loyalty. But is loyalty a specifically *moral* norm?

> Loyalty is not self-interested, because people can sacrifice, in the name of loyalty, their happiness and even their lives, and it probably is this element of potential self-sacrifice that makes most people classify motives of loyalty as moral motives…loyalty is positive and is primarily characterized by esteem and concern for the common good of one's group.[3]

Oldenquist holds that loyalty is the basis for social morality, for shared morality, and for acts that further the common good. He also makes an additional point that is worthy of note: loyalty can be lost when the object of loyalty is no longer worthy of loyalty.[4]

The Nightingale Pledge carries a two-fold loyalty: "With loyalty will endeavor to aid the physician in his work and devote myself to the welfare of those committed to my care."[5]

2.1 Primacy of the Patient's Interests

Because the nurse's primary commitment is to the patient, it carries the greatest weight and priority and consequently it trumps all other loyalties. As Corwin notes, it is the relative weight and priority accorded to each of those loyalties that is the ground for potential conflict.[6] Realistically, it supersedes all other loyalties within the professional sphere, but perhaps not in the personal sphere if the welfare of one's family is at stake—not inconvenience to the family, but its actual welfare.

Loyalty is not the whole of the relationship, for the nurse–patient relationship is much larger than loyalty. Many have captured the nature of that relationship as situated within an "ethic of care."[7] Of the various approaches to ethics, such as ethical principlism (see Chapter 3), or virtue ethics (see Chapter 5), an ethic of care has gained a degree of prominence in nursing that it has not yet achieved in other disciplines. While it is not itself a feminist theory of ethics, it has roots in feminism. Care ethics arose during the Lawrence Kohlberg–Carol Gilligan debate of the late 1970s. Kohlberg had developed a hierarchical stage theory of moral development, focusing on cognitive psychological structures, as Jean Piaget had before him. His theory proposed three levels with two stages in each level. The levels and stages of moral development are:

Level 1:   Pre-conventional
Stage 1. Obedience and punishment orientation (avoidance of punishment)
Stage 2. Self-interest orientation

Level 2:   Conventional
Stage 3. Interpersonal accord and conformity (adherence to social norms)
Stage 4. Authority and social-order maintaining orientation (obey the law)

Level 3:   Post-Conventional
Stage 5. Social contract orientation (acknowledge pluralism; mutuality of respect)
Stage 6. Universal ethical principles (principle based conscience and reasoning)[8]

Kohlberg claims that in his final stage, "universal ethical principles," moral reasoning is based on the use of abstract, universal ethical principles. It is heavily justice-centered in this stage. Based on his research, initially using only male subjects, he claimed that few people reached Stage 6, that women only tended to develop to Stage 3, and that while men employed abstract ethical reasoning at a level beyond that of women, women tended to focus instead on the welfare of family and friends and relationships. Gilligan challenged Kohlberg's theory and findings as androcentric and as formulating an inadequate account of the moral values and reasoning of women. Gilligan developed an alternate theory of moral reasoning, in three stages, based on an ethic of care that reinterpreted justice from a gendered perspective.[9] Subsequent research has shown that care-based versus justice-based approaches to ethics are not gender-based.[10]

Two streams of work and theory developed, one focused on the art and science of caring in nursing, and the other specifically on an ethic of care (not limited to nursing). The two streams intermingle at points. Those whose work has been foundational and who have furthered the theory of human care and caring, with which an ethic of care is associated, include Noddings,[11] Tronto,[12,13] Baier,[14] Benner,[15] Held,[16] Sevenhuijsen,[17] Slote,[18] Watson,[19] Leininger,[20] and Roach.[21]

A considerable amount of research and theory development, more specifically on an ethic of care, has taken place in Europe.[22] For example, the International Care Ethics (ICE) Observatory in Surrey, England (formerly the International Centre for Nursing Ethics) has the following as its overall aim: "The ICE Observatory acts as an inter-disciplinary, national and international hub of educational, organisational and research expertise and activity to revalue care and promote an in-depth understanding of, and commitment to, ethics in health and social care."[23] The ICE Observatory is the home of the first nursing journal devoted entirely to ethics, *Nursing Ethics: An International Journal for Health Care Professionals*, which began in 1994.

An ethic of care starts with the concept of relationship. This is not simply the nurse–patient relationship but rather the entire relational nexus in which the nurse and patient are situated. This would include the patient and the patient's family or close relationships. It also includes the nurse, and the healthcare team. Beyond that it includes the institution or agency in which care takes place, for the institution's policies and ethos will affect care and the ways in which it is given. And looking even farther, beyond that relationship, also includes society and its expectations for what care is and how it should be given. Even our relationships with the natural environment have a place in an ethic of care. Advocates for an ethic of care claim that an ethic of care successfully overcomes the limitations of ethical principlism. In particular, they maintain that ethical principlism sees clinical cases as conflicts or dilemmas and in doing so problematizes clinical ethical decision-making in nursing. Benner et al. assert that:

> Nursing students need to learn about critical ethics and dilemma ethics, but also everyday ethical comportment related to relational or care ethics. Students must learn everyday ethical comportment and the notions of good central to the profession. Student nurses need to learn the ethics of care and responsibility, the ethos of self-care in the profession, skills of involvement, and clinical reasoning. Students need to be able to reflect on and articulate their everyday ethical concerns, and not limit their understanding to ethical breakdowns and dilemmas.[24]

Early development of an ethic of care focused more narrowly on dyads such as mother–child or nurse–patient. Initial theoretical development was somewhat diffuse or vague and failed to specify whether care was a duty, virtue, value (end that was to be sought), emotion, feeling, or trait of personality. Gastmans argues that care is a virtue.[25] Virtues are habits of moral character that are learned and habituated and are not personality traits or feelings. Virtues predispose a person to do what is right; that is, to meet one's ethical obligations. See Chapter 5 for a discussion of virtue ethics. There was also a tendency to identify an ethic of care as intrinsically gendered.

Tronto's masterful work, *Moral Boundaries: A Political Argument for an Ethics of Care*, sets forth a theory of care that tackles some of the lingering and nagging concerns with prior formulations.[26] She, with Fisher, define care in this way:

> On the most general level, we suggest that caring be viewed as a species activity that includes everything that we do to maintain, continue, and repair our 'world' so that we can live in it as well as possible. That world incudes our bodies, our selves, and our environment, all of which we seek to interweave in a complex, life-sustaining web.[27]

Tronto explicitly rejects what has come to dominate bioethical discourse: a set of universal, impartial, value neutral, ethical principles that form the basis for moral reasoning, decision making, and action. She writes:

> [Philosopher Immanuel] Kant's notion of ethical life set…the boundaries around morality as an autonomous sphere of human life. These boundaries require that morality be derived from human reason in the form of universal principles that are abstract and formal. They require that the social and political connections to morality not be counted as central to morality itself.… And they require that…morality consists of a set of principles that are universalizable, impartial, concerned with describing what is right.

This perspective varies from the dominant approach to bioethics in nursing, called *ethical principlism* (see discussion in Chapters 3 and 6). The "four principles of biomedical ethics" (respect for autonomy, nonmaleficence, beneficence, and justice), in wide use since the 1970s, promulgated by Beauchamp and Childress in their landmark work *Principles of Biomedical Ethics*,[28] and utilized in *The Belmont Report*,[29] provide the prevailing approach to bioethics in clinical practice, on institutional ethics committees, and in the current bioethical literature in medicine and nursing. Instead, Tronto advocates for a contextual morality, an ethic of care.[30]

An ethic of care has four sequential phases: caring about, taking care of, care-giving, and care-receiving.[31] *Caring about* requires the recognition that care is necessary and an assessment of what the needs for care might be. Caring about is "culturally and individually shaped."[32] *Taking care of* "involves assuming some responsibility for the identified need and determining how to respond to it"[33] and involves concepts of agency and responsibility. *Care-giving* involves directly meeting the needs for care and generally ("almost always") involves direct contact. Providing the money for care activities "is more a form of taking care of than it is a form of care-giving." [33] *Care-receiving* requires that the object (person, recipient) of care respond to the care received. This is "the only way to know that caring needs have been met."[34] Care-receiving serves another function as well. It prevents the care-giver from making assumptions about what care is needed or how the need should be met without actually determining this in mutuality and communication with the recipient of care.[35]

While Gastmans, as noted above, views care as a virtue, Tronto maintains that care is a practice and neither a principle nor an emotion. As a practice, it involves both thought and action that are interrelated and directed toward a specified end. She calls it "practical rationality." [36] What guides this practical rationality toward care? Here, all four phases of care and the related four moral elements of care must be employed as an integrated whole for care to be demonstrated.

In addition to the four phases of care, there are four corollary moral elements: attentiveness, responsibility, competence, and responsiveness.[36] *Attentiveness* requires recognizing need; ignoring, or ignorance of, others and their need is regarded as a moral failing or moral evil. Tronto points to several issues regarding attentiveness. First, one must both be attentive to one's own needs for care, and be able to set them aside in order to see the care needs of others. Overidentification with the care recipient is also to be avoided. In an ethic of care, *responsibility* becomes "a central moral category."[37] *Responsibility* differs from *obligation* in that "responsibility is embedded in a set of implicit cultural practices, rather than a set of formal rules or series of promises. …we are better served by focusing on a flexible notion of responsibility than we are by continuing to use obligation as the basis for understanding what people should do for each other."[38] Thus, responsibility is more flexible, creative, and generous than is obligation. *Competence* is the third moral element: "how could it not be necessary that the caring work be competently performed in order to demonstrate that one cares?"[39] *Responsiveness* is the fourth moral element. It distinctively refers to the responsiveness of the care receiver to the care given as well as the responsiveness of the care-giver to the care-receiver. This dual responsiveness works to prevent both the domination and subordination that can occur in unequal relationships and any abuse of care-receiver vulnerability.[40]

Tronto takes note of the vulnerability and inequality that intrinsically exist in relationships of care. The one who needs care is made vulnerable by that very need. That vulnerability intrinsically entails a loss of autonomy to some degree, making one dependent upon another to have that need met. The use of abstract, allegedly value-neutral, universal moral principles such as respect for autonomy is at odds with Tronto's ethic of care.

Benner and Wrubel noted early on that nursing and care are both devalued. They too reject an ethics of abstract, universal, decontextualized, rational principles. They write that:

> In a highly technical society that values autonomy, individualism, and competitiveness, caring practices have always been fragile, but this societal blindness causes those who value technological advances to overlook the ways these advances are rendered dangerous and unfeasible without a context of skillful, compassionate care. The dominant view of knowledge in the Western tradition emphasizes abstract, general, theoretical knowledge while overlooking and devaluing local, specific, practical knowledge and expert skillful clinical judgments about particular clinical situations.[41]

The devaluing of care is important as it affects nursing within the institutions and agencies that employ it. However, the devaluing of care is important in the larger global context, a concern of Provisions 8 and 9. An important body of literature has developed on the devaluation of care as *intimate labor*.[42] Intimate labor is largely behind the scenes labor that is not seen as having the same economic value as, for instance, the fees for nursing care that are folded into a room charge. Nursing falls at the high end of the continuum of intimate labor while housekeeping and childcare fall at the lower end. The concerns of this body of literature are that care is socially and economically devalued. Parreñas and Boris write that "intimate labor emerges as a mechanism that maintains and reflects socioeconomic inequalities."[43] What is important here is that care activities (including nursing care) as forms of intimate labors are tied to economic structures that perpetuate inequality and support a wide range of unjust structures. Issues of social justice will be discussed under provision 9. Care, an ethic of care, and the devaluing of care must be examined beyond the immediate relational context of nursing.

One of the breakthroughs of Tronto's approach to an ethic of care is that she situates an ethic of care within the larger context of politics and the shape of society. When an ethics of care is framed within a socio-political context it has a clear touch-point with nursing's social ethics, especially its concerns for health disparities (see Provisions 8 and 9). But more specifically, she analyzes the place of care in American society as it relates to power and privilege, noting that care is "gendered, raced, and classed."[44] Tronto's ultimate goal is the political re-valuing and centering of an ethic of care.

An ethic of care takes account of the contextual realities of our human lives and, for nursing, provides a capacious moral climate for patient care as well as a perspective for the aims of nursing's social ethics. In an ethic of care, the patient is central, having her or his own contextually shaped care needs. In an ethic of care, the larger social, political and natural environments are also in need of care.

2.2 Conflict of Interest for Nurses

An ethic of care recognizes that care, even good care, involves conflict in a number of ways, not the least of which is that "often care-givers will find that their needs to care for themselves come in conflict with the care that they must give to others."[45] The classic example of this is the nurse in an emergency situation, for example, caring for injured fire fighters in an emergency department, when her or his own family may be in the wildfire evacuation area.

Care-giving may also involve other sorts of conflicts such as caring for a patient whose lifestyle is reprehensible, or caring for an enemy combatant, or caring for a patient who is deeply prejudiced and bigoted. Nurses care for patients and need not agree with or support the value structure of the patient, but work for the patient's health, healing, and well-being nonetheless.

An actual *conflict of interest* refers to situations that place the nurse in a position where a choice must be made between the nurse's own self-interest and the patient's interests. The moral presumption of the nurse–patient relationship in principle-based ethics is that the best interests of the patient will be served. In an ethic of care, conflict of interest strains the larger moral notions of attentiveness and responsibility and the overall framework of the four care phases. The existence of a conflict of interest does not, however, presume that the nurse will make a morally inappropriate choice, but only that the circumstances of the situation raise the risk of such decisions. Several important relational elements come into play in a conflict of interest: [46]

1. A relationship must exist, whether personal or professional.
2. If it is a professional relationship, then there are common role-related expectations and responsibilities.
3. A professional relationship is one of trust with an expectation of loyalty.
4. The nurse's attentiveness has led to the identification of the patient's need(s) for care.
5. Some aspect of the nurse's own self-interest comes into play.
6. The nurse can choose to exercise self-interest over the care need of the patient.
7. Both the nurse's self-interest and the patient's care need(s) conflict.

While conflicts of interest in nursing need not involve money, they often do. For example, School Nurse Davy, as the children call him, serves in three schools in a resource-poor school system. He has far more children to care for than time or resources allow but he still tries to personally involve both the young students and families in caring for their specific health needs. Due to the new state lottery, additional funds derived from the lottery will be allocated to public schools. His three schools would be given extra funding for the school health and student lunch programs if he can demonstrate that the student services quota (number of students seen) has been met. He has been asked to quickly run a number of hearing and vision tests, and also to categorize some of his classroom visits for hygiene and nutrition lectures as separate student contacts in order to raise the school's student services contacts above the quota. Interpretive Statement §2.2 acknowledges financial incentives and that "Healthcare financing and delivery systems may create conflict between economic self-interest and professional integrity."[47] Here the economic self-interest is even more complex in that it involves additional needed funding that would serve the students, and indirectly benefit the school health program. It challenges Nurse Davy's integrity and compassion— without actually putting money into Nurse Davy's pocket. In situations of conflict of interest, the 2015 Code directs nurses to "address such conflicts in ways that ensure patient safety and that promote the patient's best interests while preserving the professional integrity of the nurse and supporting interprofessional collaboration."[48]

2.3 Collaboration

This interpretive statement focuses on collaboration with others, including the patient, to meet patient needs. This differs from collaboration as discussed in the eighth provision, which is collaboration to achieve larger health goals and ends beyond the bedside (see Chapter 8). Here the focus is on the nurse's commitment to the patient and therefore to collaboration that best serves to meets the care needs of the patient. As early as the *Suggested Code* of 1926, it was recognized that more than one discipline would be necessary to achieve the aims of health care: "The key to the situation lies in the mutuality of aim of medicine and nursing; the aims, to cure and prevent disease and promote positive health, are identical, the technics of the two are different and neither profession can secure complete results without the other."[49]

In the 1950, 1957, and 1960 Codes, there is a reference to the healthcare *team*. Initially, that reference is to sustain confidence in the physician and team, then subsequently to work harmoniously with the team. These, then, are not references to collaboration but do acknowledge indirectly that more than a single discipline delivers patient care. The *team* disappears from the 1968 Code, though there are references to working with others to achieve social (rather than patient care) ends. The healthcare team again receives mention in the 1976 Code, but only in reference to the disclosure of information necessary for the team to give appropriate patient care.[50] Provision 6 in the

1985 Code contains a section (§6.3) on consultation and collaboration for patient care:

> The provision of health and illness care to clients is a complex process that requires a wide range of knowledge, skills, and collaborative efforts. Nurses must be aware of their own individual competencies. When the needs of the client are beyond the qualifications and competencies of the nurse, consultation and collaboration must be sought from qualified nurses, other health professionals, or other appropriate sources. Participation in intradisciplinary or interdisciplinary teams is often an effective approach to the provision of high quality total health services.

This is not the most rousing endorsement of collaboration, rather it is collaboration based on necessity. It is not until the 2001 Code that collaboration is more positively embraced, as both intra and interprofessional collaboration:

> Collaboration is not just cooperation, but it is the concerted effort of individuals and groups to attain a shared goal. In health care, that goal is to address the health needs of the patient and the public. The complexity of healthcare delivery systems requires a multi-disciplinary approach to the delivery of services that has the strong support and active participation of all the health professions...Intra-professional collaboration within nursing is fundamental to effectively addressing health needs of patients and the public.[51]

The 2015 revision retains this more positive view of the essential nature of collaboration for patient care:

> The complexity of health care requires collaborative effort that has the strong support and active participation of all health professions. Nurses should actively foster collaborative planning to provide safe, high-quality, patient-centered health care.... Collaboration within nursing is essential to address the health of patients and the public effectively.[52]

In the discussions of collaboration, there is a trajectory across the successive revisions of the code that reflects the social location of nursing, the scientific development of nursing and medicine, specialization, changing nursing practice and advancing nursing roles, and an increasing complexity of healthcare delivery systems. Initially discussions are about working with physicians and sustaining confidence in the physician. Then working harmoniously with the physician and other healthcare professionals emerges. This begins the shift toward using the language of "other health professionals" and a decrease in mention of the "physician." Working with others becomes *collaboration* as nursing theory and research increases the identification of the distinctive differences between nursing and medicine; that is, as nursing tries to separate itself as a profession from medicine. The language used for collaboration at this point displays an uneasy tension between nursing and medicine. As both nursing and medicine become increasingly specialized, and as healthcare systems become more complex, collaboration is embraced by both because more specialized knowledge is needed and also because failure to collaborate leads to all the hazards of the fragmentation of patient care. High-quality patient care cannot exist without welcoming and embracing both interdisciplinary and intradisciplinary collaboration in today's healthcare system.

2.4 Professional Boundaries

The fundamental nature of the nurse–patient relationship is therapeutic, not personal. In addition, the fundamental nature of the healthcare team relationships is professional, not personal. This revision of the interpretive statements is rather more direct than any previous code in its declaration: "Dating and sexually intimate relationships with patients are always prohibited…. Boundary violations can also occur in professional colleague relationships. In all communications and actions, nurses are responsible for maintaining professional boundaries."[53] The 2001 Code's allusion to more intimate relationships with team members is indirect and previous codes, where they dare, only vaguely hint at such indiscretions.

Another boundary violation, bribery, is mentioned in the first adopted code in 1950. Its Provision 10 says: "The nurse accepts only such compensations as the contract, actual or implied, provides. The professional worker does not accept tips or bribes."[54]

The language of tips and bribes then disappears from successive codes. The issue of gifts, as opposed to bribes, is different. Gifts are expressions of gratitude, bribes are "a reward given to pervert the judgment or corrupt the conduct."[55] The purposes of gifts are morally praiseworthy; the purposes of bribes are morally blameworthy. Gifts were a concern in the early modern nursing literature when nursing care was delivered in the home. They might be personal expressions of gratitude by a family or a patient, or they might be the annual or seasonal bonus that would be given to all household attendants. The same is true of private duty nursing in the hospital before hospitals employed staff nurses and instead students to staff the hospital. Discussion of gifts is minimal in the nursing literature. In hospital contexts, recommendations have traditionally been that gifts given by patients should be directed toward the staff of the unit rather than toward an individual nurse. The issue of gifts has become a concern once again but this time as an issue of cultural context, awareness, and sensitivity. The guidelines that are now offered are that "accepting gifts from patients is generally not appropriate; factors to consider include the intent, the value, the nature and the timing of the gift as well as the patient's own cultural norms. Gifting members of the healthcare team is closely linked with healing and recovery in some cultures. When a gift is offered, facility policy should be followed."[56]

Provision 2 is focused on the patient as the first allegiance of the nurse and on the primacy of the patient's interests. These are best affirmed by a deep and guiding understanding of the moral nature of the nurse–patient relationship. That understanding serves to help draw and to keep appropriate therapeutic boundaries in place. When the nurse–patient relationship is seen within an ethic of care, the more complete context of that relationship also helps to demarcate and maintain professional boundaries between and among members of the healthcare team.

Cases

Case 1

Anaya Praben, a 32-year-old woman, is in persistent vegetative state and has been for some years. The patient's outdated advance directive is confusing on the issue of food and fluid, though clear about not wanting to be on a ventilator if she were in a coma. Her husband wants the feeding tube removed, but is unable to say that it would have been the patient's wish. He says that it is his decision for her. Her two siblings and parents reject this as a possibility because, they say, "human life is sacred" and that their daughter believed this. They say their daughter is alive and should receive nursing care, including feeding. The healthcare team disagrees on what to do ethically. The parents ask the nurse if they might attend the next patient care conference.

Case 2

Hundreds of refugee immigrants have recently been relocated to a rural county leading to a significant shortage of influenza vaccine. The County Health Department has decided to temporarily restrict this vaccine only to pregnant women and elderly people who are 60 years of age or older and who are US citizens until such time as additional vaccine might become available. The potential availability of additional vaccine in the coming weeks is uncertain. The immunization clinic nurse is worried about exposure to the flu from the clinic population then taking it home and exposing his family. He figures they are at higher risk because of his job. He is considering taking some of the vaccine home to give shots to his family.

ENDNOTES

All URLs were current when accessed on January 9, 2015.

1 R. Corwin, "The Professional Employee: A Case Study of Conflict in Nursing Roles" *American Journal of Sociology* 66, no. 6 (1961): 604–15.

2 Andres Oldenquist, "Loyalties," *The Journal of Philosophy*, 79, no. 4 (April 1982): 175–76.

3 Ibid., 176.

4 Ibid., 178–79.

5 Lystra Gretter, *The Florence Nightingale Pledge* (Detroit, MI: Farrand Training School for Nurses, 1893).

6 Corwin, "Professional Employee."

7 Note that an ethic refers to a theory or system of moral values, such an "ethic of care." The term ethics (which is singular, not plural) refers to the field of study of moral analysis, choices, and behavior; that is, to philosophical or theological reflection upon morality.

8 Lawrence Kohlberg, "Moral stages and moralization: The cognitive-developmental approach," in *Moral Development and Behavior: Theory, Research and Social Issues*, ed. T. Lickona (Holt, NY: Rinehart and Winston, 1976).

9 Carol Gilligan, "In a Different Voice: Women's Conceptions of Self and Morality." *Harvard Educational Review* 47, no. 4 (1982): 481- 517.

10 Ann M. Beutel and Margaret Mooney Marini, "Gender and Values," *American Sociological Review* 60, no. 3 (June 1995): 436–448. See also: Maureen R. Ford and Carol R. Lowery, "Gender Differences in Moral Reasoning: A Comparison of the Use of Justice and Care Orientations," *Journal of Personality and Social Psychology* 50, no. 4 (1986): 777–83; Mary Rothbart, Dean Hanley, and Marc Albert, "Gender Differences in Moral Reasoning," *Sex Roles* 15, nos. 11 and 12 (1986): 645–53; D. L. Krebs, S. C. Vermeulen, K. Denton, and J. I. Carpendale, "Gender and perspective differences in moral judgment and moral orientation," *Journal of Moral Education* 23, no. 1 (1994): 17–26.

11 Nel Noddings, *A Feminine Approach to Ethics and Moral Education* (Berkeley: University of California, Berkeley Press, 1984).

12 Joan Tronto, "An Ethic of Care," in *Feminist Theory: A Philosophical Anthology*, eds. A. Cudd and R. Andreasen (Oxford, UK: Malden-Blackwell Publishing, 2005), 251–63.

13 Joan Tronto, *Moral Boundaries: A Political Argument for an Ethic of Care* (London: Routledge, 1993).

14 Annette Baier, "What Do Women Want in a Moral Theory?" *Noûs* 19, no. 1 (March 1985): 53–63.

15 Patricia Benner and Judith Wrubel, *Primacy of Caring: Stress and Coping in Health and Illness* (Reading, MA: Addison-Wesley, 1989).

16 Virginia Held, *The Ethics of Care* (Oxford, UK: Oxford University Press, 2005).

17 Selma Sevenhuijsen, *Citizenship and the ethics of care: Feminist Considerations on Justice, Morality, and Politics* (London: Routledge, 1998).

18 Michael A. Slote, *The Ethics of Care and Empathy* (London, New York: Routledge, 2007).

19 Jean Watson, *Nursing: The Philosophy and Science of Caring* (Denver, CO: University of Colorado Press, 1985). See also: Jean Watson, *Caring Science: A Core Science for Health Professions* (Philadelphia, PA: FA Davis, 2004).

[20] Madeline Leininger, ed., *Caring: The Essence of Nursing and Health* (Detroit, MI: Wayne State University Press, 1980).

[21] Simone Roach, *The Human Act of Caring* (Ottawa: Canadian Hospital Association, 1992).

[22] A brief overview of the development and an analysis of an ethics of care can be found in: Chris Gastmans, "The Care Perspective in Healthcare," in *Essentials of Teaching and Learning in Nursing Ethics: Perspectives and Methods, The Teaching of Nursing Ethics: Content and Methods,* eds. Anne Davis, Louise de Raeve, and Verena Tschudin (London: Elsevier, 2006), 135–48.

[23] More information about the International Care Ethics (ICE) Observatory can be found at this website: http://www.surrey.ac.uk/fhms/research/centres/ICE/index.htm

[24] Patricia Benner, Molly Sutphen, Victoria Leonard, and Lisa Day, *Educating Nurses: A Call for Radical Transformation* (New York: Jossey-Bass/Carnegie Foundation for the Advancement of Teaching, 2009), 222.

[25] Chris Gastmans, "The Care Perspective in Healthcare Ethics," in *The Teaching of Nursing Ethics: Content and Methods,* eds. Anne Davis, Louise de Raeve, and Verena Tschudin (London: Elsevier, 2006).

[26] Tronto, *Moral Boundaries.*

[27] Bernice Fisher and Joan Tronto, "Toward a Feminist Theory of Care," in *Circles of Care: Work and Identity in Women's Lives,* eds. Emily Abel and Margaret Nelson (Albany, NY: State University of New York Press, 1991), 40.

[28] Tom Beauchamp and James Childress, *Principles of Biomedical Ethics* (1st ed.) (Oxford, UK: Oxford University Press, 1979).

[29] The National Commission for the Protection of Human Subjects of Biomedical and Behavioral Research of the U.S. Department of Health and Human Services, *The Belmont Report: Ethical Principles and Guidelines for the Protection of Human Subjects of Research* (Washington, D.C.: DHHS/USGPO, 1979), available at http://www.hhs.gov/ohrp/humansubjects/guidance/belmont.html

[30] Tronto, *Moral Boundaries,* 27.

[31] Ibid., 106–08.

[32] Ibid., 106.

[33] Ibid.

[34] Ibid., 108.

[35] Ibid., 109.

[36] Ibid., 109.

[37] Ibid., 131.

[38] Ibid., 132.

[39] Ibid., 133.

[40] Ibid., 134–136.

[41] Patricia Benner and Judith Wrubel, *The Primacy of Caring: Stress and Coping in Health and Illness* (Menlo Park, CA: Addison-Wesley, 1989), xv.

[42] Rhacel Parreñas and Eileen Boris, *Intimate Labors: Cultures, Technologies, and the Politics of Care* (Stanford, CA: Stanford University Press, 2010), 3.

[43] Ibid., 10.

[44] Ibid., 113.

[45] Ibid., 109.

[46] Bernard Lo and Marilyn Field, eds., *Conflict of interest in Medical Research, Education, and Practice* (Washington, DC: Institute of Medicine/National Academies Press, 2009).

[47] American Nurses Association, *Code of Ethics for Nurses with Interpretive Statements* (Silver Spring, MD: ANA, 2015), 6.

[48] Ibid.

[49] ANA, "*A* Suggested Code," *American Journal of Nursing 26*, no. 9 (1926): 600–01.

[50] ANA, *Code for Nurses with Interpretive Statements* (Kansas City, MO: ANA, 1976), 6.

[51] ANA, *Code of Ethics for Nurses with Interpretive Statements* (Silver Spring, MD: ANA, 2001), 15.

[52] Ibid., 14–15.

[53] Ibid., 16.

[54] ANA, *A Code for Professional Nurses* (New York: ANA, 1950), Provision 10.

[55] *Oxford English Dictionary Online*, "Bribe," accessed on Month day, 2012, http://0-www.oed.com.patris.apu.edu/view/Entry/23151?isAdvanced=false&result=1&rskey=8CFta9&

[56] ANA, *Code of Ethics for Nurses with Interpretive Statements*(2015), 7.

Provision 3
The nurse promotes, advocates for, and protects the rights, health, and safety of the patient.

Provision 3. Advocacy's Geography

Introduction

The third provision weaves together multiple threads into a safety net for the patient. It includes protecting patient information, whistleblowing, attributes required for nursing practice, a culture of safety, and processes to address questionable practice. Historically, this provision is an amalgamation of two or more provisions from previous codes.

As to protecting patient information or preserving patient secrets, confidentiality is found in the Nightingale Pledge and every historic and contemporary code of ethics except the *Suggested Code* of 1926. The 1968 code is the first code to include the protection of human subjects in research. The acquisition of the specific attributes necessary for excellence in nursing appears in one form or another in all of the codes. A focus on patient safety is implicit in all of the codes but first receives specific mention in the 1968 Code. The issue of questionable practice first arises in the Code of 1960; however, it is not until the 2001 Code that concerns for impaired practice include the welfare of both the patient and the nurse. Unlike other provisions in this code that are more narrowly focused, this provision has a broad range of elements. Because these elements of patient safety are rather different, the development of each one will be discussed separately.

3.1 Protection of the Rights of Privacy and Confidentiality

Confidentiality and *privacy* are at the top of the list of the patient rights that nurses must protect. Concerns for confidentiality appear in the nursing codes from the start. The Nightingale Pledge, widely accepted as the first code of ethics for nurses, was not so much a code of ethics as an oath that encompassed ethical elements. It was written by Lystra Gretter in 1873 and was named to honor Florence Nightingale. Gretter sought to create an oath that was patterned after the Hippocratic Oath taken by physicians. Confidentiality is embedded in the pledge:

> I solemnly pledge myself before God and in the presence of this assembly:

> To pass my life in purity and to practice my profession faithfully. I will abstain from whatever is deleterious and mischievous, and will not take or knowingly administer any harmful drug.

> I will do all in my power to elevate the standard of my profession, and will hold in confidence all personal matters committed to my keeping, and all family affairs coming to my knowledge in the practice of my profession.

> With loyalty will endeavor to aid the physician in his work and devote myself to the welfare of those committed to my care.[1]

In holding "in confidence all personal matters committed to my keeping, and all family affairs coming to my knowledge in the practice of my profession," the focus of confidentiality is upon both the information related to the patient as well as to the patient's family even though, in that day, the patient was only the one who was ill. An understanding of the social context of the day makes clear the reason for the patient-and-family duty of confidentiality. Graduate nurses, having completed their formal education, went into the community, often referred through a registry associated with their school of nursing, and gave care to patients in their homes. Hospitals in the early days of nursing were largely staffed by students. The *Tentative Code* of 1940 makes the reason for family-based confidentiality crystal clear:

> The confidences concerning individual or domestic life, which are intrusted to the nurse by the patient, and the defects of disposition or character which are observed, should be held as a trust, and should not be revealed except when imperatively required by law, or when deemed necessary to promote the patient's welfare. In the latter case, it may be necessary to confer with the physician or those having responsibility for the patient. In such a situation a wise course of action can be taken only through the exercise of discriminating judgment.[2]

Nurses giving patient care in the home were exposed to the machinations of family life, including the affairs of the family and in some instances the sexual advances of a family member toward the nurse. The family's dirty laundry was never to be exposed, and gossip was unacceptable, even with the patient.[3] This code recognizes that at times the law demands violation of confidentiality: "confidences…should not be revealed except when imperatively required by law, or when deemed necessary to promote the patient's welfare."[4] The 1950 *Code for Professional Nurses*, the first officially adopted code, states in Provision 5: "Professional nurses hold in confidence all personal information entrusted to them."[5] By 1960, there was a greater recognition that confidentiality is not absolute and at times the law requires that patient information be divulged. Its Provision 4 states: "The nurse respects and holds in confidence all information of a confidential nature obtained in the course of nursing work unless required by law to divulge it."[6] The interpretive statement expands this:

> The nurse, as well as the physician, has a clear obligation to keep secret any information relating to a patient's illness which she obtains during the performance of her professional duties, unless the patient authorizes her to disclose this information or a competent court orders her to reveal it. This obligation is based first, on the ethics of her profession and second, on the law.[7]

All states have mandatory reporting laws for threats to public health, suspicion of domestic violence, child abuse, elder abuse, and other situations.

Confidentiality is the nondisclosure of patient secrets or information without patient authorization. *Privacy*, as a right, is the freedom not to be observed or intruded upon without authorization and to control access to one's personal information. The 1968 revision of the Code expands the provision to include privacy as well as confidentiality. This is the first appearance of *privacy* in the nursing code. The second provision states: "The nurse safeguards the individual's right to privacy by judiciously protecting information of the confidential nature, sharing only that information relevant to his care."[8]

The Code of 1976 states in Provision 3: "The nurse safeguards the client's right to privacy by judiciously protecting information of a confidential nature."[9] However, by 1976, a number of situations that require disclosure of patient information arose, including disclosure to the health team for the purposes of clinical care, for quality assurance purposes, in a court of law, and for research and nonclinical purposes. The interpretive statements comment on each of these conditions. In the 1985 iteration of the Code, Provision 3 is unchanged. However, the interpretive statements specify that information disclosed for quality assurance purposes, peer review, and third-party payment may only be disclosed "under defined policies, mandates, or protocols."[10] So now, processes are to be in place to support the obligation.

The 2001 Code changes the context of the obligation to maintain confidentiality and privacy. The corresponding Provision 3 states: "The nurse promotes, advocates for, and strives to protect the health, safety, and rights of the patient."[11] So confidentiality and privacy are removed from the provision and replaced with a broader rights approach, of which confidentiality and privacy are the first two named rights in the interpretive statements. Between 1985 and 2001, monumental changes had taken place in patient records, laboratory and test results, and more. Electronic medical records (EMR) have entered the picture. Now, in addition to confidentiality and privacy, concerns for data security must be addressed.[12] But if confidentiality refers to the duty not to disclose the secrets of another without her or his permission, how does privacy differ? What exactly is privacy? Some uses of the doctrine of privacy "have had a peculiar tendency to gravitate around sexuality: the groundbreaking cases involved contraception, marriage, and abortion."[13] Others have become a part of the discussion of recent concerns for the government surveillance of citizens.

Whereas the 2001 Code had separated confidentiality and privacy in the interpretive statements, this code brings them together. Privacy has two main understandings or uses, both of which have relevance to nursing but only one of which is relevant to this provision. Privacy as a right is understood as a basic human right and is found in the 1948 UN *Universal Declaration of Human Rights*, Article 12: "No one shall be subjected to arbitrary interference with his privacy, family, home or correspondence, nor to attacks upon his honour and reputation. Everyone has the right to the protection of the law against such interference or attacks."[14] The moral ground for the right to privacy, and the corresponding duty to protect it, is rooted in personhood, autonomy, and natural rights. This moral right is then given a legal basis, in the 4th Amendment of the US Constitution and in tort law. The 4th Amendment states:

> The right of the people to be secure in their persons, houses, papers, and effects, against unreasonable searches and seizures, shall not be violated, and no warrants shall issue, but upon probable cause, supported by oath or affirmation, and particularly describing the place to be searched, and the persons or things to be seized.[15]

The 4th Amendment originally prevented government intrusion into citizens' lives that was unreasonable or without cause. Rubenfeld distinguished between the two types of privacy that have developed. He writes that there are:

> expectations of privacy secured by the fourth amendment or with the right of privacy protected by tort law. ...[this] concept of privacy is employed to govern the conduct of other individuals who intrude in various ways upon one's life. Privacy in these contexts can be generally understood in its familiar informational sense; it limits the ability of others to gain, disseminate, or use information about oneself. By contrast, the right to privacy [that concerns the writer here]... attaches to the rightholder's own actions. It is not informational but substantive, immunizing certain conduct - such as using contraceptives, marrying someone of a different color, or aborting a pregnancy - from state proscription or penalty.[16]

In other words, the first use of the right to privacy is that of protection of information about one's self and the second use is about preventing the government (state) from interfering with private decisions or actions such as choosing to use birth control. The Haifa Center of Law and Technology has formulated a helpful, plain-language, definition of privacy that encompasses both senses of privacy:

> The right to privacy is our right to keep a domain around us, which includes all those things that are part of us, such as our body, home, property, thoughts, feelings, secrets and identity. The right to privacy gives us the ability to choose which parts in this domain can be accessed by others, and to control the extent, manner and timing of the use of those parts we choose to disclose.[17]

The first sense of privacy—protection of information—is the sense in which privacy is used in Provision 3 of the Code. However, the second use of privacy, that of state intrusion into personal life by either proscribing or penalizing behaviors, is also of interest to nursing and ethics. It is this second sense of privacy that is invoked against laws that would prevent, for example, the use of contraception. Both senses of privacy come into play in communicable disease reporting, discussions of seizure of cell phone data, library usage data, and other forms of government surveillance of the citizenry. Here the discussion is moving in the direction of concern for whether privacy can exist at all in a highly technological, technologically intertwined, society.[18] Is there any sense in which personal information is secure or secret in a digital age?

Looking at the successive revisions of the Code, the drift of confidentiality (and privacy) is clear. Originally, breaching confidentiality was only permissible when required by law. By 1976, required disclosure of secrets is a much larger world: disclosure to the health team, for quality assurance, in a court of law, for research and nonclinical purposes. In 2009, the Health Information Technology for Economic and Clinical Health Act (the HITECH Act) was enacted under Title XIII of the American Recovery and Reinvestment Act of 2009. Under this act, the Department of Health and Human Services (DHHS) has set aside almost $26 billion for the implementation of health information technology and a nationwide network of digital health records.[19] While this would allow for greater population health management, it makes the protection of privacy and confidentiality even more complex.

Now with electronic record continuing to extend nationally, and despite regulations under the 2009 Health Insurance Portability and Accountability Act (HIPAA) Privacy Rule, we must ask "Are privacy and confidentiality fictions?" When the extent of disclosure is expanded well beyond those giving direct care, privacy and confidentiality are not so much fictions as an ideal that nurses must continue to strive for.

Confidentiality and privacy are based on the bedrock of trust that must always exist in the nurse–patient relationship and so every effort must be maintained to safeguard these patient rights. The Code of 2015 states:

> Central to that [nurse–patient] relationship is an element of trust and an expectation that personal information will not be divulged without consent. The nurse has a duty to maintain confidentiality of all patient information, both personal and clinical in the work setting and off duty in all venues, including social media or any other means of communication. Because of rapidly evolving communication technology and the porous nature of social media, nurses must maintain vigilance regarding postings, images, recordings or commentary that intentionally or unintentionally breaches their obligation to maintain and protect patients' rights to privacy and confidentiality.[20]

This Code recognizes the influence and risks to information in the digital age. Even so, the digital age is still dawning and issues of privacy will only become increasingly complex over the next decade, beyond what we can even now imagine.

3.2 Protection of Human Participants in Research

The 1968 Code is the first code to include the protection of human subjects in research. Provision 6 states: "The nurse participates in research activities when assured that the rights of individual subjects are protected."[21] By 1976, the protection of human participants in research moves from the provision to the interpretive statements under Provision 7: "The nurse participates in activities that contribute to the ongoing development of the profession's body of knowledge."[22] By now the rights of human subjects in research have received wide attention and the ANA has prepared a separate publication, to which the interpretive statement refers, *Human Rights Guidelines for Nurses in Clinical and Other Research.* These guidelines would subsequently become unnecessary and national and international guidelines would be put in place for all research using human participants. (See Chapter 7.) The 1985 Code follows the same path as the 1976 Code. However, the 2001 Code moves human subjects protection back from Provision 7 on the development of the profession's body of knowledge, to Provision 3 on patient health, safety, and rights, which is essentially the same in both the 2001 and 2015 codes.

The focus of this interpretive statement is upon the rights of the individual who participates as a subject in research. Issues regarding human participants in research, Institutional Review Boards, and national and international conventions governing research will be discussed under Provision 7 which deals with the advance of the profession's body of knowledge. This provision deals with protecting the rights, health, and safety of the patient, so some patient-related considerations need to be discussed here. Interpretive Statement §3.2 addresses human participants in research, without mentioning patients specifically, as it recognizes that not all human participants in research are patients; some are students, or nurses, or the healthcare team, or others. All participants, however, have a right to accept or refuse participation, to be given all the information a person would need to make a decision regarding participation, to withdraw from a study without being subject to reprisal or untoward consequences, and to be protected from risk of harm. The DHHS has guidelines governing the use of human participants (also called human subjects) in research. These guidelines were published by the National Commission for the Protection of Human Subjects of Biomedical and Behavioral Research in *The Belmont Report*.[23] *The Belmont Report* sets forth the required ethical principles and guidelines for the protection of human participants in research.

The guidelines require the use of the ethical principles of *respect for persons, beneficence* and *justice*. The report defines respect for persons as:

> Respect for persons incorporates at least two ethical convictions: first, that individuals should be treated as autonomous agents, and second, that persons with diminished autonomy are entitled to protection. The principle of respect for persons thus divides into two separate moral requirements: the requirement to acknowledge autonomy and the requirement to protect those with diminished autonomy.[24]

The report's definition of respect for persons is a form of respect for autonomy, and is a much narrower definition than is used in a broader ethics literature. The report also defines beneficence: "In this document, beneficence is understood...as an obligation. Two general rules have been formulated as complementary expressions of beneficent actions in this sense: (a) do not harm and (b) maximize possible benefits and minimize possible harms."[25] Its definition of justice is less a definition specifically than an enumeration of various approaches to justice.

Who ought to receive the benefits of research and bear its burdens? This is a question of justice, in the sense of "fairness in distribution" or "what is deserved." An injustice occurs when some benefit to which a person is entitled is denied without good reason or when some burden is imposed unduly. Another way of conceiving the principle of justice is that equals ought to be treated equally. However, this statement requires explication. Who is equal and who is unequal? What considerations justify departure from equal distribution? Almost all commentators allow that distinctions based on experience, age, deprivation, competence, merit and position do sometimes constitute criteria justifying differential treatment for certain purposes. It is necessary, then, to explain in what respects people should be treated equally. There are several widely accepted formulations of just ways to distribute burdens and benefits. Each formulation mentions some relevant property on the basis of which burdens and benefits should be distributed. These formulations are (1) to each person an equal share, (2) to each person according to individual need, (3) to each person according to individual effort, (4) to each person according to societal contribution, and (5) to each person according to merit.[26]

Beyond *The Belmont Report*, justice is a complex and nuanced principle that gives rise to various systems of government. In addition, each of the enumerated approaches might be used under different conditions. For example in education, instructor time might be allocated on the basis of student need, but grades allocated on the basis of merit. Chapter 7 contains a discussion of research-gone-wrong and the abuse of human participants. But for the purposes of explaining why justice is important to research, the report notes that:

> Against this historical background, it can be seen how conceptions of justice are relevant to research involving human subjects. For example, the selection of research subjects needs to be scrutinized in order to determine whether some classes (e.g., welfare patients, particular racial and ethnic minorities, or persons confined to institutions) are being systematically selected simply because of their easy availability, their compromised position, or their manipulability, rather than for reasons directly related to the problem being studied. Finally, whenever research supported by public funds leads to the development of therapeutic devices and procedures, justice demands both that these not provide advantages only to those who can afford them and that such research should not unduly involve persons from groups unlikely to be among the beneficiaries of subsequent applications of the research.[27]

Justice requires that vulnerable groups receive special protection. It is not possible here to go into an extended explanation of these principles. For the best resource on this, the reader is referred to Beauchamp and Childress's excellent book *Principles of Biomedical Ethics*, now in the seventh edition.[28] This book has become the standard work for principle-based ethics, is widely read and used, and its approach is consistent with that of *The Belmont Report*. While the Code accepts a range of theoretical approaches to ethics, including ethical principlism, the requirements of *The Belmont Report* necessitate the use of ethical principles. These principles are applied to human-participant research through informed consent, assessment of risks and benefits, and a just selection of subject participants.[29] These too receive thorough explanation in Beauchamp and Childress's book.

The interpretive statement includes legal surrogates in the informed consent process. A *surrogate* is someone who acts on behalf of another when that person cannot act on his or her own behalf. Surrogates are needed for persons whose condition or status does not allow them to participate: a person in coma, an infant, a person with severe intellectual compromise. A surrogate might be appointed by a court or might be designated in an advance directive. The duty of a surrogate is to make the decision on behalf of the person or patient that they themselves would have made if they were able to do so, or if the person's wishes could not be ascertained, to make the decision in the best interests of the person or patient herself or himself.

Children pose a special case since they cannot legally give consent to participation in research. However, the *Code of Federal Regulations* (CFR) requires that researchers "solicit the assent of children" who are capable of assenting.[30] Morally, a child's refusal of assent is binding. However, the CFR further states that:

> if the IRB determines that the…intervention or procedure involved in the research holds out a prospect of direct benefit that is important to the health or well-being of the children and is available only in the context of research, the assent of the children is not a necessary condition for proceeding with the research. [31]

In addition, the CFR states that:

> if the IRB determines that a research protocol is designed for conditions or for a subject population for which parental or guardian permission is not a reasonable requirement to protect the subjects (for example, neglected or abused children), it may waive the consent requirements… provided an appropriate mechanism for protecting the children who will participate as subjects in the research is substituted…".[32]

Ethically, even young children should be included in the research process by educating them about participation to the level of their developmental understanding and capacity.

This interpretive statement also addresses whistleblowing in research; that is, reporting researchers, research projects, or clinical trials that violate patient or participant's rights. *Whistleblowing* refers to the disclosure of wrongdoing. That wrongdoing may be observed in research, academic, institutional, clinical, or any other setting. Whistleblowing is also an expectation when research results have been falsified or academic standards for honesty, particularly plagiarism or theft of the work of another, have been violated. Whistleblowing presents a moral quandary; it is important, yet whistleblowers are often treated as pariahs and face reprisal. However, federal regulations require that policies and procedures developed by institutions to handle allegations of misconduct must include provisions for "undertaking diligent efforts to protect the positions and reputations of those persons who, in good faith, make allegations."[33] The Government Accountability Project has created an excellent and quite thorough handbook for those concerned about whistleblowing, which is available online.[34]

It is the responsibility of administrators in nursing, education, or research to provide a culture of safety for reporting violations or perceived violations of the rights of human subjects, falsification of research results, or theft of the work of another. Nursing educators should include basic materials on whistleblowing in discussions of academic dishonesty as well as in courses on research. Introductory materials on whistleblowing are available online,[35] and there is even an online site for the protection of whistleblowers in civil service.[36]

3.3 Performance Standards and Review Mechanisms

The 2001 Code contains a section on standards and review mechanisms in Interpretive Statement 3.4 of Provision 3. The 2015 Code moves much of that material to Interpretive Statement 7.2 on standards of practice and their relationship to the development of the profession's body of knowledge. What is retained under this provision is directly related to the patient's safety.

Nurses must demonstrate the requisite knowledge, skill, and dispositions that provide the basis for the protection and advocacy for patient rights, health, and safety. This requires the ongoing assessment of knowledge, skill, and dispositions prior to entry into practice (as a student) and after one enters practice. This, of course, pertains both to basic as well as advanced practice. Curriculum and clinical laboratories are designed to lay a foundation of knowledge and skill. Dispositions are a bit different. Dispositions are an intrinsic state of being or qualities of mind or character, in which one has a habit or inclination to act in a specific way. *Moral dispositions* incline a person to behave in a specific way morally. Dispositions are shaped by virtues. Examples would be curiosity of mind, appreciation of beauty, use of imagination or creativity, honesty in character, perseverance in the face of obstacles, and so forth. These dispositions are shaped and formed throughout life based on the persons who model them in our lives and the environments that have fostered, cultivated, and rewarded them. Sometimes positive dispositions develop because of adversity or observations of what one wants *not* to be. Nurse educators must evaluate students for knowledge and skill, and seek to create a positive environment for the development of positive dispositions. Administrators and supervisors are likewise responsible for similar evaluation of nurses in practice, whatever the role, and for the creation of environments that foster continued growth of knowledge and skill and the cultivation of moral dispositions.

3.4 Professional Responsibility in Promoting a Culture of Safety

Previous codes contain information of reporting errors in their interpretive statements. However, the concept of a *culture of safety* enters the Code with this revision. This section of the interpretive statements is specifically focused on reporting errors or near misses.

The corollary of whistleblowing in research is that of reporting error or near misses in clinical practice. One can create a syllogism, a form of logical argument, for error:

All humans make errors.

All nurses are humans.

All nurses make errors.

We cannot live error-free lives; it is a part of the human condition. However vigilant, conscientious and competent, it is still impossible to go through one's nursing career without ever making an error. It is a high-stakes environment, as errors have the potential for significant, perhaps even grave harm. We can only hope that errors are minor and of little or no consequence for patients' safety or well-being. Given that errors will occur, there must be processes and guidelines for prompt reporting and remedying, and for disclosure to the patient, whether the error is one's own or that of a co-worker. Some errors occur because system factors contribute to their creation. System factors, too, should be reported and remedied, preferably before they contribute to error. Under no circumstances should error be concealed or condoned. Error should not be punished unless absolutely warranted by bad judgment or negligence. Cover-up should be subject to disciplinary action.

Communication should follow the chain of authority within the institution or agency, working from "the level closest to the event and should proceed to a responsive level as the situation warrants."[37] If the institution is unresponsive and the error is of substance and significance, it may be important to go beyond the institution to the appropriate authoritative body, such as an accrediting or quality assurance body. Here, reporting becomes whistleblowing. However, one would hope that it need not go that far. Institutions should have policies and procedures for handling error, and should also provide a transparent, clear, and unambiguous report of the investigation and its outcomes.

3.5 Protecting Patient Health and Safety by Action on Questionable Practice

This interpretive statement deals with questionable practice, whether impaired, incompetent, illegal, or unethical. Concerns for questionable practice first arise as an issue in the 1960 Code. Its Provision 17 states: "The nurse refuses to participate in unethical procedures and assumes the responsibility to expose incompetent or unethical conduct in others to the appropriate authority."[38] The same concern appears in more abbreviated form in Provision 4 of the Code of

1968: "The nurse acts to safeguard the patient when his care and safety are affected by incompetent, unethical, or illegal conduct of any person."[39] The provision in 1976 removes the masculine pronoun and changes the provision to be gender neutral: "The nurse acts to safeguard the client and the public when health care and safety are affected by the incompetent, unethical, or illegal practice of any person."[40] The change in the 1985 Code provision is subtle but important—it changes *health care* to *health*. Its Provision 3 reads: "The nurse acts to safeguard the client and the public when health and safety are affected by the incompetent, unethical, or illegal practice of any person."[41] In 2001 and 2015, incompetent, unethical, and illegal practice are removed from the provision and it is strengthened and made more positive. This is a welcome change. Provision 3 of the 2001 Code reads: "The nurse promotes, advocates for and strives to protect the health, safety and rights of the patient"[42] and its slight reordering in 2015 is "The nurse promotes, advocates for, and protects the rights, health, and safety of the patient."[43]

Questionable practice includes incompetent, unethical, illegal, or impaired practice. While they are all forms of questionable practice, the means of remedying each may and perhaps should involve different processes, policies, and procedures. Incompetent practice is evaluated against standards of practice for general as well as specialist nursing. The ANA publication *Nursing: Scope and Standards of Practice*[44] and additional standards for specialty practice (discussed at length in Chapter 7) are such standards and are foundational documents for professional practice. The standard for the ethical practice of nursing is this Code.[45] It is a non-negotiable standard of practice. Illegal practice is measured against the state nurse practice act (different in each state) and federal regulations. It may be that the reporting mechanism and lines of communication may be the same for each of these though approaches to addressing the situation may differ. All may involve warning, termination, or reporting to the appropriate external authority such as a state board of nursing (or other professional state board) or to the local police or sheriff's department.

In general, incompetent, unethical, or illegal practice involves the principle of fair warning and requires speaking to the person involved first. However, flagrantly incompetent, unethical, or illegal practice may warrant going past the person involved directly to a more senior authority in the institution. Where the patient's safety or well-being is jeopardized, immediate intervention may be necessary.

While whistleblowers should be protected by institutional policy, nurses must also support those who call attention to unethical, incompetent, illegal, or impaired practice. Where necessary, state nurses' associations should step up to the challenge of questionable practice to advise and support nurses and to evaluate processes and policies for reporting questionable practice, perhaps even to formulate generic model policies and processes: "the professional organization has a responsibility to protect the practice of those nurses who choose to report their concerns through formal channels."[46] Uncovering questionable practice serves not only patient safety, but also the integrity of the profession, and more broadly the social institution of health care.

3.6 Patient Protection and Impaired Practice

Impaired practice is a bit different from incompetent, unethical, or illegal practice in that the nurse is capable of functioning competently, ethically, and legally, but by reason of impairment cannot now do so. *Impairment* raises the issue of impaired practice due to substance abuse but this is not always the case. Impaired practice may arise from illness, exhaustion, grief, burnout, or any number of causes including those of substance abuse or drug or alcohol intoxication. Insofar as nursing seeks a caring environment for patients, it must also do so for its own.

Impairment is a matter of compassion and care when the impaired person is a patient. It should be the same when the impaired person is a colleague— or one's self. Intervention is required but it should be compassionate and caring and should seek not only assessment and treatment but where possible, restoration to practice.

Where impaired practice is a consequence of substance abuse or addiction, it can be appropriate for the nurse to enter a *diversion program,* which can divert nurses from criminal or disciplinary structures to rehabilitative programs. Diversion programs differ between and among states. A number of states have diversion programs. The New Mexico Board of Nursing notes that:

> It is estimated that 14% of all licensed nurses are dependent on alcohol and/or other mind-altering drugs. Historically, a disciplinary approach to problems with addiction was the normal course of action in the nursing profession, as well as in other health care professions. In the early 1980s, the nursing profession began to proactively address the problem of addiction in its ranks. They began to examine the issues of chemical dependency and addiction in nurses from a rehabilitative, rather than a disciplinary, approach. The first two alternative diversion programs were established in California and Florida. New Mexico became the third in the country to establish a diversion program.[47]

The National Council of State Boards of Nursing has a useful comprehensive video about substance use in nursing.[48] In 1982, the ANA House of Delegates approved Action on Alcohol and Drug Misuse and Psychological Dysfunctions Among Nurses.[49] Then, in 1984, the ANA studied and proposed ways to address nurses with addictions or psychological dysfunction.[50] In 1994, the National Council of State Boards of Nursing published *Model Guidelines: A Nondisciplinary Alternative Program for Chemically Impaired Nurses.*[51] To assist nurses, the ANA has created an Impaired Nurse Resource Center:

> ANA recognizes that a nurse's duty of compassion and caring extends to themselves and their colleagues as well as to their patients. Nurses who are challenged with substance abuse problems not only pose a potential threat to those for whom they care; they have neglected above all to care for themselves.

> At ANA, we care about nurses. That's why we've developed the Impaired Nurse Resource Center; an online repository of information aimed at helping suffering nurses get help.

> Additionally, we strongly support the peer assistance programs offered by most — but not all — of the state boards of nursing. These programs offer comprehensive monitoring and support services to reasonably assure the safe rehabilitation and return of the nurse to her or his professional community. To determine whether your state has adopted the "alternative to discipline" model, check with your specific state's Board of Nursing.[52]

The resource center provides position statements and related resources.

Cases

Case 1

You have been hired as a recently graduated acute care nurse practitioner. You feel that your graduate program and its preceptors provided you with a modern, progressive set of practice skills. As you get oriented, you are told that people here work on a team and may often be providing care to patients who are cared for by other providers. That is not a problem most of the time, but you note that patients who have been worked up and have their care plan written primarily by Virginia, another APRN, are not being cared for by state of the art protocols and sometimes are being handled in ways that are not validated by the nursing research literature. You are not sure what to do, for Virginia is one of the senior staff and, though a peer, is irritable and doesn't communicate well in team meetings.

Case 2

You are a case manager making a home visit to a patient who was discharged after having a stroke and falling. This fall caused a hip fracture and the patient still has significant pain, but you believe that he should be able to begin more ambulation. You review the charting by the visiting nurse indicating that he is taking narcotic pain medication several times a day. As you begin your assessment, the patient complains of excessive pain and wishes to stop the ambulation exercises you are doing with him. You determine that he is having significant pain and ask him if he thinks that he needs more of his prescription pain medicine. He says, "I haven't taken any pain medicine since last week except Tylenol. That's all the nurse says I need." By your assessment, the patient is clear, aware, and not forgetful. You then examine all his medications and find there is no bottle of prescription meds for pain, only Tylenol.

Case 3

You work closely with several people at your small clinic and have started meeting socially to have a few drinks. You notice one of your fellow nurses, Brad, tends to drink more than the rest of the group. He lives nearby, walks home, and never seems abusive, so you never mention it until one day as you are returning from lunch, you see Brad leaving a bar and headed back to work at the clinic. In the clinic, you return a patient record to Brad and you smell alcohol on his breath. He takes the record, smiles, and says, "Thanks. I needed this record. I'm seeing her in ten minutes."

ENDNOTES

All URLs were current when accessed on January 9, 2015.

1. Lystra Gretter, *The Florence Nightingale Pledge* (Detroit, MI: Farrand Training School for Nurses, 1893).

2. American Nurses Association, "A Tentative Code," *American Journal of Nursing* 40, no. 9 (1940): 978.

3. H. C. C., "Ethics in nursing: A nurse's duty to herself: Talks of a superintendent with her graduating class," *The Trained Nurse and Hospital Review* 2, no. 5 (May 1889): 179. (The author's full name is not given. She was a female superintendent of a school of nursing in Brooklyn, NY.)

4. American Nurses Association, "A Tentative Code." *American Journal of Nursing* 40, no. 9 (1940): 978.

5. American Nurses Association, *A Code for Professional Nurses* (New York: ANA, 1950).

6. American Nurses Association, *A Code for Professional Nurses* (New York: ANA, 1960).

7. Ibid., 8.

8. American Nurses Association, *A Code for Professional Nurses* (Kansas City, MO: ANA, 1968).

9. American Nurses Association, *Code for Nurses with Interpretive Statements* (Kansas City, MO: ANA, 1976).

10. American Nurses Association, *Code for Nurses with Interpretive Statements* (Kansas City, MO: ANA, 1985), 5.

11. American Nurses Association, *Code of Ethics for Nurses with Interpretive Statements* (Silver Spring, MD: ANA, 2001), 16.

12. Ibid., 17.

13. Jed Rubenfeld, "The Right of Privacy," *Faculty Scholarship Series*, Paper 1569 (1989): 738, http://digitalcommons.law.yale.edu/fss_papers/1569

14. United Nations, *Universal Declaration of Human Rights* (General Assembly, 1948), http://www.un.org/en/documents/udhr/

15. U.S. Constitution, Bill of Rights, 4th Amendment, http://www.archives.gov/exhibits/charters/bill_of_rights_transcript.html

16. Rubenfeld, "Right of Privacy," 740.

17. Yael Onn, Michael Geva, Yaniv Druckman, Ariel Zyssman, Rom Timor, Inbal Lev, Arz Maroun, Tamar Maron, Yossi Nachmani, Yaniv Simsolo, Saar Sicklai, Adi Fuches, Maor Fishman, Shai Packer, and Lotem Pery, "Privacy in the Digital Environment," Haifa Center of Law and Technology Publication Series no. 7 (2005): 1–12, http://weblaw.haifa.ac.il/he/Research/ResearchCenters/techlaw/DocLib/Privacy.pdf

18. Students of the Interdisciplinary Law and Technology workshop, Faculty of Law, University of Haifa, *Privacy in the Digital Environment* (Haifa, Israel: Haifa Center of Law and Technology, 2005), 1–175, http://books.google.com/books?id=yeVRrrJw-zAC&printsec=frontcover#v=onepage&q&f=false

19. "HITECH Act Rulemaking and Implementation Update," Department of Health and Human Services, http://www.hhs.gov/ocr/privacy/hipaa/understanding/coveredentities/hitechblurb.html

[20] American Nurses Association, *Code of Ethics for Nurses with Interpretive Statements* (Silver Spring, MD: ANA, 2015), Interpretive Statement 3.1, 9.

[21] ANA, *A Code for Professional Nurses* (1968).

[22] ANA, *Code of Ethics for Nurses with Interpretive Statements,* (1976).

[23] The National Commission for the Protection of Human Subjects of Biomedical and Behavioral Research of the U.S. Department of Health and Human Services, *The Belmont Report: Ethical Principles and Guidelines for the Protection of Human Subjects of Research* (Washington, D.C.: DHHS/USGPO, 1979), http://www.hhs.gov/ohrp/humansubjects/guidance/belmont.html

[24] Ibid.

[25] Ibid.

[26] Ibid.

[27] Ibid.

[28] Tom Beauchamp and James Childress, *Principles of Biomedical Ethics* (7th ed.) (Oxford, UK: Oxford University Press, 2013).

[29] DHHS, *Belmont Report.*

[30] Public Welfare, Part 46: Protection of Human Subjects, *Code of Federal Regulations,* title 45 (June, 2005), Subpart D, 46.401–409.

[31] M. E. Broome, E. Kodish, G. Geller, and L. A. Siminoff, "Children in research: New perspectives and practices for informed consent," *IRB: Ethics and Human Research* (supplement) 25, no. 5 (September–October 2003): S20–25.

[32] Ibid.

[33] Research Triangle Institute, James S. Lubalin, Mary-Anne E. Ardini, and Jennifer L. Matheson, *Consequences of Whistleblowing for the Whistleblower in Misconduct in Science Cases* (Washington, D.C.: RTI, 1995), 2, http://ori.hhs.gov/sites/default/files/consequences.pdf

[34] Tom Devine, *The Whistleblower's Survival Guide: Courage Without Martyrdom,* Parts 1-4, http://www.whistleblower.org/reports-publications. See more at: http://www.whistleblower.org/reports-publications#sthash.yfQKiiQR.dpuf

[35] James Peterson and Dan Farrell, *Whistleblowing: Ethical and Legal Issues in Expressing Dissent* (Dubuque, IA: Kendall/Hunt Publishing, 1986), http://ethics.iit.edu/publication/WhistleBlowing_Peterson1.pdf

[36] Tom Devine, interview by Whistleblower Insider, *History of GAP: An Interview with Tom Devine,* http://www.whistleblower.org/history-gap-interview-tom-devine, February 2014.

[37] ANA, *Code of Ethics for Nurses with Interpretive Statements* (Silver Spring, MD: ANA, 2015), 12.

[38] ANA, *Code of Ethics for Nurses with Interpretive Statements* (1960).

[39] ANA, *Code of Ethics for Nurses with Interpretive Statements* (1968).

[40] ANA, *Code of Ethics for Nurses with Interpretive Statements* (1976).

[41] ANA, *Code of Ethics for Nurses with Interpretive Statements* (1985).

[42] ANA, *Code of Ethics for Nurses with Interpretive Statements* (2001), 16.

[43] ANA, *Code of Ethics for Nurses with Interpretive Statements* (2015), v.

[44] American Nurses Association, *Nursing: Scope and Standards of Practice* (2nd ed.) (Silver Spring, MD: ANA, 2010).

45 ANA, *Code of Ethics for Nurses with Interpretive Statements,*(2015).

46 Ibid.

47 "Diversion Program FAQs," New Mexico Board of Nursing, http://nmbon.sks.com/FAQs_and_Forms.aspx

48 "Substance Use Disorder in Nursing," National Council of State Boards of Nursing, https://www.ncsbn.org/cps/rde/xchg/ncsbn/hs.xsl/333.htm

49 ANA House of Delegates, *Action on Alcohol and Drug Misuse and Psychological Dysfunctions among Nurses* (Kansas City, MO: ANA, 1982). http://www.nursingworld.org/MainMenuCategories/WorkplaceSafety/Healthy-Work-Environment/Work-Environment/ImpairedNurse/Response.pdf

50 American Nurses Association, *Addictions and Psychological Dysfunctions in Nursing: The Profession's Response to the Problem* (Kansas City, MO: ANA, 1984), 2.

51 National Council of State Boards of Nursing, Inc., *Model Guidelines: A Nondisciplinary Alternative Program for Chemically Impaired Nurses* (Chicago, IL: Author, 1994).

52 "Impaired Nurse Resource Center," American Nurses Association, http://www.nursingworld.org/MainMenuCategories/WorkplaceSafety/Healthy-Work-Environment/Work-Environment/ImpairedNurse

Provision 4
The nurse has authority, accountability, and responsibility for nursing practice; makes decisions; and takes action consistent with the obligation to promote health and to provide optimal care.

Provision 4. The Expectations of Expertise

Introduction

This provision is about authority, accountability, responsibility, and delegation. It is customary to address accountability and responsibility together. While they are intimately related, they are not the same. *Accountability* means to be *answerable*, or to give an account or defense to oneself and others for one's own choices, decisions and actions as measured against a standard such as the ANA Scope and Standards of Practice,[1] the ANA Code of Ethics,[2] nursing specialty standards, the Federal Policy for the Protection of Human Subjects (the "Common Rule"),[3] accreditation standards, and international standards such as those promulgated by the United Nations. In addition, nurses are accountable and responsible for adhering to the standards relevant to their particular role and domain of nursing practice. Accountability also includes performance of professional activities at a level commensurate with one's education and in compliance with applicable laws. Nurses are always answerable for judgments, choices, decisions, and actions.

Responsibility, however, differs from accountability. Responsibility refers to the blameworthiness or praiseworthiness that one bears for one's conduct or the performance of duties. It is often expressed as liability for one's actions and may be apportioned in degree based on circumstances. Nurses are always answerable for their actions, but some circumstances create situations of shared responsibility. This will be explained in greater detail under the interpretive statements.

Accountability and responsibility are always linked to standards, as there must be something against which one's decisions or actions must be measured. Without a standard by which to measure, it cannot be known if one has fallen short or even exceeded expectations. From the earliest days of modern nursing in the United States, nursing's leaders were concerned about standards. The original 1896 Articles of Incorporation of the ANA mention standards in the purposes of the organization:

> The object of the Association shall be: to establish and maintain a code of ethics, to the end that the standard of nursing education be elevated; the usefulness, honor, and interests of the nursing profession be promoted; public opinion in regard to duties, responsibilities, and requirements of nurses be enlightened; emulation and concert of action in the profession be stimulated; professional loyalty be fostered, and friendly intercourse between nurses be facilitated.[4]

One of the first tasks of organized nursing was to take control of nursing education in order to standardize it both for content and quality. At the fourth annual convention of the American Society of Superintendents of Training Schools for Nurses in 1897, approximately 75 attendees tackled this issue. They held that the:

> object of this society is to further the interests of the nursing profession, by establishing and maintaining a universal standard of training, and by promoting fellowship among its members by meetings, papers and discussion on nursing subjects, and by interchange of opinions. Heretofore all the training schools had been conducted on their own peculiar plans, independent of any other institutions, there being no standards of curriculum. The need of a common curriculum is badly felt, and this society undertakes to supply it.[5]

In 1912, this group came to be known as the National League for Nursing Education, later becoming the National League for Nursing. Standards of practice were still in the future. It would take several years to secure the quality of nursing education. In 1919, the Rockefeller Foundation funded the Committee for the Study of Nursing Education. The committee included Annie Warburton Goodrich, M. Adelaide Nutting, and Lillian Wald. The report of the committee was published in 1923, and is known as the Goldmark Report.[6] The report concluded that the quality of nursing education was inadequate on a number of counts including the use (or exploitation) of students for service at the expense of education. It recommended that future nursing educators have a university education.

There were a number of other issues that would need to be addressed before standards of practice could be formulated. A system of accreditation of schools of nursing would need to be put in place. Licensure would need to become mandatory and the title Registered Nurse protected in its use. A licensure exam would need to be created then ultimately made uniform across the states. A code of ethics would need to be formulated and adopted by the

ANA House of Delegates (this occurred in 1950). Nursing research would need to grow and expand. The inception of the journal *Nursing Research* in 1952 would help to cement this focus. The scope of this work is breathtaking and remarkable for the speed with which it took place. In 1973, the ANA published its *Standards of Nursing Practice*.[7] Though delegation receives brief mention under resource utilization, issues of accountability and responsibility are not raised in these standards, but do appear in the code of ethics of that day.[8] *Accountability* and *responsibility* do not appear in the early codes. They are first addressed in the Code of 1960 in two provisions in particular:

> "7. The nurse participates responsibly in defining and upholding standards of professional practice and education"; and

> "8. The nurse assumes responsibility for individual professional actions and judgment, both in dependent and independent nursing functions, and knows and holds laws which affect the practice of nursing."[9]

By 1968, when the Code is revised, the concept of delegation is added. The two provisions that are important to this discussion are:

> "3. The nurse maintains individual competence in nursing practice, recognizing and accepting responsibility for individual actions and judgments"; and

> "5. The nurse uses individual competence as a criterion in accepting delegated responsibilities and assigning nursing activities to others."[10]

By 1976, when the Code receives a thorough revision, accountability, responsibility, and delegation all appear in the provisions, which are reiterated in the 1985 revision of the Code:

> "4. The nurse assumes responsibility and accountability for individual nursing judgments and actions"; and

> "6. The nurse exercises informed judgment and uses individual competence and qualifications as criteria in seeking consultation, accepting responsibilities, and delegating nursing activities to others."[11]

In the 2001 revision of the Code, another thorough revision, accountability, responsibility and delegation finally meet in the same provision:

> "4. Nurse is responsible and accountable for individual nursing practice and determines the appropriate delegation of tasks consistent with the nurse's obligation to provide optimal patient care."[12]

So now, in the 2015 revision, *delegation* is removed from the provision and receives extensive discussion in the interpretive statements. The reason for its removal is that delegation is only one of many of the decisions and actions that a nurse makes and need not be singled out in the provision itself. The new provision reads:

> "4. The nurse has authority, accountability, and responsibility for nursing practice, makes decisions, and takes action consistent with the obligation to promote health and to provide optimal care."[13]

This may seem circuitous, and to some extent it is, but it is necessary. In this trajectory a subtle but extremely important shift takes place and needs to be noted.

Many early nursing books and journal articles discuss the responsibilities of the nurse. By this they mean the duties assigned to the nurse or ordered by the physician and executed by the nurse. These are what have been historically regarded as *dependent functions*, as they depend upon the direction of others, meaning physicians. The nurse is responsible for following and implementing orders faithfully with knowledge, skill, and competence. By the time we get to the Code of 1960, however, the nurse is *accountable* and *responsible* for individual nursing judgments and actions. This signals a monumental and historic change in nursing, for accountability and responsibility in this sense require nursing autonomy. Now nurses even "determine appropriate delegation." Even more, the 2015 revision acknowledges that the nurse has *authority*, accountability, and responsibility.[14] This shift in language is so faint and muted that it would be easy to pass it by, but it is an indication that nursing has at last come of age as a profession with authority, accountability, responsibility, and autonomous judgment!

4.1 Authority, Accountability, and Responsibility

The current edition of ANA's *Nursing: Scope and Standards of Practice* makes the following observation:

> All nursing practice, regardless of specialty, role, or setting, is fundamentally independent practice. Registered nurses are accountable for nursing judgments made and actions taken in the course of their nursing practice, therefore, the registered nurse is responsible for assessing individual competence and is committed to the process of lifelong learning. Registered nurses develop and maintain current knowledge and skill through formal and continuing education and seek certification when it is available in their areas of practice.[15]

The reference here is not to independent practice in the sense that actions are carried out in indirectly supervised or unobserved settings, but instead it means *independent* in the sense that nurses make independent, evidence-informed, professional judgments, rooted in nursing science, to which nurses must be committed to keeping current. Not only are accountability and responsibility linked to standards, they are also closely tied to professional growth, competence, and ongoing learning. The sources of authority of the knowledgeable, skilled nurse are three-fold: (a) the law, specifically state nurse practice acts, and (b) employing agencies and organizations, and (c) immersion and currency in the ever-developing art and science of nursing. All of these concepts, then—accountability, responsibility, authority, standards, competence, and autonomy—are inextricably intertwined and separable only for the purposes of discussion.

Neither nursing science nor the scope and standards of nursing practice are static. The same is true of nursing roles and functions, a fact that is recognized legislatively. As one of several examples, the California State Legislature amended the Nurse Practice Act with the following statement:

> The Legislature recognized that nursing is a dynamic field, continually evolving to include more sophisticated patient care activities. It declared its intent to recognize the existence of **overlapping functions** between physicians and registered nurses and to permit **additional such sharing** and to provide **clear legal authority** for those functions and procedures which have common acceptance and usage. Prior to this, nurses had been educated to assume advanced roles, and demonstration projects had proven their ability to do this safely and effectively. Thus, legal amplification of the role paralleled the readiness of nurses to assume the role and recognized that many were already functioning in an expanded role.[16] [bold in original]

As the scope of nursing practice expands, and as new roles and specializations develop in nursing, both the ANA and existing as well as emerging specialty practice associations will develop standards collaboratively for those roles and specializations. Currently, the scope and standards of nursing practice of 22 specialties have been formulated, adopted, and published cooperatively. They include nursing specialties such as addictions, corrections, faith community, forensic, holistic, intellectual and developmental disabilities, neuroscience, nursing informatics, and school nursing. It is not beyond of the realm of possibility to expect one day to see specialty scope and standards for space/aeronautics, policy/legislative, natural disaster, fitness, and global health nursing, all of which are arenas in which nurses are now involved.

4.2 Accountability for Nursing Judgments, Decisions, and Actions

The second interpretive statement declares that: "To be accountable, nurses follow a code of ethical conduct that includes such moral principles as fidelity, loyalty, veracity, beneficence and respect for the dignity, worth, and self-determination of patients, as well as adhering to the scope and standards of nursing practice."[17] While we have already looked at standards of practice, it must be noted that the Code is itself a binding standard of practice. As a standard of practice it predates other published nursing standards by approximately 25 years. The Code gives guidelines for meeting ethical obligations, creating an environment in which virtues can flourish, and for the values that ought to be affirmed and sought, and much more. The Code does not subscribe to one particular theoretical approach to ethics but instead leaves the door open for multiple approaches to ethics. The Code is hospitable to principle-based ethics, but also to an ethic of care, a virtue-based ethics, as well as deontological, teleological, and other approaches to ethics. It must, of necessity, affirm at least those principles detailed in *The Belmont Report*,[18] but it may go beyond it to embrace other principles and approaches as well.

A new addition to the interpretive statements is that "nurses are accountable for their practice even in instances of system or technology failure."[19] There is the story that is told of the healthcare team standing around the patient's bed, looking at the patient's chart (it's an old story!). The patient is now deceased and the team, peering intently at the chart and not the patient, says, "This is wonderful. Your lab reports and tests indicate that you are doing so much better." In 1978, Reiser, in *Medicine and the Reign of Technology*, examines the rise and effect of the use of technology in clinical medicine, tracing that rise from stethoscope and microscope through radiology, ventilators, antibiotics, renal dialysis, and more. Reiser argues that the clinical use of technology has created a distance between clinician and patient and lead to a process that made the physician's understanding of the patient's condition or disease independent from the patient's subjective description of her or his experience of the illness. Physicians viewed their use of technology as actually providing more accurate information than that provided by the patient, which leads to both a reliance upon technology and a loss of clinical dialogue. Reiser cites William Cullen, who cautioned clinicians not to completely disregard patient accounts "however fallacious," although some 30 years later there was an exhortation from René Laennec calling for a complete dismissal of patient testimony, "as we are almost always sure of being misled by their prejudice and ignorance."[20] Reiser states that "the physician has become a prototype of technological man…the environment of medical institutions can encourage a dependence on machines and specialists that erodes a physician's self-confidence, and distracts him from considering the patient as a whole person."[21]

In 1978, when his book was published, clinical diagnosis and care had not yet seen the massive changes in medicine that would result from computerization and an even greater escalation of technology. Reiser's work serves as a cautionary tale—technology must not supplant clinical dialogue, must not devalue patient testimony, and must never replace clinical judgment. As a crucial element of evidence-informed practice, nurses should trust their well-informed judgment and know that they remain accountable and responsible for clinical judgment and action even when all systems are down.

4.3 Responsibility for Nursing Judgments, Decisions and Actions

Nurses are responsible for their judgments, decisions, and actions—Period. *Responsibility*, however, may be shared. Responsibility apportions praiseworthiness or blameworthiness (liability). A nurse who, last Thursday, practiced below standards for safety and committed an error is accountable and responsible for that error. However, the fact that patient census and acuity escalated at the same time that two experienced nurses called in sick and were replaced by a new graduate with no experience in that specialty, means that some of the responsibility for the situation falls upon nursing administration as well.

Even in this context, ANA's scope and standards of nursing practice (which applies to all registered nurses) make it clear that there is a difference between what is expected of the novice or generalist nurse when compared with the expert, specialist nurse, or advanced practice registered nurse (APRN).[22] For each standard of practice competencies are listed that are basic competencies and applicable to all nurses no matter what their experience or level of knowledge. However, after specifying these competencies, there are "additional competencies for the graduate-level prepared specialty nurse and the APRN." [23] However, as a standard of practice, compliance with the *Code of Ethics for Nurses with Interpretive Statements* is not based on experience or level of knowledge. Its ethical expectations are for all nurses in all settings.

When a nurse fails to meet an obligation or carry out a duty, or fails to meet a standard of practice, he or she is liable. There is a distinction between legal liability and moral blameworthiness:

> Legal liability can take several forms. The legal action can be administrative as in a licensure proceeding; civil as in a malpractice action; criminal if the conduct of the nurse is defined in criminal law; or employment related. Legal liability stems from violations of the law and breaches of legal duty, and not necessarily from moral or ethical obligations. Often, the law and ethics overlap, especially in areas of health care such as care at the end of life, privacy and confidentiality,

and human rights. Ideally, the legal system would follow ethical thinking and consensus. Unfortunately, what is ethical may not be either covered in law or inadequately covered in law. In fact, some laws may actually be unethical. The law is useful as a consideration of fact and precedent for ethical decision making; however, laws do not direct or control nursing ethics or morals. The *Code of Ethics for Nurses* is a statement of moral obligations and duties intended to guide the practice of nursing; it is not a legal document. [24]

The requirements of the law and ethics are not coextensive. In general, the law requires the non-infliction of harm (nonmaleficence), while ethics requires both the non-infliction of harm as well as doing good (beneficence). That is, in general, the demands of ethics exceed the demands of the law. The law also carries a *coercive force*—one can be fined or incarcerated for violations of the law. The coercive force of ethics is that of *moral suasion.* Moral suasion, from the same root as *persuasion,* is "persuasion exerted or acting through and upon the moral nature or sense."[25] It is peer or community pressure placed upon one to conform to moral expectations and may include reprimand, rebuke, censure, shaming, shunning, exclusion from a community or association, and the like. For example, ethics violations by members of Congress may result in expulsion, censure, reprimand, or suspension. It may also involve public humiliation: for example, censure requires a member of the House of Representatives to "stand at the well" of the chamber to receive a verbal rebuke as the resolution of censure is read aloud by the Speaker of the House. Those House members who receive a reprimand must "stand in his place" but not in the well of the chamber.[26] In addition, the Office of Congressional Ethics posts "public disclosures" on its web page. [27] Even without fine or imprisonment, moral suasion carries a coercive force that can be significant. At one time, the ANA had published *Suggested Guidelines for Handling Violations of the Code for Professional Nurses,* and had distributed them to every state and territorial association, but those guidelines have since fallen out of print.[28]

The relationship between law and ethics can fall into one of four categories. An action may be legal and morally permissible, illegal and morally permissible, legal and morally impermissible, or illegal and morally impermissible. (See the table below.) Presuming *informed consent, patient wishes,* and *medical indication* (and a US context), *note that the moral permissibility of some clinical interventions, per se, is contested* so that their placement on the grid below would be contested (and therefore may be listed more than once simply to provide examples). In addition, some actions governed by state law *may be illegal in one jurisdiction, and legal in another.*

Relationship		Examples
legal &	morally permissible	abortion, amputation, hysterectomy, vasectomy, circumcision, separation of conjoined twins, sex reassignment, rendering first aid, required vaccination, withholding or withdrawing nutrition or hydration, assisted suicide, withdrawal of life-sustaining treatment
legal &	morally impermissible	abortion, vasectomy, sex reassignment, eugenic sterilization (historically), hemicorpectomy, withholding or withdrawing nutrition or hydration, assisted suicide, withdrawal of life-sustaining treatment
illegal &	morally permissible	abortion, assisted suicide, conscientious objection
illegal &	morally impermissible	eugenic sterilization (today), euthanasia, assisted suicide, female genital mutilation, forced medication, forced feeding, use of restraints

The Relationships Between Law and Ethics: Four Categories

The Code is clear that "nurses must not engage in practices prohibited by law".[29] Conscientious objection (see Provision 5) would be the sole exception to this declaration.

Sometimes the inner conflict that a nurse must grapple with is that of personal values that come into conflict with the law or with those of the employing institution. Consider, for example, military nurses whose firmly held values and beliefs come into conflict when ordered to force feed political detainees at a detention facility. Or consider the conflict of values experienced by a nurse practitioner working in student health in a conservative religious college that does not permit the prescription of birth control pills even for non-reproductive conditions such as endometriosis. Provision 2 states that the "nurse's primary commitment is to the patient".[30] This school nurse is in an untenable position where institutional constraints obstruct the primary commitment to the patient. The nurse is accountable and responsible for nursing care, even in the face of those constraints—and "must bring forward difficult issues related to patient care and/or institutional constraints upon ethical practice for discussion and review."[31]

Nursing has a distinctive sphere of knowledge and experience, a sizable body of research, and honorable and lengthy ethics tradition. In short, nursing has a significant perspective that must be brought to the table and inform practice. It is morally impermissible for the nurse to remain outside of or silent about patient care or institutional policy decisions. "Nurses are obliged to actively engage in, and contribute to, the dialogue and decisions made."[32] Not only are nurses accountable and responsible for judgments, decisions, and actions, they also bear accountability and responsibility for failing to participate in decisions, for failing to express a professional opinion.

As noted in the introduction, authority, accountability, responsibility, autonomy, standards, and competence are intertwined. Nurses must assess their own competence, competencies, knowledge, skill, and abilities. They must seek additional education, or consultation, or collaboration where necessary to meet the needs of the patient. That is, nurses must not exceed their limits, but at the same time must seek constantly to expand their repertoire of nursing knowledge and skill. They are not alone in this: "Educational resources should be provided by agencies or organizations and used by nurses to maintain and advance competence."[33]

4.4 Assignment and Delegation of Nursing Activities or Tasks

Like accountability and responsibility, delegation is also one of the hallmarks of the growth in autonomy experienced by the profession and its members. Early modern nursing largely took place in the home and did not move into hospitals fully until World War II and after. Even then, nurses were hired as private duty nurses for individual patients within the hospital context. This practice continued even into the 1970s. In this structure, there was no one to whom the nurse would or could delegate. For delegation to become a part of nursing, specific conditions must exist including at least some degree of autonomy of nursing practice, a degree of supervisory hierarchy, and differing levels of responsibility, preparation, and specialization. In addition, there must eventually be legal or regulatory support for delegation—eventually because the law often lags behind practice and must then play catch-up and authorize it. (For example, in California in the 1960s, it was illegal for a nurse to "pierce the skin" yet nurses routinely—and illegally—administered injections and started IVs!) There must also be a need for delegation. The need for delegation can be created by a national shortage of nurses and a lack of workforce sustainability so that in absolute numbers, there are not enough nurses to go around. The need for delegation also arises when tasks that once were restricted to medicine now accrue to nurses because of overlapping nurse practice acts, thus increasing the nursing task-load. In addition, an escalation in the number of tasks generated by advances in medicine, nursing, and technology also generate an increased task-load and a concomitant need for delegation. And finally, the ability to sustain life at higher and higher levels of nursing and medical complexity also contributes to the need for delegation. The Joint Statement on Delegation by the ANA and the National Council of State Boards of Nursing (NCSBN) acknowledges that delegation exists in circumstances where there is more demand than supply:

> There is more nursing to do than there are nurses to do it. Many nurses are stretched to the limit in the current chaotic healthcare environment. Increasing numbers of people needing health care combined with increasing complexity of the therapies create a tremendous demand for nursing care. More than ever, nurses need to work effectively with assistive personnel. The abilities to delegate, assign, and supervise are critical competencies for the 21st century nurse.[34]

Several terms are defined and clarified within this joint document. There is some identification of precise definitions that have differed between the ANA and the NCSBN in previously published separate position statements.

> Although there is considerable variation in the language…both defined delegation as the process for a nurse to direct another person to perform nursing tasks and activities. NCSBN describes this as the nurse transferring authority while ANA calls this a transfer of responsibility. Both mean that a registered nurse (RN) can direct another individual to do something that that person would not normally be allowed to do. Both papers stress that the nurse retains accountability for the delegation.[35]

Both papers define *assignment* as the distribution of work that each staff member is responsible for during a given work period. The NCSBN uses the verb "assign" to describe those situations when a nurse directs an individual to do something the individual is already authorized to do, e.g., when an RN directs another RN to assess a patient, the second RN is already authorized to assess patients in the RN scope of practice:

> Both papers consider supervision to be the provision of guidance and oversight of a delegated nursing task.[36]

The ANA and the NCSBN have different constituencies. The ANA speaks directly to and for nurses. The NCSBN "is an independent, not-for-profit organization through which boards of nursing act and counsel together on matters of common interest and concern affecting public health, safety and welfare, including the development of nursing licensure examinations."[37] In addition to assignment and delegation within the confines of the state's nurse practice acts, and the evaluation of the competencies and skills of the person to whom a task is assigned or delegated, what is pivotal to understand is that the Code directs that "[n]urses may not delegate responsibilities such as assessment and evaluation; they may delegate selected interventions according to state nurse practice acts."[38] In the ANA's use of the terms, and in the Code, the nurse always retains accountability and responsibility for judgments, decisions and actions including for delegation and assignment per se, and for delegated and assigned tasks, in all nursing roles and settings.

> Nurses who function as managers or administrators have a particular responsibility to facilitate appropriate assignments and delegation. This is sometimes complicated by difficult institutional policies around staffing, and can be compounded by a nursing shortage. The role of the manager or charge nurse, past and present, takes on one of the highest levels of delegation in the nursing profession. Nightingale in *Notes on Nursing* (1869) states that being in charge is not just about doing nursing tasks by oneself or appointing tasks to others, but also includes ensuring that others complete the duties to which they were appointed.[39]

Nightingale could not have foreseen the remarkable evolution of autonomy within nursing, nor the levels of complexity of care that would one day be given. As to accountability and responsibility—she would have expected no less.

Cases

Case 1

Mr. William Boggs is a nurse manager for a busy ICU. He cannot cover all three shifts with the nurses he has available. He knows that if he does not have additional nurses, the RN working nights would be unable to leave the unit for breaks, or for any other reason. Bill has repeatedly voiced concerns to the Vice President of Nursing over the ongoing issue of short-staffing, but is simply told to deal with it. So Bill institutes a change in the night shift patient-to-staff ratio. The RN on the unit will need to work without relief, and will have one CNA instead of another RN. Following a serious incident on the night shift, a disgruntled staff nurse anonymously reports Bill's actions as unsafe practice to the State Board of Nursing. As a result of the investigation by the Board, Bill talks to the state hospital licensing agency and the local newspaper about the staffing patterns at the hospital. Consequently, the hospital receives bad press and is contacted by the hospital licensing authority. Bill is fired.

Case 2

Blythe Seymour, RN, is working in a group practice dermatology clinic. The workload has increased and the physicians have decided to hire another RN. When Kate, the new RN, begins her orientation, Blythe tells her she will have to learn how to use the laser machine to remove tattoos. Kate hesitates and explains that she had thought that her responsibilities included assisting the dermatologist in the tattoo removal procedure, not doing it by herself. Blythe says, "This is why we hired you. I am sure that it's OK: the doc showed me how and I can show you." Blythe and Kate continue the orientation. When Kate goes home, she sends an email to the Board of Registered Nursing and asks if this falls within the RN scope of practice.

ENDNOTES

All URLs were current when accessed on January 9, 2015.

[1] American Nurses Association, *Nursing: Scope and Standards of Practice* (2nd ed.) (Silver Spring, MD: ANA, 2010).

[2] American Nurses Association, *Code of Ethics for Nurses with Interpretive Statements* (Silver Spring, MD: ANA, 2015).

[3] The Federal Policy for the Protection of Human Subjects or the 'Common Rule," in CFR 45 part 46 outlines protections and specifies requirements when humans participate in research. Research animals are protected by the Animal Welfare Act (1966), administered by the U.S. Department of Agriculture.

[4] Convention of Training School Alumni Delegates and Representatives from the American Society of Superintendents of Training Schools for Nurses, *Proceedings of the Convention, Manhattan Beach, November 2–4, 1896* (Harrisburg: Harrisburg Publishing; 1896).

[5] "To Meet Here Next Week: The American Society of Superintendents of Training Schools for Nurses," *Baltimore American* 1802, no. 33 (February 1897): 9, center column.

[6] Committee for the Study of Nursing Education, *Nursing and nursing education in the United States* (New York, NY: MacMillan Company, 1923).

[7] American Nurses Association, *Standards of Nursing Practice* (Kansas City, MO: ANA, 1973).

[8] ANA, *Nursing: Scope and Standards* (2nd ed.), 140.

[9] ANA, *A Code for Professional Nurses.* (New York: ANA, 1960), 10-11.

[10] ANA, *A Code for Professional Nurses.* (Kansas City, MO: ANA, 1960), pp. 4, 6.

[11] ANA, *Code* (1960), 1.

[12] ANA *Code of Ethics for Nurses with Interpretive Statements.* (Silver Spring, MD: ANA, 2001), 7.

[13] ANA *Code of Ethics for Nurses with Interpretive Statements.* (Silver Spring, MD: ANA, 2015), 15.

[14] Ibid.

[15] ANA, Nursing: Scope and Standards of Practice (2nd ed.) 24.

[16] Board of Registered Nursing, *An Explanation of the Scope of RN Practice Including Standardized Procedures*, sec. 2725 (reviewed January 2011), http://www.rn.ca.gov/pdfs/regulations/npr-b-03.pdf

[17] ANA, *Code of Ethics* (2015), Interpretive Statement 4.2, 15–16.

[18] National Commission for the Protection of Human Subjects of Biomedical and Behavioral Research of the U.S. Department of Health and Human Services, *The Belmont Report: Ethical Principles and Guidelines for the Protection of Human Subjects of Research* (Washington, D.C.: DHHS/USGPO, 1979), http://www.hhs.gov/ohrp/humansubjects/guidance/belmont.html

[19] ANA, *Code of Ethics* (2015), Interpretive Statement 4.2, 15–16.

[20] Stanley Joel Reiser, *Medicine and the Reign of Technology* (Cambridge, UK: Cambridge University Publishing, 1978). See also discussions of that period on the *technological imperative*—the "irresistible" pressure to use technology if it is available, even to the detriment of patients; Langdon Winner, *Autonomous Technology: Technics-out-of-Control as a Theme in Political Thought* (Cambridge, MA: MIT Press, 1978).

[21] Reiser, op cit.

[22] ANA, Nursing: Scope and Standards of Practice (2nd ed.), (2010).

[23] Ibid., 32–33.

[24] Laurie Badzek, "Provision Four," in *Guide to the Code of Ethics for Nurses: Interpretation and Application*, ed. Marsha Fowler (Washington, DC: ANA, 2010), 47–48.

[25] *Oxford English Dictionary* "Suasion," http://0-www.oed.com.patris.apu.edu/view/Entry/192401?redirectedFrom=suasion&

[26] "Process," Office of Congressional Ethics, http://oce.house.gov/process.html; "Citizen's Guide," Office of Congressional Ethics, http://oce.house.gov/citizens-guide.html

[27] "Office of Congressional Ethics," OCE, last modified November 10, 2014, http://oce.house.gov

[28] American Nurses Association, *Suggested Guidelines for Handling Alleged Violations of the Code for Professional Nurses* (New York: ANA, 1964).

[29] ANA, *Code of Ethics for Nurses with Interpretive Statements* (2015), Interpretive Statement 4.3 16.

[30] Ibid., Provision 2, v.

[31] Ibid., Interpretive Statement 4.3, 16–17.

[32] Ibid.

[33] Ibid.

[34] American Nurses Association and the National Council of State Boards of Nursing, *Joint Statement on Delegation* (press release Sept 26, 2006), http://nursingworld.org/DocumentVault/Position-Statements/Unlicensed-Assistive-Personnel/ana_ncsbn_jointdelegation14459.pdf

[35] Ibid.

[36] Ibid.

[37] "Home Page," National Council of State Boards of Nursing, https://www.ncsbn.org/index.htm

[38] ANA, *Code of Ethics for Nurses with Interpretive Statements* (2015), Interpretive Statement 4.4, 17.

[39] Badzek, "Provision 4," 50.

Provision 5

The nurse owes the same duties to self as to others, including the responsibility to promote health and safety, preserve wholeness of character and integrity, maintain competence, and continue personal and professional growth.

Provision 5. The Nurse as Person of Dignity and Worth

The *Suggested Code* of 1926 states that "the most precious possession of this profession is the ideal of service, extending even to the sacrifice of life itself."[1] This somewhat overwrought statement does correctly identify the central moral motif of the profession: the ideal of service. And yet, it also presents us with one of the central tensions of the profession: serving without extending one's self too far in service or risking harm to self. Should service extend even to the sacrifice of life itself? On the absolutely practical side, this would be a serious hindrance for nurse recruiters! Setting aside extraordinary circumstances under which nurses might *choose* to risk their lives, nurses do have a duty to tend to their own well-being, not to place themselves in harm's way, or, as the provision asserts, nurses have duties to self that ought to be observed.[2] A principle of duties to self (sometimes called a principle of self-regarding duties) can be divided into five main features: a duty of moral self-respect; a duty to preserve one's health, safety, and well-being; a duty to maintain wholeness of character; a duty to preserve one's integrity; and a duty to grow professionally and to maintain competence. These are collectively understood as a single duty of *duties-to-self*.

Introduction

Early nursing ethics has sometimes been characterized as more concerned with etiquette than with ethics; however, this is a misunderstanding.[3] Early nursing ethics focused on the character of the moral agent, refusing to separate personal from professional behavior. Its seeming focus on "good conduct" was in reality a focus on what the nurse *was,* not on what the nurse *did.* The presumption was that good character (the virtues) would produce right action, i.e., that virtue accomplished duty. Concerns for what appeared to be questions of etiquette were part of the larger concern for right conduct as it emerged from right character. It would not be out of place, then, that early nursing ethics texts included sections on personal hygiene, physical self-care, saving for old age, diet and sleep, recreation, and even dating behaviors. Reading more deeply into the nursing ethics literature the major emphases were on more substantive concerns such as confidentiality. Nursing was predominantly, sometimes exclusively, a female profession. It is important to note that the number of men in nursing has moved from 2.7% in 1970 to 9.6% in 2011.[4,5] However, what was regarded as "right character" for nurses in the late 1800s and even into the 1960s or 1970s was always conditioned by what society understood to be the "proper" comportment and role of women in its day.

So, within the social context of 1900 and the social location of women in that day, Isabel Robb quotes a letter she received asking for the recommendation of a nurse to fill a head-nurse position in a hospital. That letter concludes "in short, we require an intelligent saint."[6] This does, in fact, capsulize Robb's own understanding of the ideal nurse. It also ran counter to the cultural norm of women as bearers of the "finer sensibilities" and men (not women) as the possessors of intelligence. In this period it was claimed that higher education of women undermined the human species as it could reduce female fertility, even causing withering of the reproductive organs. Contrary to this cultural sensibility, Robb argues vigorously for the higher education of women as nurses.[7] Though her perspective would not today be seen as "feminist," in its day it was almost radically so.

Nursing students in that era were seen to be morally unformed. The task of the nursing school was, in part, the moral formation of the student, to equip the student for patient care (in the home in that period), and for participation in addressing the ills of society. The training school was tasked with shaping students into moral beings so that they could be trusted to deliver care, unsupervised, as graduates working in patient homes. Because the school was a place of moral formation to build moral character, every aspect of the student's life was subject to moral scrutiny. Students were to be morally equipped not simply with an ethics at the bedside, but also for a social ethics that addressed broader social problems. (See the chapter on Provision 9.)[8]

Robb, Parsons and many of the early nurses writing about nursing ethics held the view that nurses also exercised a moral influence upon patients. Parsons writes that "only the character that is built on a foundation of generosity and sweetness (if linked to intelligence, common sense, and humor) is safe in any exigency that may arise. This character foundation is seldom inherited, but must be built up by training and practice."[9] It was the task of the nursing faculty to build up this character foundation through training and practice within the school of nursing.

The emphasis on the character of the moral agent, otherwise known as "virtue ethics," was not unique to nursing, but rather reflected the prevailing societal virtue-oriented perspective on ethics. In a review of the nursing ethics literature from 1873 to 1975, the virtues expected of the nurse included:

absolute accuracy, accepts criticism, adaptable, agreeable, alert, appreciative, calm, charitable, cheerful, Christian, clean, comforting, competent, conscientious, considerate, contented, controlled, cooperative, courageous, courteous, cultured, decisive, decorous, dependable, devoted, dignified, disciplined, discreet, discriminating, eager, economical, economizing, efficient, emotionally mature, enduring, enthusiastic, even temperament, ever ready, faithful, fealty, fidelity to duty, finesse, firm, friendly, gentle words, gentle, gentler virtues, good reputation, good breeding, good grammar, good memory, good posture, gracious, healthy, healthful, helpmeet, high thinking, honest, humanitarian, humble, humorous, impartial, industrious, ingenious, inspires confidence, inspiring, intelligent, intuitive, joyful, kind, liberal of thought, likes people, longsuffering, loving, loyal, maintains dignity, meek, mentally fit, morally pure, neat, noble, nonmalevolent, obedient, open minded, patient, patriotic, peaceable, perceptive, perfect woman, physically fit, plain living, pleasant personality, poised, praiseworthy, principled, protective, prudent, public spirited, punctual, pure manner, pure speech, pure heart, quickness, quietness, readiness, reassuring, refined, reliable, resourceful, reserved manner, resistant to infection, respectful of authority, responsible, restful, right living, righteous, satisfied, scientific attitude, seeks perfection, self-controlled, self-respect, self-reliant, self-sacrificing, selfless, sense of fittingness, sincere, skilled, smiling, soft hand, spiritual, spontaneous, stable, strong, studious, sweet, sympathetic, systematic, tactful, tasteful dress, teachable spirit, team worker, tender heart, thorough, thoughtful, thrifty, tolerant, truthful, uncomplaining, unobtrusive, unselfish soul, versatile, vigilant, virtuous, warm, watchful, welcomes criticism, wholesome, womanly.[10]

Nurses were to demonstrate all of these, to all patients, in all settings, at all times! These were the virtues that were considered essential to the character of the nurse, those that made for a "morally good nurse." While it is hard to delete some of the more amusing "virtues" from the list, reducing the list to actual virtues or excellences expected of the nurse in days past (as opposed to sociocultural expectations of women) leaves: benevolence, care, compassion, competence, courage, devotion, faithfulness, honesty, integrity, justness, kindness, knowledgeableness, love, loyalty, nonmalevolence, prudence, skill, teachableness, temperance, tolerance, trustworthiness, wisdom, understanding, truthfulness.[11] One would hope to see these in nurses today.

In the late 1960s, nursing began shifting from a virtue-based ethics to a duty-based ethics. This shift was a consequence of both societal changes and the rise of the field of bioethics. However, both a virtue- and a duty-based approach to ethics are essential. If duties are to have any power and if virtues are to have any direction, both must be operative. The problem of a duty-based ethics is that obligations are empty if the person does not possess the moral character to meet those obligations. The problem of a virtue-based ethics is that it runs the risk of abuse through unwarranted intrusion into the private life of the individual, an intrusion that was amply evident in early nursing schools, even into the 1960s.

In addition to the shift from a virtue-based to an obligation-based ethics, there is another shift, that of the moral inter-relationship of personal and professional behavior. Because early nursing ethics into the 1960s was virtue-ethics based, it saw no separation between the personal and the professional or the private and public spheres of ethics. It was inconceivable that one could be a rogue, scoundrel, liar, and cheat in private life and not be the same in public life. Nurses were reminded that what they did in private life would reflect upon the honor and standing of the nursing profession, so they should act accordingly. Through the successive codes, until nursing moves to an ethics of obligation, both the personal and professional life of the nurse are addressed. The Nightingale Pledge includes the oath to "pass my life in purity and to practice my profession faithfully."[12] The *Tentative Code* of 1940 is explicit about the nurse's personal and professional conduct:

> It is the responsibility of the nurse to: conduct herself as a woman of high ideals, to use every means to maintain the dignity and standards of her profession…. Integrity, tolerance, and sympathetic understanding are characteristics which influence the personal conduct and social responsibility of the nurse. They are not the concern of the nurse alone, but have a definite influence on the standing of the nursing profession.[13]

By 1950, the first adopted code, the *Code for Professional Nurses* states in Provision 13 "the nurse in private life adheres to standards of personal ethics which reflect credit upon the profession," and in Provision 14, "in personal conduct nurses should not knowingly disregard the accepted patterns of behavior of the community in which they live."[14] However, by 1960, the revised Code states that "the nurse adheres to standards of personal ethics which reflect credit upon the profession."[15] The 1968 revision significantly shortens the Code and it is reduced from 17 to 10 provisions. Mention of the private or personal ethics of the nurse disappears from the Code and remains gone until 2001. Through the 1976 and 1985 versions of the Code, society shifted away from a virtue ethics and was developing an ethics focused on obligation. Bioethics, deeply influenced by the landmark book *Principles of Biomedical Ethics* by Beauchamp and Childress,[16] became and to some degree remains oriented toward ethical principlism; that is, the use of principles to analyze issues and cases and to guide decision-making. While the argument between virtue and obligation emerges in medicine, nursing moves in the direction of other approaches to ethics including feminism, an ethic of care, and to some degree, virtue ethics, while still retaining some of the clinical usefulness of principle-based ethics. Behind all this is the social context in which the misdeeds of politicians are uncovered by the media and the public argument takes place over whether one can be a rogue and scoundrel in private life and still be a good president, legislator, governor, etc.

Formation, including moral formation, is still a necessary part of nursing education. While early nursing saw the task of education as the full moral formation of young women into moral beings, specifically morally good nurses, contemporary moral formation is less expansive. It is assumed that students come to nursing school with a moral compass and that moral formation in today's nursing education includes creating an educational milieu in which the virtues necessary to be a morally good nurse will be fostered and cultivated and that the values espoused by the profession will become more integral to the lives of nurses-to-be. These virtues and values would then issue into comportment; that is, the outward bearing and manner of a morally good nurse, which would give evidence of the values and virtues within. From an ethical perspective it is important that students come to *be* nurses rather than persons who *do* nursing; that is, that they embrace nursing as a vocation or a profession in the old sense of *vocare* (to call; calling or to profess), and that they come to find their identity in nursing.

In the 2001 Code, the interrelatedness of virtue and obligation are reclaimed. Provision 5 is introduced into that Code and emphasizes the range of self-regarding duties incumbent upon the nurse. When first introduced in the 2001 draft of the Code, this provision and Provision 9 (on the moral role of nursing associations) were the most controversial. Interpretive Statement 5.3 of the 2001 Code emphasizes moral character and the consequent and mutual interaction of personal and professional ethics. It states: "Nurses have both personal and professional identities that are neither entirely separate, nor entirely merged, but are integrated. In the process of becoming a professional, the nurse embraces the values of the profession, integrating them with personal values."[17]

The 2015 Code extends the concerns of the analogous provision in the 2001 Code and reaches back into nursing's past to retrieve a fuller version of self-regarding duties. Patients are persons of worth and dignity. Nurses are as well.

5.1 Duties to Self and to Others

This section introduces the duty and grounds it in the self-inclusiveness of universal duties: what I owe to others as moral duties, I likewise owe to myself as a moral duty. Without so stating, this would mean that all of the provisions that apply to patients would also apply to oneself. For instance, Provision 1 states that "the nurse practices with compassion and respect for the inherent dignity, worth and unique attributes of every person." Self-respect, then, becomes one of the many duties owed oneself.

The first and only substantive work on an obligation of duties to self in the nursing literature is Andrew Jameton's chapter "Duties to Self: Professional Nursing in the Critical Care Unit."[18] Jameton notes that some philosophers, such as John Stuart Mill, have denied "that it is meaningful to talk of duties to self," but that others, including Aquinas, Kant and Hume "assert the meaningfulness of speaking of duties to oneself."[19] The arguments against a notion of duties to self center around our inability to enforce such duties; that is, that it is not meaningful to speak of self-coercion. In addition, they focus on our inability to release ourselves from such duties. Arguments for a notion of duties to self emphasize that while I cannot force myself to meet such a duty, even so, I am answerable for not meeting them and that duties to self are an instrumental good, a good that serves to support my duties to others. Note that duties to self differ from self-centeredness or entitlement in that they specifically support my moral duties to others. The strongest argument for a notion of duties to self resides in the concept of universal obligations. If an obligation applies to everyone, then I am not exempt from the collective "everyone," and those duties apply to me as well. Immanuel Kant's second formulation of the categorical imperative (his rule for moral rule-making) makes clear the inclusion of one's self in the universal: "Act so that you treat humanity, *whether in your own person* or in that of another, always as an end and never as a means." [italics added.][20]

The focus of the interpretive statements is the explanation of easily distinguished aspects of duties to self that are areas of concern. Jameton has identified three such aspects of duties to self: integrity, self-regarding duties, and identity. *Identity* refers to the coherent integration of one's personal and professional identity—what I am morally as a person, I am morally as a nurse. According to Jameton, identity includes concerns for maintaining ideals, the meaningfulness of work, expression of one's opinion, concern for wrongs committed by others, and participation in moral judgment in the work setting. *Self-regarding duties* refer to "duties [that] have a content that affects or applies to oneself primarily" (here competence is of specific concern). *Integrity* includes wholeness of character, attention to one's own welfare, or self-care, and emotional integrity reliant upon maintaining relational boundaries.[21]

The current provision (and its predecessor in the 2001 Code) is indebted to Jameton for his pioneering work, and incorporates his three aspects in somewhat different divisions.

Nursing ethics literature since the 1800s has affirmed an obligation of duties to self. One of the earliest such references is found in *Trained Nurse and Hospital Review*, July 1889. The article by H. C. C. (an otherwise unidentified superintendent of a training school in Boston) is entitled "Ethics in nursing: A nurse's duties to herself: Talks of a superintendent with her graduating class."[22] The focus of the article is on rest and bodily care as essential to the health of the nurse, for the sake of the ability to meet her (in that period nurses were exclusively female) duties to patients. Particular concern is directed toward the dedicated, energetic nurse who may overextend and risk personal health in the course of care-giving. H. C. C. writes "Please remember I am only speaking to the good nurses—the enthusiastic ones—poor nurses, lazy nurses, have no temptation to overwork themselves. They may die of indigestion but they will not die of exhaustion."[23] Many of the early nursing ethics books echoed this emphasis on duties to self. Isabel Robb's oft reprinted *Nursing Ethics: For Hospital and Private Use* (1900) places considerable emphasis on a range of duties to self.[24]

This emphasis on self-regarding duties remains prominent in the nursing ethics literature, including the earliest codes, for decades. The *Tentative Code* of 1940, one of the early, but never adopted, codes for nursing, includes a section on the nurse's responsibilities to herself (the Codes used the feminine pronoun). It states: "A nurse is to keep herself physically, mentally, and morally fit, and to provide for spiritual, intellectual and professional growth. She should institute savings plans which will bring her financial security in her old age."[25] While the emphasis on duties to self persists in the nursing literature, especially in textbooks, as noted above, it departs from the later codes. The incorporation of a provision on self-regarding duties in the 2001 Code was a reappearance rather than something new. The 2015 Code reorganizes the provision and more finely divides its content.

5.2 Promotion of Personal Health, Safety, and Well-Being

This section is both something old and something new. It is new in this Code but it is old in our nursing ethics tradition, as has been hinted at already. There is a two-fold moral thrust here. First, nurses have a duty to themselves to promote and preserve their own health—for their own sake. Second, nurses should "practice what they preach" and model health promotion and health maintenance for others. (Practicing a healthy lifestyle has a direct relationship to a healthy work environment, which will be addressed in Provision 6.)

However, nurses face particular risks. The first is the risk of fatigue and particularly compassion fatigue. Smart et al. find that:

> Providing care, compassion, and empathy for patients can enrich the lives of caregivers, both personally and professionally. Compassion satisfaction has been identified as a construct that measures these affirmative experiences. Conversely, in the course of performing their jobs, healthcare professionals may experience profound emotional reactions as they witness the suffering of others, and thus gradually lose the ability to demonstrate compassion and empathy (Sabo, 2006). Compassion fatigue is considered to be the progressive and cumulative product of prolonged, continuous, and intense contact with patients, and exposure to stress.[26]

Neville and Cole note that "health promotion behaviors were shown to be positively associated with compassion satisfaction and inversely related to both burnout and compassion fatigue."[27]

The second risk that nurses face are those hazards intrinsic to the care of people who are ill, especially that of risk by exposure to pathogens, but also other risks such as patient violence, latex or chemical allergies, lifting injuries, and so on. The Hewletts' poignant article "Providing Care and Facing Death: Nursing During Ebola Outbreaks in Central Africa" identified three themes from their interviews of nurses:

> …(a) lack of protective gear, basic equipment, and other resources necessary to provide care, especially during the early phases of the outbreaks; (b) stigmatization by family, coworkers, and community; and (c) exceptional commitment to the nursing profession in a context where the lives of the health care workers were in jeopardy.[28]

Nurses *do* show exceptional commitment and great courage in contexts where their own lives might be imperiled, as in an outbreak of Ebola Viral Disease (EVD) or in a natural disaster (extraordinary care contexts). Nurses also risk exposure daily to a wide range of communicable and infectious diseases. The duty to self includes taking all precautions that are available and to be vigilant in their use. Where there is a "lack of protective gear, basic equipment, and other resources necessary to provide care," nurses who nonetheless provide care do so as a matter of *supererogation.* Supererogatory acts are morally good and praiseworthy acts that go beyond what is strictly required. Historically, supererogation has been a hallmark of nursing—and of heroism.

Section 5.3 Wholeness of Character

Can a person who is a rogue, scoundrel, liar, and cheat in personal life be a virtuous nurse in professional life? It is unlikely. What we are personally, we are professionally. Our personal and professional identities are not separate; they are integrated and deeply commingled, mutually influencing each other. The person who has become a nurse, as opposed to the person who "does nursing," is one who has incorporated and integrated the values of the profession with personal values. The *Suggested Code* of 1926 notes that the "nurse who fails to find happiness in her work is not truly a nurse."[29] The person who does not has been and remains of special concern to nursing educators. It is unfortunate that some nursing students are misplaced in nursing, finding little congruence with the values of the profession, and having insufficient personal insight to see the conflict between their personal identity and their budding professional identity. Indeed, some students never fully become nurses; in fact, some are alienated toward nursing, and yet they develop the knowledge and skills to complete a nursing education with considerable success and to pass the NCLEX Board exams with flying colors.

Consider the quandary of Professor Svetlana Scythe. Senior student Allison Baxter has come into her Nursing Issues and Trends class. Allison has a GPA of 3.8, is technically proficient in clinical, has reasonable communication and interpersonal skills in patient care, is able to prioritize and manage a patient load, and is generally quite capable in nursing theory and practice. But she hates nursing. She wanted to be a paramedic with the fire department but could not get in because of the exceptionally competitive application process and the very long waiting list. In the end, her father pushed her into nursing school. For all her ability, she does not identify with nursing, nor does she want to and indeed, in discussions in the Issues and Trends class, has a negative attitude toward nursing and speaks ill of the profession among her friends. Prof. Scythe and other faculty members over the years have tried to counsel Ms Baxter out of the nursing program, but she will not leave in part because of parental pressure, in part because she does not want to start all over in school, and partly because it will shortly afford her an acceptable income. The faculty are very concerned about graduating this student, but don't know if they can refuse to graduate a student who has an excellent academic record but an anti-nursing attitude.

In the realm of the law, the law only demands that it be obeyed, and not that one be a good person besides. Ethics, of course, demands that we be good persons, beyond the expectations of what is strictly required. Course and program requirements of schools function like the law—you must meet them but they cannot demand that you be a "good nurse" in the sense of affirming nursing and embracing a nursing identity. However, where a student clearly fails to identify with nursing, vigorous and consistent attempts should be made from the earliest point onward to counsel the student out of the program. Early-out means earlier into another more suitable discipline, and less time lost. In addition, faculty can decline to give letters of recommendation if there is no evidence of change. In situations such as this, it is more than likely that the graduate will not find work meaningful, and in fact may come to hate it, and may leave the profession. She may also stay in this "bad marriage," but that is a matter of her choice.

Not everyone is suited to nursing, and admissions criteria and screening should be sufficiently rigorous to ascertain a student's fit with nursing. Post-admission follow-up and advising must be vigilant to redirect students when necessary. A more intentional and hearty emphasis on embracing the values and ethics of the profession, including the Code, from the earliest courses on would strengthen the curriculum and might serve as a deterrent to those who in the end will not become nurses in the moral sense. There is also an important place for courses on nursing history in this endeavor. While the case presents a moral quandary for nursing educators, as the 1985 Code makes evident the moral quandary, it is in the 2001 Code and then the 2015 Code that Allison's failure to come to congruence between personal and professional identity indicates an unfortunate failure in duties to self and forecasts an unhappy professional future for her. (See also Provision 7, Interpretive Statement 7.2.)

As an additional example, a similar situation sometimes can occur in nursing in some accelerated generic master's degree programs that take in persons with baccalaureates in non-nursing disciplines. Consider the case of Bob, an aerospace engineer with a master's degree who was laid off in the last defense-contract cycle of lay-offs. He saw a colleague apply to nursing school, asked about entry level salaries, and decided that nursing would be a quick and easy fix to his situation. He entered an accelerated generic program. He easily mastered the essential and technical skills and did exceptionally well academically and moved very rapidly through the program. However, he did not become socialized into the value structure of the profession. The program, though accelerated, did attend to professional socialization and the values of the program, but Bob did not. He retained the value structure of his prior discipline, rocket science, and consistently remarked that "nursing is not rocket science." His relationship with patients was one of superiority and "hard facts," lacking warmth and compassion. In these days of outsourcing, not all persons come into nursing with altruistic or pristine motives. And they need not. However, in nursing education it is crucial that attention be given to formation. Nursing values must be cultivated and inculcated in these adult learners, and integrated into their personal value structure so that they are nursing-identified, if they, the patient, and the profession are to be well served.

We bring our whole selves to nursing, not just our professional identity. That means that we bring our personal and our professional moral values in one package to the issues, concerns, and dilemmas that confront us in practice. The 2015 Code states: "Authentic expression of one's own moral point of view is a duty to self."[30] Sometimes this moral point of view is more professional than personal, and sometimes more personal than professional in derivation.

To further elucidate the principle of duties to self, consider Father Mac James, a patient on dialysis for polycystic kidney disease. It is expected that he will have to remain on dialysis for the rest of his life. He tells his nurse, APRN Abby Rhys, that he wants to give up, but as a retired Episcopal priest, also feels an obligation to continue treatment. One day he tells her that he wants to stop dialysis on July 23, following the 40th anniversary of his ordination. He says that his quality of life is unacceptable and probably will not improve, and that he has lived long enough. He says he has "a sense of peace" about his decision. The family is deeply distressed and tries to convince him to change his mind. After all, "he isn't that old," they say. In the clinical care conference, all agree that they think Father Mac should continue his dialysis. Except Abby. She has had several discussions with him and believes that his is a reasoned, reflective position, consistent with his beliefs and values. Abby needs to persuade the team to hear his perspective.

As the only member of the team who supports the patient's position, should she speak up? Yes. This does not mean that her view will prevail or that they are guaranteed to listen. Even when persons of moral goodwill come together to discuss life and death issues, there may be disagreement. One does not have a duty to self to express personal values so that others might be persuaded differently. The duty to self is to express one's professional moral point of view, to preserve one's authenticity, to be true to one's self. In addition, doing so maintains open moral dialogue that is not achieved if different views are suppressed. In some cases, this moral expression may be the only explicitly nursing moral voice, a voice that might not be heard is the nurse fails to speak up. Sometimes, however, the moral point of view being expressed arises from the nurse's personal values in a professional context.

Expressing one's moral opinion is one element of authenticity, as is the expression of who one really is within moral boundaries. Consider Michael Tucker, a hospice nurse and a lifelong Evangelical Christian in a largely Jewish facility. For Michael, issues of faith are as much matters of life and death as cancer is. In the hospice setting, Michael has ample opportunity to present his faith to his patients and he is ready to do so, but wonders what is or is not morally appropriate. Stan Grossman is his patient. He was reared without religious influences but identifies as Jewish. He is acutely anxious as he sees his life drawing to a close and is reaching out for answers. Another patient, Miriam Swartz, also Jewish, also seeking answers, yet not so panicked as Stan, asks

Michael about his faith and if it works for him. Sophie Adleman knows that her faith is of support to her as she is dying and wants Michael to pray with her and to call the *Bikur Cholim* to visit because "the Rabbis teach us that visiting a sick person removes $1/60$th of his or her illness" and she figures that she needs "only 58 more visitors to be healed." Michael needs to know if he can speak of his faith to Stan or Miriam. Is it a violation of his own values to call the *Bikur Cholim* for Sophie and to pray with her?

Morally, should Michael speak of his own Christian faith with panicked Stan? Probably not. Given Stan's anxious state of mind, it is quite possible that Michael's expression of his own faith would be coercive to Stan. If Michael judges that Stan is looking for spiritual answers, he should start with the answers closest to Stan's own background, and, if after adequate exploration it does not suffice, he can enlarge the discussion if Stan so requests. Michael ought to consider the nature and depth of the conversation and secure a professional chaplain for Stan, if warranted and welcome. Vulnerable patients may not be evangelized. Doing so is not an expression of a duty to self to be who one is; rather, it is taking unfair advantage of a wounded individual; many religions take a dim view of this. May Michael permissibly respond to Miriam with an expression of his personal faith? Probably yes. Miriam has asked a personal question of Michael and looks for a personal answer. Michael is free to authentically express who he is, even in matters of religious faith—or politics—if asked. Miriam has asked a question inviting a religious response and explanation. Michael may give this freely, yet only in a way that preserves Miriam's freedom, i.e., without attempting to proselytize her.

We bring our whole selves to patient care. Michael is a nurse, but he is also a Christian nurse, and that is who he must be for the patient who inquires of him, and that is who he must be for himself. In some instances, being one religion or another need not be made explicit to be consistent with one's self identity. In many instances the religion can be transparent to the patient, and remain the ground and motive for caring for others. What about Sophie? Does Michael jeopardize his faith commitment or values by supporting Sophie's explicitly Jewish religious needs? Can he pray with her and remain authentic? Michael has two kinds of religious commitments: those of his own faith and spirituality, and those of his faith that would extend the faith to others. Sophie is not interested in his faith; she is interested in her own. Given this, Michael does not jeopardize or deny his own Christian identity by supporting Sophie in her religion, even in praying with her. His duty to self in preserving his own wholeness of character is not affected by doing so. Since Sophie is not interested in having his faith extended to her, Michael may not do so; however, he may be a person of faith with another person of faith, bringing their separate faiths together for Sophie's good. In this, Michael does not deny his religious value of the extension of the faith; rather, he affirms that the extension of the faith is for those who choose to receive it. Like information in informed consent, it is to be offered, not imposed.

In not offering where it is not welcome, Michael does not violate any duty to self. Indeed, by refraining from offering faith where it is not welcome, Michael affirms the freedom that must exist in faith. Michael can call the *Bikur Cholim* to visit her, he can pray with Sophie, and he can refrain from evangelism and still remain authentically who he is. Early codes made explicit the demand that nurses respect the religious and other beliefs of the patient. Later codes broadened to include a respect for large range of personal attributes including religious and cultural values.

While this case focuses on religion as an aspect of "wholeness of character" of the nurse, religion is but one example. Some nurses are not religious; what if the nurse in this case were atheist? Any strong, enduring commitment that forms a part of who the nurse is as a person plays a role in wholeness. Whether politics, vegetarianism/veganism, ecofeminism, pacifism, atheism, agnosticism, or any other strongly held commitment, all are a part of who the nurse is authentically and may be shared, or must be withheld, on the same sorts of grounds as religion: nurses "are generally free to express an informed personal opinion as long as this maintains appropriate professional and moral boundaries and preserves the voluntariness or free will of the patient."[31] The role of the nurse is to assist patients in reflecting on their own values, not those of the nurse.

Patients request other kinds of personal information from nurses as well. Increasingly, patients demonstrate well-developed internet skills in sleuthing health problems and illness treatments. Greater or lesser degrees of discernment of the quality of the information make their way to the nurse in health and illness counseling and patient education. Nurses will be asked about alternative or adjunctive therapies, the orange pill in the TV ad, herbals, therapeutic teas, and a virtually endless range of treatments. Is the nurse free to offer an opinion?

Nurses have relationships with patients. If this is not the case, then the patient could just as well ask the question of a computer. But patients do not want a computer, they want a living, breathing, human nurse. Nurses are generally free to express their *informed* personal opinion in the face of patient inquiries on matters related to health and illness. In professional relationships, the boundaries are professional, and must be maintained. Patient freedom must also be maintained; that is, expressions of personal professional opinion must preserve patient voluntariness. Duties to self demand that nurses be who they authentically are—and that patients be supported in and permitted to be who they authentically are.

Section 5.4 Preservation of Integrity

Integrity is an internal quality, differing from honesty, which is interpersonal in nature. Integrity is, thus, primarily a self-concern and a self-regarding duty.

Preservation of integrity as a duty to self requires a lived conformity with the values that one holds dear, both personal and professional. Professional values, the values of nursing, while individually held, are shared by and among nurses so that a duty to self that is jeopardized in the work setting for one nurse may by circumstances apply to all nurses in that setting.

For much of the history of modern nursing, staffing patterns for "general duty" nursing have posed problems for nurses. In a report on the nursing supply in the 1920s, Burgess wrote the following in 1928:

> General floor duty is often the last resort of the desperate private duty nurse. There are reasons for this. In all too many hospitals the superintendent of nurses is expected to get along with an inadequate number of assistants. The result is that the nurses on floor duty are working under tremendous pressure, and as the number of patients swells above normal it is inevitable that much of the nursing service on the ward will be inadequate and improperly given. Good nurses refuse to work that way. …the fact is that general duty [i.e., hospital nursing] is not considered respectable. It is despised not only by the nurses themselves but by the hospital authorities. Some hospitals actually pay the servants and maids and orderlies on their wards as much as they pay graduate nurses.[32]

Too many patients, inadequate number of assistants, overworked, pressure cooked—a description from the 1920s that sounds remarkably contemporary!

The 1985 Code makes clear the responsibility of the nurses and the nursing profession to participate (individually and collectively) in establishing "conditions of employment that (a) enable the nurse to practice in accordance with the standards of nursing practice and (b) provide a care environment that meets the standards of nursing service."[33] The concern in Provisions 9 and 10 of the 1985 Code are for the preservation of the integrity of nursing. The Code of 2001 furthers the concerns of "integrity" by applying them to the preservation of the integrity of the nurse, especially the nurse placed in an economically constrained environment that pressures the nurse to practice in ways that violate the nurse's professional integrity. Like the *Tentative Code*, the 2015 Code overtly recognizes the moral threats posed by economic constraints in the practice setting, an observation that is lacking in the 1985 and other codes.

The 2001 Code also introduces two concepts that are new: that of integrity-preserving compromise, and that of "conscientious objection." In raising the notion of integrity-preserving compromise, the 2015 Code recognizes the competing values that confront the nurse, and that the nurse's nursing values might not prevail. However, the nurse need not bow to all other values. Nursing values, the nurse's values, are to be preserved and the nurse is to negotiate compromises that will preserve them. This requires, of course, a "community of moral discourse," where the nurse speaks up, and where one profession's values do not trump those of others. (See Provision 6 for more on the community of moral discourse.)

The second new concept is not actually new but rather the introduction of new terminology that is continued, intact, in the 2015 Code. In the 2001 Code, and now in the 2015 Code, "refusal of assignment" is given its more formal designation, *conscientious objection*. Conscientious objection is most frequently applied to the refusal on moral or religious grounds to bear arms or to go to war. Prior to the American Revolution, conscientious objectors in this country often came from "peace churches" such as the Quakers, Mennonites, and Brethren. As a consequence, these churches have a long tradition of scholarly literature on conscientious objection and pacifism. When not applied to war or to bearing arms, conscientious objection refers to the morally or religiously based refusal to participate in an activity otherwise required, perhaps even by the law. Thus, in nursing, conscientious objection would be the refusal to participate in some aspect of patient care on moral or religious grounds. This refusal might be based on a moral or religious objection to a specific intervention categorically (e.g., abortion, sex reassignment surgery, lethal injections in capital punishment, force-feeding prisoners), or moral objection to a particular intervention with a specific patient (as in requiring Father Mac above to continue dialysis), or a moral objection to a pattern of behavior (e.g., habitual short staffing that forces sub-standard nursing practice that endangers patient wellbeing).

Australian nurse-ethicist Johnstone identifies five conditions for conscientious objection. They are: (a) moral motivation; (b) an autonomous, informed, and critically reflective choice, (c) a last resort, (d) admission by the objector that others may have equal and opposing claims, and (e) situations with moral uncertainty.[34]

Conscientious objection, whether expressed individually or collectively, always involves the refusal to violate a deeply held moral value, personal or professional. Previous codes have always provided a "moral way out" for nurses who were confronted with any one of the conditions noted above. These codes specified that where there is a categorical objection to a particular intervention (e.g., abortion) that such objection should be made known at the time of employment and that, in no case, should the nurse abandon the patient. This 2015 Code enlarges the discussion, gives it a conceptual framework in conscientious objection, and rightly expresses it as an aspect of duties to self. It also notes that conscientious objection does not protect a nurse against consequences for having refused to participate in an aspect of nursing practice or patient care.

The benefit of clearly identifying an ethical rule of conscientious objection is that it gives nurses a way to conceptualize and articulate a "refusal to care," more accurately a "refusal to participate" in a specific aspect of patient care. In the days before advance directives, when patients were full code because a Do-Not-Resuscitate order was not written when it should have been (e.g., no statistical chance of success, or the patient did not want it), nurses might remind the physician to write one only to encounter foot-dragging. When the patient went into cardiac arrest, some nurses felt the only way out of the dilemma was to engage in a "slow code." Conscientious objection provides a way out of this bind by affording nurses an opportunity to make a strenuous objection known on moral grounds, and then to make it stick. In other words, conscientious objection permits nurses to preserve their integrity in the face of a clinical activity or situation to which they have moral objections to participation.

Section 5.5 Maintenance of Competence and Professional Growth

Previous Codes have included a responsibility for ongoing professional growth, reaching back to *A Suggested Code* of (1926) and *A Tentative Code* of (1940). The *Suggested Code* states:

> Professional growth and development are promoted by membership in professional organizations, both state and local, by attendance at meetings and conventions and by constant reading on professional subjects. Yet further growth may be assured by attendance on institutes and postgraduate courses.[35]

Though the context is that of professional growth as a duty to self, it does not so much discuss professional growth as it does how one might go about growing professionally.

The *Tentative Code* of 1940 is not quite so specific; it declares a "requirement of continuous study and growth" and a duty for the nurse "to provide for spiritual, intellectual and professional growth," as noted above.[36] In several Codes, such as that of 1950, the nurse is responsible for "continued reading, study, observation, and investigation," not strictly as a duty to self, but rather as a duty to the profession in order that the social–professional status of nursing, and the status of the individual nurse as a professional, may be maintained.[37] Notice, however, that it moves beyond continued study and reading for self-development, or even to better serve the patient; instead, it casts the duty in terms of maintaining the stature of nursing as a profession, maintaining the social prestige of nursing. Nursing is, of course, in a struggle in these and ensuing years for the social recognition accorded professions. The *Tentative Code* even opens with the assertion "Nursing is a profession," and then goes on to defend that assertion with a sizable amount of material that is not actually appropriate to a code of ethics.[38] Here, the concern is for the profession and its professionalism, not for the nurse, so it could be argued that in this particular statement formulation it may not be a duty to self.

The emphasis upon professional growth as an aspect of duties to self shifts over the years in two ways. First, it shifts from a duty to self to a duty to the profession for the sake of the profession. Second, it shifts in the direction of an increasing concern for competence, mostly for the sake of the profession, but also for the sake of the patient. Though they have been used as if interchangeable, professional growth and competence are not the same. Competence is the rock bottom level of acceptable practice, the level below which no practitioner should fall. Professional growth moves the nurse beyond basic entry education and mere competence, as a minimum standard of practice, toward excellence and is thus directed toward an ideal of practice. The Code of 1985 merges professional growth and competence and their ends:

> For the client's optimum well-being and for the nurses' own professional development, the care of the client reflects and incorporates new techniques and knowledge in health care as these develop, especially as they relate to the nurse's particular field of practice. The nurse must be aware of the need for continued professional learning and must assume personal responsibility for currency of knowledge and skills.[39]

Though the Codes have presented professional growth as necessary to competence for the sake of the profession's stature, and for the welfare of the recipient of nursing care, Jameton argues that competence is instead a self-regarding duty, primarily directed toward oneself. He writes:

> Competence is...primarily...an attribute of self to be cultivated, and secondarily as a means of affecting patients.... Nursing, as a practice, provides a set of "internal" goods that are satisfying in themselves. Internal goods are the intrinsic excellences of good nursing practice, as distinguished from external rewards such as salary, the gratitude of patients, and so forth. The existence of intrinsic conceptions or excellence makes it possible for nurses to regard development of competence as a matter of self-development rather than simply a matter of achieving external rewards through affecting others.[40]

Without denying that competence affects others, the 2001 Code more clearly and vigorously casts competence as a self-regarding duty, essential to self-respect and self-esteem, professional status, and the meaningfulness of work.[41] It ties professional growth to a commitment to life-long learning reminiscent of the early nursing ethics literature. Professional growth is not limited to the knowledge and skill necessary for patient care, but also includes "issues, concerns, controversies, and ethics."[42]

Emphasis upon competence, per se, is repeated and reinforced in the 1960 Code and in succeeding codes. Provision 8 of that 1960 Code states: "The nurse maintains professional competence and demonstrates concern for the competence of other members of the nursing profession."[43] Over the next several decades, competence as articulated in the Codes has four emphases: the professional competence of the nurse; the competent nurse forced by circumstances (e.g., staff reductions) to practice less competently; the duty to act upon observed incompetence of nurses, physicians or others; and the duty to delegate tasks only in accord with the competence of others. Only the first and second of these refers to a self-regarding duty of competence. As a self-regarding duty, the Code of 2001 and the Code of 2015 call for ongoing and authentic self-evaluation and peer review as a means of evaluating one's performance.

5.6 Personal Growth

The requirement for personal growth is by no means new to nursing's ethics, but it has been neglected in recent decades. Interestingly, the 2001 Code mentions personal growth in the provision itself but does not address it in the interpretive statements. Instead it focuses on professional growth. The 2015 Code rectifies this omission. After noting that personal and professional, private and public ethics, values, and virtues are brought together in one person, in wholeness of moral character, Interpretive Statement 5.6 actually notes that "[n]ursing care addresses the whole person as an integrated being; nurses should also apply this principle to themselves."[44] Finally! The nurse is a whole person. Now, if nurses can just remember that. Professional growth is specific to one's vocation. Personal growth interacts with professional growth but is a much larger domain covering all of the nurses' interests, knowledge, world and self-understanding, as well as the totality of the nurse's well-being. The Code does not simply grant permission to develop personally—it expects it.

Conclusion

Nursing has historically maintained that the nurse owes the same duties to self as to others. In this provision, the 2015 Code develops the material that was newly reintroduced in 2001. Unlike early discussions of duties to self that focused on the physical health of the nurse, continued education, and savings for old age, this more contemporary Code directly extends the discussion into areas of wholeness of character, identity and integrity, and wholeness of person not seen in the earlier literature or codes. As with the 2001 Code, it holds competence to be a self-regarding duty and not simply an instrumental good in service to others. Indeed, this provision focuses on the full range of duties to self as nurse-focused, rather than nursing- or patient-focused. At first glance, this provision might seem an innovation, and in some ways it was in 2001. But it is not—it only reclaims what has been crowded out. It is something old, something renewed, something borrowed from history, and something true.

Cases

Case 1

Ms Natalicio is a newborn intensive care unit (NICU) nurse. She is skilled at feeding and caring for medically stable infants, but is much less proficient with infants who are critically ill or whose condition changes rapidly. Nurse Natalicio has a reputation in the NICU that she can teach almost any infant to take oral feedings. As one physician says, "She can successfully feed a rock." The nurse manager of the NICU is encouraging her to expand her skills through continuing education, and has made continuing education an element of the annual performance appraisal for all RNs on the unit. Ms Natalicio argues that she is good at what she does and does not have time or energy to pursue more continuing education.

ENDNOTES

1   American Nurses Association, "A Suggested Code," *American Journal of Nursing* 26, no. 8 (August 1926): 599–601.

2   For a more complete discussion of the obligation or option to care in the face of risk to the nurse, see the ANA Position Statement "Risk and Responsibility in Providing Nursing Care" (Washington, DC: ANA, revised June 21, 2006).

3   This section on nursing ethics history is adapted and modified from A. Davis, M. Fowler, and M. Aroskar, *Ethical Dilemmas and Nursing Practice* (5th ed.) (Upper Saddle River, NJ: Pearson Education, 2010), 30–42.

4   "Men in Nursing Occupations," U.S. Census, https://www.census.gov/newsroom/releases/pdf/cb13-32_men_in_nursing_occupations.pdf

5   Peter McMenamin, "More Men Are Being Educated as Registered Nurses," *ANA Nursespace*, last modified May 15, 2013, http://www.ananursespace.org/BlogsMain/BlogViewer/?BlogKey=3b170d0f-2c76-426f-bdbb-b4a10aa98234&ssopc=1

6   I. A. H. Robb, *Nursing Ethics: For Hospital and Private Use* (New York: E. C. Koeckert, 1900), 40. Reprinted without revision in 1911, 1916, 1920.

7   Ibid., 22–38, 40–47.

8   Marsha Fowler, *Ethics and Nursing, 1893–1984: The Ideal of Service, the Reality of History* (Los Angeles: University of Southern California, 1984), 1–420.

9   Sara E. Parsons *Nursing Problems and Obligations*. (Boston: Whitcomb, 1916), 8.

[10] Fowler, *Ethics and Nursing,* 412–13. For an example of articles naming virtues essential to the graduate nurse, see also: Adeline S. Weis, "Our Professional Balance," *American Journal of Nursing* 28, no. 10 (1928): 1025–26.

[11] Fowler, op cit, 412–413.

[12] Lystra Gretter, *The Florence Nightingale Pledge* (Detroit, MI: Farrand Training School for Nurses, 1893). Photocopy of autograph manuscript.

[13] American Nurses Association, "A Tentative Code", *American Journal of Nursing* 40, no. 9 (1940): 977–980.

[14] American Nurses Association, *A Code for Professional Nurses* (New York: ANA, 1950), Provisions 13 and 14.

[15] American Nurses Association, *A Code for Professional Nurses* (New York: ANA, 1960), Provision 12.

[16] Tom Beauchamp and James Childress, *Principles of Biomedical Ethics* (1st ed.) (Oxford, UK: Oxford University Press, 1979).

[17] American Nurses Association, *Code of Ethics for Nurses with Interpretive Statements* (Silver Spring, MD: ANA, 2001), 24.

[18] Andrew Jameton, "Duties to Self: Professional Nursing in the Critical Care Unit," in *Ethics at the Bedside,* eds. Marsha Fowler and June Levine-Ariff (Philadelphia: JB Lippincott, 1985), 115–35.

[19] Ibid., 117–18.

[20] Immanuel Kant, *Groundwork of the Metaphysics of Morals,* ed. Mary J. Gregor (Cambridge, England: Cambridge University Press, 1998).

[21] Jameton, "Duties to Self," 120–32.

[22] H. C. C., "Ethics in nursing. No. II: A nurse's duty to herself: Talks of a superintendent with her graduating class," *The Trained Nurse and Hospital Review* 3, no. 1 (July 1889): 1–5.

[23] Ibid., 2.

[24] Robb, *Nursing Ethics.*

[25] American Nurses Association, "A Tentative Code," 980.

[26] D. Smart, A. English, J. James, M. Wilson, K. B. Daratha, B. Childers, and C. Magera, "Compassion Fatigue and Satisfaction: A Cross-Sectional Survey among US Healthcare Workers," *Nursing & Health Sciences* 16, no. 1 (2014): 3.

[27] Kathleen Neville and Donna Cole, "The Relationships Among Health Promotion Behaviors, Compassion Fatigue, Burnout, and Compassion Satisfaction in Nurses Practicing in a Community Medical Center," *The Journal of Nursing Administration* 43, no. 6 (June 2013): 352.

[28] Bonnie Hewlett and Barry Hewlett, "Providing Care and Facing Death: Nursing During Ebola Outbreaks in Central Africa," *Journal of Transcultural Nursing* 16, no. 4 (2005): 289.

[29] American Nurses Association, "A Suggested Code," 600.

[30] ANA, *Code of Ethics for Nurses with Interpretive Statements* (Silver Spring, MD: ANA, 2015), 20.

[31] Ibid.

[32] Mary Ayers Burgess, "The Hospital and the Nursing Supply," in *Transactions of the American Hospital Association* (Chicago: AHA, 1928): 440–14.

[33] ANA, *Code of Ethics for Nurses with Interpretive Statements* (Kansas City, MO: ANA, 1985), 14.

[34] Megan-Jane Johnstone, *Bioethics: A Nursing Perspective* (4th ed.) (London: Churchill Livingstone, 2004): 329–30.

[35] American Nurses Association, "A Suggested Code," 599–601.

[36] ANA, "A Tentative Code", 977, 980.

[37] ANA, *A Code for Professional Nurses* (1950).

[38] ANA, "A Tentative Code", 977–78.

[39] ANA, *Code of Ethics for Nurses with Interpretive Statements* (1985), 9.

[40] Jameton, "Duties to Self," 124.

[41] ANA, *Code of Ethics for Nurses with Interpretive Statements* (2001), 18.

[42] Ibid.

[43] ANA, *Interpretation of the Statements of the Code for Professional Nurses* (New York: ANA, 1960), 11.

[44] American Nurses Association, *Code of Ethics for Nurses with Interpretive Statements* (2015), Interpretive Statement 5.6.

Provision 6

The nurse, through individual and collective effort, establishes, maintains, and improves the ethical environment of the work setting and conditions of employment that are conducive to safe, quality health care.

Provision 6. The Moral Milieu of Nursing Practice

Introduction

The work environment in which nursing care is provided is of paramount importance in this provision. While this provision emphasizes the ethical environment specifically it extends to the whole of the work setting and the ways in which it is conducive to safe, quality health care. This provision has a long and somewhat contested history in its evolution to the present provision. Its roots lie deep in the concern for the economic and general welfare of the nurse. *A Suggested Code* (1926) notes that "self-development can best be nurtured in the soil of economic self-respect."[1]

There is an uneasy tension however, one that persists to this day. The concern for the economic welfare of the nurse, that is, nursing self-interest, is always held in tension with concern for the welfare of patients. Thus the *Suggested Code* also states that "[n]o worker is welcome to the ranks of nursing who does not put the ideal of service above that of remuneration."[2] This must be understood in the light of the early employment settings of nursing. Into the 1930s, hospitals were staffed by students who were gradually replaced by graduate nurses as staff nurses. Until the 1940s, much of nursing (by graduate nurses) took place in the home. In the 1940s, as nursing began to shift more fully into hospitals, nurses still served as private duty nurses hired by the patient or the patient's family to give care in the hospital; hospitals were transitioning into employing graduate nurses as staff nurses. The development of staff nurse positions was not uniform across the states and it is likely that California developed staff nursing prior to other states.[3] In addition to low wages, nurses were subject to arbitrary schedules including split shifts, rotating shift schedules, and uncompensated overtime, no health or retirement benefits, and no sick or personal leave. Maternity leave was not considered and does not emerge until the late 1960s.[4]

From the late 1800s through the *Tentative Code* of 1940 (and beyond), it was clear that both nursing students and graduate nurses could be and were subject to exploitation. Students were used for service at the expense of education and graduate nurses were underpaid and at times unremunerated. *A Tentative Code* is abundantly clear that this is unacceptable. It states:

> In some instances, the economic status of the patient will undoubtedly command the gratuitous services of nurses; but officers of endowed institutions and hospitals…have no claim upon the nurse for unremunerated services…. If an institution organized to provide adequate service for the sick, including nursing, for any reason cannot fulfill this obligation, it should not expect to commandeer the unremunerated, or markedly underpaid, services of nurses.[5]

A brief word about collective bargaining is important here. One of the original purposes of the ANA, articulated in its bylaws of 1897, was to "promote the usefulness and honor, the financial and other interests of the nursing profession."[6] For decades, however, nurses were unable to secure satisfactory wages and working conditions and could not engage in collective bargaining. Following the end of World War II,

> [t]he severe nursing shortage that developed during the war had not abated and salaries of registered nurses were low, lagging far behind those of other workers. Many believed that both the quality and quantity of nursing care were suffering because of unsatisfactory personnel policies and inadequate wages. In addition, nurses were restless and wanted changes in their working conditions. In response to active recruitment, some were joining labor unions as a means to improve their economic status.
>
> The ANA initiated the Economic Security Program in an attempt to rectify these pressing dilemmas. The program…endorsed collective bargaining and maintained that state nurses' associations should be the sole representatives for nurses in labor relations. The initial response of nurses to the ESP was positive…. ANA's new ESP followed the example of the California State Nurses Association's (CSNA) ESP, which had already been successful in winning pay raises for California nurses during World War II.[7]

Nursing constituted a huge population of workers that was largely unrepresented in collective bargaining. The ANA, through its State Nursing Associations (SNAs), sought to represent nurses in collective bargaining. By 1950, the ANA formally adopted a "no-strike policy." Strikes were regarded as inconsistent with the professional ideal of service. In addition, many nurses saw collective bargaining, itself, as inconsistent with the profession's values and ideals. Because the no-strike policy weakened the ANA negotiating position, and because the progress in wages and work conditions that had been made was inadequate, the ANA rescinded its no-strike policy in 1968.[8] Thereafter, more nurses joined SNAs, thus strengthening them.

Nurses were, of course, too large a population to go unnoticed by labor unions, who would come to vie with the ANA for the authority to represent nurses. This is a contentious issue both historically and in the present day that deserves separate attention beyond what can be afforded here. Nonetheless, it is important to note the balance that the ANA strives to achieve in its collective bargaining:

> Some constituent member associations of ANA serve as an advocate for the nurse by seeking to secure just compensation and humane working conditions for nurses by engaging in collective bargaining on behalf of nurses. While seeking to assure just economic and general welfare for nurses, collective bargaining, nonetheless, seeks to keep the interests of both nurses and patients in balance.[9]

By 1950, when the Code is no longer in narrative format but instead enumerates a series of provisions, Provision 9 states: "The nurse has an obligation to give conscientious service and in return is entitled to just remuneration."[10] However, by the 1960 revision of the Code, the provision (now 10) becomes "the nurse, acting through the professional organization, participates in establishing terms and conditions of employment."[11] Several issues are hidden in this shift in language. They include an expansion of concern for remuneration to the larger context of conditions of employment and work setting conditions as well; perspectives on collective bargaining to secure a just wage and satisfactory working conditions; disagreement over who should conduct collective bargaining on behalf of nurses; the tension between professional self-interest and the interests of patients; and the permissibility of nurses striking.

By 1968, the comparable Provision 8 reads: "The nurse, acting through the professional organization, participates in establishing and maintaining conditions of employment conducive to high quality nursing care."[12] Though the provision intrinsically contains a concern for the Economic and General Welfare (E&GW) of the nurse, it also heightens the notion that satisfactory working conditions for the nurse contribute to high quality of nursing care, to the benefit of the patient. By 1976, however, the corresponding provision (9) reads: "The nurse participates in the profession's efforts to establish and maintain conditions of employment conducive to high quality of nursing care."[13] The professional organization has been dropped from the provision in recognition of the success of unions in taking over collective bargaining from the professional associations. The interpretive statement refers specifically to the E&GW of the nurse, standards of practice and the quality of nursing care, collective action through assistance from the professional association in negotiating employment conditions and professional standards, and individual agreements for the provision of nursing care. Interpretive Statement 9.2 (1976) states, in part:

> Defining and controlling the quality of nursing care provided to the client is most effectively accomplished through collective action.... The Economic and General Welfare program of the professional association is the appropriate channel through which the nurse can work constructively, ethically, and with professional dignity. This program, encompassing commitment to the principle of collective bargaining, promotes the right and responsibility of the individual nurse to participate in determining the terms and conditions of employment conducive to high quality nursing practice.[14]

By 1985, the analogous Provision 9 is identical, though the interpretive statements change. Underneath the provision is a concern that the shift of collective bargaining to unions that represent non-professional health workers as well as nurses with a worker-oriented focus could be at odds with concerns for standards of practice, nursing ethics, and the quality of nursing care:

> Nurses may participate in collective action such as collective bargaining through the state nurses' association to determine the terms and conditions of employment conducive to high quality nursing care. Such agreements should be consistent with the profession's standards of practice, the state law regulating nursing practice, and the Code for Nurses.[15]

There is a hint here about concern for the moral standards of the work environment that become pronounced in the succeeding code. By 2001, Provision 6 is modified slightly but the interpretive statements shifts the focus to an emphasis on the moral environment in which care is rendered. The provision reads: "The nurse participates in establishing, maintaining, and improving healthcare environments and conditions of employment conducive to the provision of quality health care and consistent with the values of the profession through individual and collective action."[16]

Note that the provision adds in "improving healthcare environments" and "consistent with the values of the profession." The first section of the interpretive statement (Interpretive Statement 6.1) focuses on the "[i]nfluence of the environment on moral virtues and values" and the second (Interpretive Statement 6.2) is about the "[i]nfluence of the environment on ethical obligations." [17]So, between 1985 and 2001 what happens to bring about this shift?

In the years between 1950 and 2001, significant progress was made in the E&GW of the nurse with improvement in working conditions and wages. "Improvement" does not mean "solved," as some issues persist, such as salary compression, absence of breaks, unpaid overtime, and nurse–patient ratios. But with these issues improving, nurses could turn their attention toward concerns about the environment of practice, specifically the moral environment.

In 1974, Marlene Kramer published *Reality Shock: Why Nurses Leave Nursing*.[18] Her book is the report of her research that examines the movement of new nursing graduates into the workforce. Its focus is "mainly on the discrepancy and the shock like reactions that follow when the aspirant professional perceives that many professional ideals and values are not operational and go unrewarded in the work setting."[19] Kramer uses a sociological method and perspective to examine the effect of discordant value structures upon nurses, the value structure of the nursing profession against the value structure of bureaucratic health care that employs the nurse. She states "the goal of adaptation in a reality shock situation is the creation of a viable habitat in which one can be productive, effective, and content for a longer and probably indefinite period of time."[20] Adaptation to reality shock, then, requires some change in the environment. While Kramer uses a sociological method, it is clear from the cases that she cites that the values and ideals that are challenged are in fact moral values and ideals. Her work, thus, prefigures that of Jameton on moral distress.

In *Nursing Practice: The Ethical Issues*, Jameton identifies three categories of moral concern: moral uncertainty, moral dilemma, and moral distress. *Moral uncertainty* occurs when one does not know whether a troubling situation is moral or not and, if it is, what values or obligations pertain. *Moral dilemma* occurs when one is confronted with a conflict of values or a conflict of obligations that pose conflicting courses of action. *Moral distress* "arises when one knows the right thing to do, but institutional constraints make it nearly impossible to pursue the right course of action."[21] It is important to note that the distress arises from having certainty about what is the right action to take yet being obstructed from taking that action by the institutional constraints that are operative. The distress of *moral distress* does not arise from discomfort intrinsic to the case itself. Since 2000, there has been an escalation of interest in moral distress in the nursing research literature, across settings, roles, and even countries. Storch and colleagues note:

> Within Canada's fast-paced, ever-changing healthcare environment, providers are experiencing difficulty practising according to their professional ethical standards, leading many to experience moral or ethical distress. Limited attention has been paid to improvements in the ethical climate in healthcare settings in research focusing on

nurses' workplaces. In this three-year study, we focused on how the ethical climate in healthcare delivery can be improved.... Together, we developed strategies for taking action, aimed at improving the quality of the work environment.[22]

While not all issues that trouble nurses in the United States are universal, some are certainly shared despite national boundaries.

The nursing literature has many research articles on verbal abuse of nurses by physicians, sexual harassment, bullying, mobbing, workplace violence against nurses and nursing students and other issues that characterize frankly reprehensible moral behavior. There is no ambiguity, uncertainty, or even disagreement about the rightness or wrongness of these behaviors. In recent years institutional policies have been developed to address these issues, and in some cases laws have undergirded action on these behaviors. Institutional policy can and should be developed to address issues of moral environment. These policies need to address structures that limit moral action—for example, a lack of reporting structures for moral concern, or a failure to provide protection from reprisal for reporting. Policies also need to address systemic structural inequalities that privilege some healthcare professionals over others; for example, committees related to the quality of patient care, standards of care, committee leadership, and the like should include significant nursing representation.

Institutional policies can only go so far in bringing about change. Just as anti-segregation laws cannot eradicate racism and white exceptionalism, institutional policies cannot eradicate medical exceptionalism. That is to say that the longstanding differential of power, prestige, and privilege between medicine and nursing and the notion that medicine is somehow qualitatively superior, not just socially but morally as well cannot be righted through institutional policy alone.

For nursing to be fully co-participating in the entire enterprise of health, from patient care to policy, nursing must be active on the national and global stage. The Institute of Medicine (IOM) report *The Future of Nursing: Leading Change, Advancing Health*[23] hints at some of the changes that must take place. Three of its recommendations are:

Recommendation 1: Remove scope-of-practice barriers.[24]

Recommendation 4: Increase the proportion of nurses with a baccalaureate degree to 80 percent by 2020.

Recommendation 5: Double the number of nurses with a doctorate by 2020.[25]

Recommendation 7: Prepare and enable nurses to lead change to advance health.[26]

For nurses to practice at a level commensurate with their education and experience, barriers to practice that exclude nurses from reimbursement structures, that out-price liability insurance, that prevent nurses from engaging in fee-for-service practice, that anti-competitively and unduly restrict or regulate nursing practice must be removed. The IOM report calls upon the Commission on Collegiate Nursing Education and the National League for Nursing Accrediting Commission to require "all nursing schools to offer defined academic pathways, beyond articulation agreements, that promote seamless access for nurses to higher levels of education."[27] Nursing education must be advanced to move nurses toward eventual educational parity with medicine. The report also calls upon these bodies to "monitor the progress of each accredited nursing school to ensure that at least 10 percent of all baccalaureate graduates matriculate into a master's or doctoral program within five years of graduation."[28] The report further recommends that "[p]ublic, private, and governmental health care decision makers at every level should include representation from nursing on boards, on executive management teams, and in other key leadership positions."[29]

Moral distress in a hospital or agency that obstructs right action is a microcosm of the social power differential that exists in society. Though medicine and nursing are both changing, nursing remains a female dominant occupation (90.4%);[30] is seen to engage in the "dirty" and "intimate labor" often socially assigned to women;[31] suffers from multiple entry points; and is often granted only a token place at the table at the institutional as well as the national level. For example, the President's Commission on Bioethics (variously renamed over the years) serves in an advisory capacity to the President of the United States. The early committees were predominantly male physicians and attorneys, researchers, and ethicists.

In another example, the National Commission for the Protection of Human Subjects in Biomedical and Behavioral Research, created by Congress in 1974, had eleven members: three physicians, two psychologists, three lawyers, two ethicists and one person in public affairs.[32] The 1979 iteration of the commission included "three physicians, three biomedical or behavioral researchers…and five…from law, sociology, economics, and philosophy, as well as a homemaker and a businessman."[33] Nursing was either absent or under-represented on subsequent committees. Today, in 2015, the Presidential Commission for the Study of Bioethical Issues has achieved gender balance, minority representation—and one nurse member, Christine Grady, who has a PhD in philosophy.

The IOM recommendation to increase the number of nurses with doctorates will ultimately afford nursing greater access to advisory and policy bodies, board positions, and other places at the table. While it is important to seek to ameliorate moral distress within institutions and agencies through the promulgation of institutional policy, the larger social context of moral distress arising as it does from the perpetuation of structural differentials in power must be tackled. The social location of women, persisting patriarchal architecture of the public and private spheres, pay inequity affecting women and minorities, the feminization of poverty, domestic violence, and a host of gender- and race-based issues ultimately sustain conditions of moral distress well beyond the hospital walls. Nurses in hospitals as well as nurses in national and world organizations must work toward institutional as well as social changes that will undermine those social conditions that perpetrate and perpetuate moral distress.

> Empowerment involves the transformation of power relations by which women move from being objects within relationships of subordination to becoming subjects, controlling their own lives. It addresses those power structures that subordinate women at different societal levels—household, community, nation—and which must be transformed so that women can take full control over their lives.[34]

"Take full control over their lives"—and over the conditions that produce moral distress—there is every reason to believe that, united, nurses can accomplish this!

6.1 The Environment and Moral Virtue

Normative ethics can be divided into two large domains: norms of obligation and norms of value. *Norms of obligation* specify what is right or wrong to do. *Norms of value* specify what is good or evil to be or to seek as an end. Thus normative ethics has four moral terms: *right* and *wrong, good* and *evil.*

Norms of obligation specify what is right or wrong to do. These norms are called norms of obligation because they tell us what our moral obligations and duties are. There is a wide range of ethical theories that have been developed across the centuries that take different approaches to determining obligation. The oft discussed Utilitarianism and Kantian formalism are two frequently cited and discussed examples of theories that specify methods to arrive at obligation. A moral dilemma occurs when there is a conflict of norms of value or norms of obligation. For this section of the Code, however, we must look at norms of value, the other domain of normative ethics.

Norms of value specify what is good or evil in *persons* as moral agents or what we are to seek as *ends.* Technically those norms that specify what we are *to be* are *norms of moral value* and are called *virtues.* Virtues are habits of character that predispose us to do what is right. They should not be confused with traits of personality. Immediately it becomes evident that virtue and obligation are related. Obligation tells us what our ethical duties are and virtue enables us to meet those obligations. The fact that they can be habituated—learned and practiced—is important. The opposite of virtues, that is what we ought *not* to be, are called *vices*. Virtues are *universal*, meaning that they are norms for all people. Virtues answer the question "What is a 'good' person in a moral sense?" Virtues include such things as justice, humility, temperance, generosity, prudence, and courage. (Vices, incidentally, would include gluttony, avarice, greed, lust, pride, and sloth.) There is a subset of virtues, called *excellences*, that are habits of character that predispose a person to do a specific job or task well. Excellences answer the question "What is a 'good' nurse in a moral sense?" Excellences would include knowledge, skill, wisdom, patience, compassion, caring, kindness, and integrity. Today they are often named or included when discussing virtues. Nurses do not come to the work setting *tabula rasa.* The virtues and values that they possess have been shaped by many things including family and friends, education, spiritual or religious communities, voluntary associations such as civic clubs, and life experience. Some of these virtues and values will have a natural fit with nursing and will be further developed within the context of nursing education and practice.

What is good or evil in the ends that we seek are sometimes referred to by their Greek name *telos* (singular) or *teloi* (plural) in the ethical literature. The ends/*teloi* that nursing seeks include such things as health, well-being, dignity, care, respect, mercy, and justice. Some ends, such as human dignity, are *intrinsic goods*; they are good in themselves and should be sought for their own sake. Other ends are *instrumental goods* that are sought so that other goods might be realized. For example, health can be considered an instrumental good because it allows persons to reach other ends such as productivity, fulfillment, and satisfaction.[35]

Interpretive Statement 6.1 is chiefly concerned with virtue. Virtues, as learned habits of character, are formed, cultivated, maintained, and flourish when the moral environment models and fosters them. For example, for honesty to flourish in nursing studies or in clinical practice or in research, there must be an expectation of honesty, and an intolerance of dishonesty in any form. Transparency becomes an important element in the process, whether in grading, hiring or employment practices, or data analysis. Other elements that must be operative within an environment that fosters virtue include respect and dignity so that people are and feel valued; communication and moral equality so that all persons participate in the *community of moral discourse*; and generosity so that the diverse contributions of members of the team, class, committee, or group are welcome and recognized. These are but a few; there are, of course, other elements of a moral milieu that can cause virtues to flourish.

6.2 The Environment and Ethical Obligation

Where the moral milieu is constructed so as to foster virtue, its members will be equipped as moral agents to do what is right, to meet their moral obligations. Sometimes those obligations are discussed in terms of principles, specifically bioethical principles. The best known list, that of Beauchamp and Childress,[36] includes respect for autonomy, nonmaleficence, beneficence, and justice. Others would specify these and additional principles such as fidelity and reparations. Some would call these rules, not principles. The distinction between *rules* and *principles* is that principles are basic and rules are derived from principles. Disagreement about what is a principle versus a rule is a technical argument and is not a disagreement about what is important. Principles and rules are both used to specify moral obligations; they serve as moral guidelines.

The principle of *respect for persons* at its simplest holds that human beings have intrinsic, inherent, and unconditional moral worth and should always be regarded and treated as such. *Intrinsic* worth means worth as a part of the very essence or nature of the person. *Inherent* worth means that the worth "sticks to" (from the Latin) the person even if they, for example, deteriorate cognitively. *Unconditional* worth means that the person has worth without qualification such as education, socioeconomic status, or having a place to live. This principle guides us in two directions: to respect persons as morally autonomous beings, and to extend protection to those of diminished capacity for autonomy.[37] From this broader principle, the principle of *respect for autonomy* generally obligates nurses to respect autonomous patient decisions. Some patients are unable to be autonomous, for example, infants, persons in a coma, someone who is inebriated, a patient with severe Alzheimer's disease, and so on. Some patients (e.g., minors) are, by law, not legally autonomous, though they may be morally autonomous. Note that the principle is *respect for autonomy*, and not a principle of autonomy—we are obligated to respect autonomy, not to *act with* autonomy. The principle of *nonmaleficence* obligates nurses not to inflict harm. Sometimes, for the sake of discussion, nonmaleficence is separated from beneficence, though in clinical practice they can be considerably harder to separate. *Beneficence* is the obligation to do good for others and includes preventing harm, removing harmful conditions and taking affirmative action to benefit another. *Justice*, as an ethical principle, deals with fairness in the distribution of social burdens and benefits. Social benefits include legislative representation, education, public health, and fire protection. Burdens, in modern society, include taxation and punishment. The principle of *reparations* obligates us to make amends for harm that has been inflicted.[38] *Gratitude* is a principle that guides us to be thankful and grateful for a kindness received and to respond in like manner. The principle of *duties to self* is a self-regarding, collective duty that includes self-improvement, maintenance of integrity, and self-regard. The principle of *fidelity* obligates us to act with loyalty and includes rules such as keeping promises, honoring agreements, performing competently, and so forth. There is a wide range of rules that are important such as confidentiality, full informedness, and free consent. These principles and rules—and many more—guide our obligations in nursing practice and are affirmed by this section of the 2015 Code and by various ethical position statements and global moral standards. These principles and rules can be subtle and complex, with considerable nuance, and require reading, study, reflection, and discernment for understanding.

The thrust of Interpretive Statement 6.2 is that the moral environment in which nurses practice, whatever the role or setting, must be such that it supports nurses in meeting their moral obligations:

> Nurses, in all roles, must create a culture of excellence and maintain practice environments that support nurses and others in the fulfillment of their ethical obligations.

Environmental factors contribute to working conditions and include but are not limited to: clear policies and procedures that set out professional expectations for nurses; uniform knowledge of the Code of Ethics for Nurses with Interpretive Statements; Code and associated ethical position statements.[39]

Note that the Code goes beyond a foundation of support for nurses; it seeks to construct a culture of excellence wherein meeting ethical obligations is an everyday expectation.

6.3 Responsibility for the Healthcare Environment

The ANA Nurse's Bill of Rights addresses environmental concerns of the workplace. It states: To maximize the contributions nurses make to society, it is necessary to protect the dignity and autonomy of nurses in the workplace. To that end, the following rights must be afforded:

1. Nurses have the right to practice in a manner that fulfills their obligations to society and to those who receive nursing care.

2. Nurses have the right to practice in environments that allow them to act in accordance with professional standards and legally authorized scopes of practice.

3. Nurses have the right to a work environment that supports and facilitates ethical practice, in accordance with the *Code of Ethics for Nurses with Interpretive Statements*.

4. Nurses have the right to freely and openly advocate for themselves and their patients, without fear of retribution.

5. Nurses have the right to fair compensation for their work, consistent with their knowledge, experience and professional responsibilities.

6. Nurses have the right to a work environment that is safe for themselves and for their patients.

7. Nurses have the right to negotiate the conditions of their employment, either as individuals or collectively, in all practice settings.[40]

It is not always easy to ascertain the quality of moral environment prior to employment. However, it is wise to speak with nurses who are current employees to see if one can get a feel for the organization. Look particularly for expressions of job satisfaction, commitment to keeping abreast of developments in nursing science, nurse collegiality and the quality of relationships within an institution, whether there is a degree of shared governance, the quality of nursing leadership, effectiveness of communication, established standards of excellence, whether there is collaboration between nurses and physicians, and other factors such as these. The American Nurses Credentialing Center Magnet Recognition Program®:

> recognizes health care organizations for quality patient care, nursing excellence and innovations in professional nursing practice. Consumers rely on Magnet designation as the ultimate credential for high quality nursing. Developed by ANCC, Magnet is the leading source of successful nursing practices and strategies worldwide…. American Nurses Credentialing Center (ANCC) evaluates the environment in which nursing is practiced as well as compliance with standards promulgated by the American Nurses Association.[41]

Magnet recognition is one indicator of a positive and healthy work environment for nurses.

In the study *Silence Kills: Seven Crucial Conversations for Healthcare*, the researchers

> found that seven categories of conversations are especially difficult and, at the same time, especially essential for people in healthcare to master. These seven conversations include: broken rules (including dangerous shortcuts), mistakes, lack of support, incompetence, poor teamwork, disrespect, and micromanagement. The study showed that a majority of healthcare workers regularly see colleagues take dangerous shortcuts, make mistakes, fail to offer support, or appear critically incompetent. Yet the research reveals fewer than one in ten speak up and share their full concerns.[42]

A morally supportive environment and a culture of excellence does not just happen. It has to be constructed and crafted with intentionality. Nurses work both individually and collectively to construct an ethical environment, and to remove barriers to its development and maintenance. Nurses are aided in this task by a knowledge of theories of organizational development and change. Change is a process of innovation and nurses must actively participate in moving that process forward:

> the diffusion of innovation refers to the process that occurs as people adopt a new idea, product, practice, philosophy, and so on. Rogers mapped out this process, stressing that in most cases, an initial few are open to the new idea and adopt its use. As these early innovators 'spread the word' more and more people become open to it which leads to the development of a critical mass. Over time, the innovative idea or product becomes diffused amongst the population until a saturation point is achieved.[43]

Institutional Review Boards and institutional ethics committees are examples of the process of innovation and adoption. They began slowly, with some resistance, and are now an accepted—and mandated—part of healthcare institutions, agencies and research institutions. Nurses played a part in their development and now sit on these committees.

What is being sought for the moral milieu of practice is a "community of moral discourse."[44] Gustafson envisions two necessary forms of discourse. The first is *prophetic*: "Prophets with their sensitivities to the presence of injustice, to the evil that lurks in the world, use their rhetoric of moral indignation to call attention to issues which less acute persons miss, or only dimly see."[45] The second is *technical policy discourse*, or *politic discourse* "that defines human problems in manageable empirical terms, and propos[es] and pursue[s] courses of action."[46] Over the years, prophetic voices have arisen within nursing—voices of caring, feminism, postcolonialism, and more. Those voices call us to what Gustafson identifies as a requirement in any community of moral discourse—"critical sophistication," that moral judgments should be carefully examined and thought through, carefully argued, with rational justification and attention to the nursing tradition from which it arises.[47]
This points to the need for rigorous ethics education, both in basic and graduate nursing programs and in clinical contexts. Such education would be focused on bioethics and the nursing ethical tradition. There are differing roles for nurses who seek to construct and maintain a moral milieu that furthers the community of moral discourse. Some nurses will be prophetic, some politic, but both are essential.

What characterizes an environment that supports a community of moral discourse? The essential elements include respect, mutuality, openness, transparency, and moral equality. Such a community must be welcoming of all participants and of diverse of perspectives.

Unfortunately, some institutions with toxic moral environments are also refractory to change. Hirschman identifies three options for response: *exit, loyalty,* and *voice.*[48] Rusbult et al. add *neglect* as an additional response.[49,50] However, as the *Silence Kills* study above indicates, *neglect* is a deadly option. The study links the ability or inability "of health professionals to discuss emotionally and politically risky topics in a healthcare setting to key results like patient safety, quality of care, and nursing turnover, among others."[51] Setting aside neglect, one can leave (*exit*) the workplace with or without expressing concern (*voice*), or one can stay (*loyalty*) with or without expressing concern. When choosing *neglect* one stays in place and simply gives up hope of change, and allows conditions to continue to deteriorate. Nurses have an obligation to attempt to change a moral environment that is harmful to moral standards or values, that is, to engage in loyalty with voice. However, one stays and expresses concern only when there is both a hope of change and no fear of reprisal. If repeated attempts have been made individually and collectively to bring about change, and the institution or agency is refractory to change, the Code calls for nurses to exit so as not to become morally blameworthy or complicit in furthering an ethically unacceptable environment. Do you exit with or without voice? The expectation is that if the concerns were of sufficient gravity that a nurse would leave a position, then they are sufficiently egregious that action should be taken by reporting to the proper authorities or reporting body such as a regulatory agency. The nurse who leaves a position because of a morally unacceptable environment should make an honest attempt to rectify the conditions but need not pursue it to the bitter end. At some point one has to move on.

Fortunately, these sorts of environments are not the norm. Even more fortunately, nurses who walk with one another, who are united, are a formidable and knowledgeable force for good change. A positive and affirming moral environment, one of respect, mutuality, dignity, and moral equality, fosters the virtues and excellences and causes them to flourish. It also potentiates moral action to meet moral obligation, and ultimately positively affects both work satisfaction and excellence in patient care.

Cases

Case 1

Three months ago, a new, extremely well-known specialist physician was granted privileges. The medical staff is elated that this physician has agreed to join them and see her as both a clinical plus and public relations boost for the hospital. The physician asks that the nurses not speak up during patient rounds because it would delay rounds. They were instructed to make their comments and ask their questions after rounds were made. The nurses have become increasingly frustrated and feel cut out of collaborative care. They believe that the level of medical care remains high, but they also perceive that the goal of high-quality nursing care is being obstructed. The nurse manager and the unit CNS have both spoken with the physician, but she will not budge. The second time they attempt to raise concerns on behalf of the nursing staff, the physician becomes increasingly arrogant and demeaning.

Case 2

A nursing school initiates a mentoring program whereby all undergraduate students meet in assigned groups with a faculty mentor each semester in their program. However, one of the three groups of junior students in pediatrics is experiencing distress. Their mentor, a senior faculty member and department chairperson, has a research grant and asks for "volunteers" to work in his "community health program," where they are expected to do well-child health assessments without supervision. The students believe that refusing to volunteer will have negative consequences, so they comply. The students know that they are not qualified to do this and they feel coerced. This is a powerful faculty member; other faculty refuse to discuss this with the students. One of the students commented "We are doing our clinicals in a Magnet hospital and the nurses love working there. I wish that we were in a Magnet school of nursing."

Case 3

Marisol Santiago is the director of nursing in a retirement village with multilevel care. Her assisted care units are staffed primarily with licensed practical nurses and nursing assistants. Recently several nursing assistants have come to her complaining about unequal treatment in assignments and privileges. She knows that there are some racial tensions among the staff, who are predominantly from the Somali and Hmong communities. She suspects that possible inter-cultural tensions may be contributing to the conflict. The retirement village has a zero tolerance policy for prejudicial behavior. She knows that this is a complex inter-cultural situation and that the local university could provide an inservice program aimed at reducing cultural tension in the workplace. The board of directors does not feel this is necessary, and the staff are resistant.

ENDNOTES

1   American Nurses Association, "A Suggested Code," *American Journal of Nursing* 26, no. 9 (August 1926): 599–601

2   Ibid.

3   Marilyn E. Flood, "The Troubling Expedient: General Staff Nursing in United States Hospitals in the 1930s" (PhD diss., University of California, Berkeley, 1981).

4   L. Berger and J. Waldfogel, "Maternity Leave and the Employment of New Mothers in the United States," *Journal of Population Economics* 17, no. 2 (2004): 331–49. See also: M. O'Connell, B. Downs, and K. Smith, "Maternity Leave and Employment Patterns: 1961–1995," *Current Population Reports* 70, no. 79 (2001): 1–21.

5   American Nurses Association, "A Tentative Code," *American Journal of Nursing* 40, no. 9 (1940): 977–980

6   Nurses' Associated Alumnae of the United States and Canada, *Constitution and Bylaws.* (Baltimore, MD: author, 1897).

7   Victoria T. Grando, "The ANA's Economic Security Program: The First 20 Years," *Nursing Research* 46, no. 2 (March/April 1997): 112. See also: L. Lawson, K. Miles, R. Vallish, and S. Jenkins, "Labor Relations: Recognizing Nursing Professional Growth and Development in a Collective Bargaining Environment," *Journal of Nursing Administration* 41, no. 5 (May 2011): 197–200; K. Darr, M. Schraeder, and L. Friedman, "Collective Bargaining in the Nursing Profession: Salient Issues and Recent Developments in Healthcare Reform," *Hospital Topics* 80, no. 3 (Summer 2002): 21.

8   ANA. Commission on economic and general welfare recommendation regarding ANA no-strike policy 1968, May 1968 (Memo). See also: Flanagan, L. (1986). Braving new frontiers: ANA's Economic and General Welfare Program, 1946-1986. Kansas City: ANA; Grando, victoria T. The ANA's Economic Security Program: The ffirst 20 Years. *Nursing Research, 46*(2), March/April 1997, 111-115.

9   "Collective Bargaining," NursingWorld.http://www.nursingworld.org/MainMenuCategories/WorkplaceSafety/Healthy-Work-Environment/Work-Environment/Collective-Bargaining

10 American Nurses Association, *A Code for Professional Nurses* (New York: ANA, 1950); American Nurses Association, *A Code for Professional Nurses, amended* (New York: ANA, 1956).

11 American Nurses Association, *A Code for Professional Nurses* (New York: ANA, 1960).

12 American Nurses Association, *A Code for Professional Nurses* (Kansas City, MO: ANA, 1968).

13 American Nurses Association, *Code of Ethics for Nurses with Interpretive Statements* (Kansas City, MO: ANA, 1976).

14 Ibid., 17.

15 American Nurses Association, *Code of Ethics for Nurses with Interpretive Statements* (Kansas City, MO: ANA, 1985), 14–15.

16 American Nurses Association, *Code of Ethics for Nurses with Interpretive Statements* (Silver Spring, MD: ANA, 2001), 25.

17 Ibid.

18 Marlene Kramer, *Reality Shock: Why Nurses Leave Nursing* (St. Louis, MO: CV Mosby, 1974).

19 Ibid., vii.

20 Ibid., 9.

21 Andrew Jameton, *Nursing Practice: The Ethical Issues* (New Jersey: Prentice Hall, 1984), 6.

[22] Storch, Jan, Patricia Rodney, Colleen Varcoe, Bernadette Pauly, Rosalie Starzomski, Lauren Stevenson, Lyle Best, Howard Mass, Timothy R. Fulton, Barb Mildon, F. Bees, Andrew Chishom, Sandra MacDonald-Rencz, A.S. McCutcheon, Judith Shamian, Christopher Thompson, Kara Shick Macaroff, and Linsey Newton, "Leadership for Ethical Policy and Practice (LEPP): Participatory Action Project," *Canadian Journal of Nursing Leadership* 22, no. 3 (2009): 68.

[23] The Institute of Medicine, *The Future of Nursing: Leading Change, Advancing Health* (Washington, D.C.: National Academies Press, 2014).

[24] Ibid., 278.

[25] Ibid., 281.

[26] Ibid., 282.

[27] Ibid.

[28] Ibid.

[29] Ibid., 283.

[30] "How many nurses are there? And other facts," The Truth About Nursing, http://www.truthaboutnursing.org/faq/rn_facts.html

[31] Eileen Boris and Rhacel Parrenas, *Intimate Labors: Cultures, Technologies, and the Politics of Care* (Palo Alto, CA: Stanford University Press, 2010).

[32] Office of Technology Assessment, Congress of the United States, *Biomedical Issues in U.S. Public Policy* (Washington DC: USGPO, February 1993), 9.

[33] Ibid., 13

[34] U.N. Division for the Advancement of Women, "Empowerment of Women Throughout the Life Cycle as a Transformative Strategy for Poverty Eradication" (report presented at the Expert Group Meeting in New Delhi, India, November 26–29, 2001), 27.

[35] Marsha Fowler, "Introduction to Ethics and Ethical Theory: A road map to the Discipline," in *Ethics at the Bedside*, eds. Marsha Fowler and June Levine-Ariff (Philadelphia: JB Lippincott, 1987), 24–38.

[36] Tom Beauchamp and James Childress, *Principles of Biomedical Ethics* (7th ed.) (NY: Oxford University Press, 2012).

[37] National Commission for the Protection of Human Subjects of Biomedical and Behavioral Research of the U.S. Department of Health and Human Services, *The Belmont Report: Ethical Principles and Guidelines for the Protection of Human Subjects of Research* (Washington, D.C.: DHHS/USGPO, 1979), available at http://www.hhs.gov/ohrp/humansubjects/guidance/belmont.html

[38] W. D. Ross, *The Right and the Good*, ed. Philip Stratton-Lake (New York: Oxford University Press, 2002). Note that Beauchamp and Childress specify four ethical principles. W. D. Ross's list is longer and includes principles that Beauchamp and Childress would identify as rules.

[39] American Nurses Association, *Code of Ethics for Nurses with Interpretive Statements* (Silver Spring, MD: ANA, 2015), 23–24.

[40] "Nurses' Bill of Rights," NursingWorld, http://nursingworld.org/MainMenuCategories/WorkplaceSafety/Healthy-Work-Environment/Work-Environment/NursesBillofRights/default.aspx

[41] "Magnet Recognition Program Overview," American Nurse Credentialing Center, http://www.nursecredentialing.org/Magnet/ProgramOverview

[42] David Maxfield, Joseph Grenny, Ron McMillan, Kerry Patersons, and Al Switzler. *Silence Kills: The Seven Crucial conversations in Healthcare*, (2005), http://www.silenttreatmentstudy.com/silencekills/SilenceKills.pdf. See also: David Maxfield , Joseph Grenny, Ramón Lavandero, and Linda Groah, *The Silent Treatment: Why Safety Tools and Checklists Aren't Enough to Save Lives* (2010), http://cms.vitalsmarts.com/d/d/workspace/SpacesStore/259079c0-eb09-4066-a003-26d2ff434be4/The%20Silent%20Treatment%20Report.pdf?guest=true

[43] June Kaminski, "Diffusion of Innovation Theory: Theory in Nursing Informatics Column," *Canadian Journal of Nursing Informatics* 6, no. 2 (June 2011), http://cjni.net/journal/?p=1444

[44] James Gustafson, "The University as a Community of Moral Discourse," *Journal of Religion* 53, no. 4 (October 1973): 397–409. See also: B. Jennings, "Possibilities of Consensus: Toward Democratic Moral Discourse," *The Journal of Medicine and Philosophy* 16, no. 4 (1991): 447–63; Thomas Schwandt, "Recapturing Moral Discourse in Evaluation," *Educational Researcher* 18, no. 8 (November 1989): 11–16, 35.

[45] Gustafson, "University as a Community," 397.

[46] Ibid.

[47] Ibid., 397–401.

[48] O. Hirschman, *Exit, Voice, and Loyalty: Responses to Decline in Firms, Organizations, and States* (Cambridge, MA: Harvard University Press. 1970), 1–162.

[49] Caryl E. Rusbult, Dan Farrell, Glen Rogers, and Arch G. Mainous III. "Impact of exchange variables on exit, voice, loyalty, and neglect: An integrative model of responses to declining job satisfaction," *Academy of Management Journal* 31 (1982): 599–627; Michael J. Withey and William H. Cooper, "Predicting Exit, Voice, Loyalty, and Neglect," *Administrative Science Quarterly* 34, no. 4 (December 1989), 521–539.

[50] Michael J. Withey and William H. Cooper "Predicting Exit, Voice, Loyalty, and Neglect," *Administrative Science Quarterly*, Vol. 34, No. 4 (Dec., 1989), 521–539

[51] Maxfield et al., *Silence Kills*, op. cit.

Provision 7

The nurse, in all roles and settings, advances the profession through research and scholarly inquiry, professional standards development, and the generation of both nursing and health policy.

Provision 7. Diverse Contributions to the Profession

Introduction

The 1960 *Code for Professional Nurses* with its interpretive statements gives considerable attention to continually improving the standards that guide nursing education and practice. It also mentions research, somewhat in passing. Provision 13 (of 17) of that Code notes: "The nurse may contribute to research in relation to a commercial product or service, but does not lend professional status to advertising, promotion, or sales."[1] The accompanying *Interpretation of the Statements of the Code for Professional Nurses* explicates the provision largely in terms of the public trust vested in nursing, and the hazards to the profession when nurses enter into the marketplace of competition and commercialism. Research is mentioned only in relation to commercial products and services (in the provision itself) and only once, negligibly, in the interpretive statement in relation to dissemination of findings through suitable channels. In subsequent revisions of the Code, research receives such vigorous attention that its lack of attention in the 1960 Code is surprising. However, the 1960 Code also fails to emphasize development of the body of knowledge of nursing—often accomplished through research—so it is not as surprising as it might seem at first blush.[2]

The vacuum was soon to be filled. By 1968, the Code devotes an entire provision, substantively not nominally, to research. It says that the "nurse participates in research activities when assured that the rights of individual subjects are protected."[3] In its interpretive statement, the provision is not yet linked to developing nursing's body of knowledge. Rather it focuses upon the "nurse practitioner," that is, the nurse clinician (not in the contemporary sense of a Nurse Practitioner), who is responsible for patient care within the context of a research setting. It acknowledges that nurses also serve as investigators in their own right, but defers that discussion and refers the reader to the ANA publication *The Nurse in Research: ANA Guidelines on Ethical Values.*[4] The nurse practitioner is responsible for quality nursing care and for the protection of the patient/subject's rights of "privacy, self-determination, conservation of personal resources, freedom from arbitrary hurt and intrinsic risk of injury, and the special rights of minors and incompetent persons."[5] The nurse may also participate only when the research is officially sanctioned by a research committee. Remember that research review boards are only beginning in the mid-1960s and will continue to evolve for some years until they reach their final specifications. These specifications are given in and governed by the Department of Health and Human Services Code of Federal Regulations Title 45, Part 46.[6]

By 1976, we arrive. There is now a provision that speaks to developing the profession's body of knowledge that is tied to *nursing* research. In this provision's interpretive statement, the nurse practitioner still receives mention but much less and the focus shifts to the nurse as researcher. The provision states: "The nurse participates in activities that contribute to the profession's body of knowledge."[7] The entire interpretive statement of the provision is focused on research as the means to the development of the profession's body of knowledge. It states "Every profession must engage in systematic inquiry to identify, verify, and continually enlarge the body of knowledge which forms the foundations for its practice."[8] Again, this provision refers the reader to an external document: *Human Rights Guidelines for Nurses in Clinical and Other Research.*[9] The section on human rights refers the reader to the same document but does identify "the right to freedom from intrinsic risks or injury and the rights of privacy and dignity. Inherent in these rights is respect for each individual to exercise self-determination, to choose to participate, to have full information, to terminate participation without penalty."[10]

The 1985 Code retains the tie between nursing knowledge and nursing research. It reorganizes the provision but retains the provision intact and much of the content in the interpretive statement as well. The revisions in this Code are minor. The first interpretive statement does acknowledge both scientific and humanistic knowledge and research and the development of theory as being indispensible.[11]

Nursing knowledge has blossomed in the past several decades and the nursing body of knowledge has expanded in many directions. In the process it has become apparent that knowledge development takes place through a variety of means that include but are not limited to research. Knowledge can also be developed through abstract conceptualization, critical reflection, clinical innovation, and other means. By 2001, the Code takes into account multiple means of generating knowledge and expanding nursing's body of knowledge. Thus the provision on body of knowledge and research changes: "The nurse participates in the advancement of the profession through contributions to practice, education, administration and knowledge development."[12] The duty shifts considerably and now the emphasis is on advancing the profession; nursing knowledge development is in the background.

At the time of the revision for what would become the 2001 Code, the Task Force for the Revision of the Code wanted to revise the Code so that it would apply more evenhandedly to all nurses in all settings and all roles. To do this they expanded from *knowledge development* to *advancing the profession* more generally. In this way nurses in administration, education, practice, self-employment, and research could be included. The provision identifies involvement in healthcare policy, implementing professional standards throughout nursing, and knowledge development as the three means to advancing the profession. However, in its intent to be inclusive, research gets lost. The only mention that it receives is that "nurse researchers are responsible for active contribution to the body of knowledge supporting and advancing nursing practice."[13] The section on knowledge development does not mention research per se but calls upon nurses to "engage in scholarly inquiry to identify, evaluate, refine, and expand the body of knowledge that forms the foundation of [the] discipline and practice."[14] It also notes that "nursing knowledge is derived from the sciences and humanities."[15] Scholarly inquiry does, of course, include research but is not limited to research. However, this collapse of the research section leads to a loss of emphasis on the ethical and human rights issues in research and thereby fails to provide nurse researchers with strong ethical guidance. This does not mean that nurse researchers are now unrestrained by fundamental ethical principles in their research, but it does mean that they would have to turn elsewhere for that guidance.

This revised 2015 Code successfully brings together concerns for inclusiveness, for multiple ways to advance the profession, knowledge development, and the ethical concerns of research. In fact, the 2015 Code reclaims research in the provision itself, and reorganizes the interpretive statements to put research and scholarly inquiry, advancing the body of knowledge, and concerns for human and animal participants in research together in the first of the interpretive statements.

7.1 Contributions through Research and Scholarly Inquiry

Research and scholarly inquiry are both systematic and rigorous forms of investigation. Further differentiation between the two is complicated by various uses and various definitions, as well as by prevailing prejudices. Newton-Smith has written:

> The overwhelming popularity of this image of science arises in part at least from the great successes of recent science.... How else are the

successes of "hard" science to be explained except on the assumption that there…must be something special about the method and the community in order to account for the superior achievements of science.… If only the philosopher and his compatriots in the Kingdom of Darkness would emulate the scientist he would acquire the capacity "to solve those problems that in earlier times have been the subject of guesswork."[16]

As this statement would indicate, scientists have to some extent disdained the research conducted by humanists—that is those researchers in the humanities—regarding it as "not really research." What are the humanities? The National Foundation on the Arts and the Humanities Act (1965) defines *humanities* thus:

The term 'humanities' includes, but is not limited to, the study of the following: language, both modern and classical; linguistics; literature; history; jurisprudence; philosophy; archaeology; comparative religion; ethics; the history, criticism and theory of the arts; those aspects of social sciences which have humanistic content and employ humanistic methods; and the study and application of the humanities to the human environment with particular attention to reflecting our diverse heritage, traditions, and history and to the relevance of the humanities to the current conditions of national life.[17]

The humanities, including ethics, are the academic disciplines that study human culture, its continuity, change, and interpretation. The humanities use methods that are primarily critical-analytical, or speculative, and often include an historical element. Research in the humanities is referred to as *scholarly inquiry* or *scholarly research* as the research takes place in the *schola*, the school. It relies heavily upon documents and libraries. Unlike scientific research that is heavily reliant on experimental design and recent studies, humanities research reaches as far back as ancient texts and everything in between to build upon the work of prior scholars. As in this book itself, old codes of ethics in nursing are important to understanding the current Code. In the sciences, however,

The Science Citation Index consistently demonstrates that about 90 percent of the millions of references cited each year were published sometime in the past three decades. And 50% involve papers published in the last ten years.… The vast majority of citations are to relatively recent papers. Nevertheless, authors continue to cite relatively older works.… This percentage might even increase in the future as more electronic legacy files are created. What people read is not necessarily what they cite when publishing. Nevertheless, electronic access to the full texts of the older journals significantly increases its use.[18]

While these results were from the 2003 analysis, recent communication with Science Citation Index/Institute for Scientific Information confirms that these results still hold today.[19] The vast majority of citations in the sciences are to relatively recent papers.

Historically there has been disagreement between the sciences and the humanities as to which constituted the best method of knowledge production and which would best guide human understanding and action. However, this dichotomy is unnecessary, counterproductive, and imprudent. Nursing needs both scientific and humanities research if it is to care for patients effectively, to develop the nursing body of knowledge, and to guide policy. The Carnegie report *Educating Nurses: A Call for Radical Transformation*, which has called for all nurses to be educated at a minimum of the bachelor's degree, is clear that nursing education needs to be strengthened and that "the need for better nursing education in science, humanities, social sciences, problem solving, teaching, and interpersonal capacities is…acute."[20] The humanities and the sciences are equally necessary to nursing. Thus, nurse-researchers interested in science and nurse-researchers interested in the humanities, both, can find a home in nursing.[21]

The Code states that all "nurses must participate in the advancement of the profession through knowledge development, evaluation, dissemination, and application to practice."[22] That does not mean that all nurses must conduct research. However, all nurses must, in one way or another, interact with research, whether as researchers, or through research utilization in the application of research to practice, or through reading to keep abreast of research findings generally but especially those related to one's own area of practice.

In the conduct of nursing research, human participants must be shown respect and must be protected from potential harm. There are a number of mechanisms that must be used so that the human participant is protected. The first step is to make certain that the research is necessary, soundly constructed, significant, worthwhile, and that all necessary resources are available (e.g., a statistician, methodological consultant, content experts). The research must be constructed so as to minimize risk to the participants. In addition, researchers employing randomized clinical trials are expected to equiponderate, to employ the *principle of clinical equipoise. Equiponderate* is a melodious word from the Latin *aequus* equal + *ponder re* to weigh.[23] It means to be in a state of equipoise where alternative options appear to carry equal weight. This is important to experimental design:

> Clinical equipoise is the assumption that there is not one 'better' intervention present (for either the control or experimental group) during the design of a randomized controlled trial. A true state of

equipoise exists when one has no good basis for a choice between two or more care options. Clinical equipoise has also been called an honest null hypothesis and/or a state of uncertainty…. Clinical equipoise provides the principled basis for medical research involving patients randomly assigned to different treatment arms of a clinical trial, and is considered a necessary feature for clinical service practitioners to ethically enroll patients into clinical trials. This assumption of a state of uncertainty has been identified as the central ethical principle for human experimentation. In fact, the majority of the literature and discussion on clinical equipoise is grounded in its theoretical value toward reducing an ethical dilemma of trial design.[24]

The moral relevance of the principle of equipoise is that human participants may not be placed in any group where a known inferior treatment option is employed—a stricture that was violated in a number of the morally questionable research projects that will be addressed below.

Where human or animal subjects are involved, the research proposal must be reviewed by one or more institutional review boards (IRBS). The WHO has developed standards for ethics review of research using human participants that includes guidance for individual researchers as well as for IRBs.[25] Customarily the initiating site's IRB and the IRB of other sites that are involved will need to review and approve the proposal. Where animals are used, the proposal must be approved by both the IRB and the Institutional Animal Care and Use Committee (IACUC).[26]

There are international regulations governing the use of human subjects in research. These arise, in good part, from the deadly research on involuntary human subjects that was conducted on prisoners during World War II. The Nuremburg Code of 1947, to which the United States is signatory, dictates that "the voluntary consent of the human subject is absolutely essential."[27] Of the ten provisions, the first states:

The voluntary consent of the human subject is absolutely essential. This means that the person involved should have legal capacity to give consent; should be so situated as to be able to exercise free power of choice, without the intervention of any element of force, fraud, deceit, duress, over-reaching, or other ulterior form of constraint or coercion; and should have sufficient knowledge and comprehension of the elements of the subject matter involved, as to enable him to make an understanding and enlightened decision. This latter element requires that, before the acceptance of an affirmative decision by the experimental subject, there should be made known to him the nature, duration, and purpose of the experiment; the method and means by which it is to be conducted; all inconveniences and hazards reasonably to be expected; and the effects upon his health or person, which may possibly come from his participation in the experiment. ... The duty and responsibility for ascertaining the quality of the consent rests upon each individual who initiates, directs or engages in the experiment. It is a personal duty and responsibility which may not be delegated to another with impunity.[28]

In addition, the World Medical Association *Declaration of Helsinki* (1964) regulates international research involving human subjects in medical research. It requires review of the research proposal prior to initiation of the research project, minimization of risk, special protection of vulnerable groups or individuals, preservation of privacy and confidentiality, informed consent, and more.[29]

It was not only the World War II research atrocities that drove changes in research regulations and oversight. In 1966, Henry Beecher's landmark paper on ethics in human research was published.[30] Beecher, an anesthesiologist, identifies twenty-two medical research projects that were conducted from prestigious universities, published in respected medical journals, and were deeply ethically questionable. The paper makes for very disturbing, even frightening, reading. In addition to the 22 experiments that Beecher identifies in the paper (and many others that were not in the paper), there were a number of studies that became well-known and roused public ire. Four such studies included the Willowbrook experiment, the Tuskegee experiment, the Tearoom Trade experiment and the Milgram obedience experiment. The reader is urged to read Beecher's article as well as the easily accessible details of each of these four studies.

In the Willowbrook hepatitis studies, experimentation was conducted over a period of 15 years with over 700 mentally disabled children in the Willowbrook State School. Some of the children were deliberately injected with hepatitis to track the progression of the disease.[31] The Tuskegee Institute syphilis experiment was a 40 year study that was conducted from 1932 to 1972 by the US Public Health Service. It sought to chronicle the progress of untreated syphilis. The subjects were 600 rural African-American men, 399 with syphilis and 201 without. The men were given to understand that they were being treated for "bad blood," a nonspecific local term that was used for a range of ailments such as fatigue. Their syphilis was not treated, even when the drug of choice, penicillin, became available in 1947.[32] The Tearoom Trade Experiment, a doctoral dissertation in sociology, studied anonymous male sexual/homosexual encounters in public toilets in the mid-1960s in an attempt to challenge prevailing sexual stereotypes. The researcher, who concealed his identity as a researcher, volunteered to "stand guard" while two subjects engaged in a sexual encounter. He subsequently used their license plate numbers to find their identity and residence. A year later, in disguise, he interviewed them in their homes, representing himself as a health service interviewer and obtaining follow-up personal information.[33] The Milgram experiment in social psychology sought to examine obedience to authority figures in relation to personal conscience. The study involved

> ordering a naive S[ubject] to administer increasingly more severe punishment to a victim in the context of a learning experiment. Punishment is administered by means of a shock generator with 30 graded switches ranging from *Slight Shock* to *Danger: Severe Shock.* The victim is a confederate of the E[xperimenter]. The primary dependent variable is the maximum shock the S is willing to administer before he refuses to continue further. 26 Ss obeyed the experimental commands fully, and administered the highest shock on the generator. 14 Ss broke off the experiment at some point after the victim protested and refused to provide further answers. The procedure created extreme levels of nervous tension in some Ss. Profuse sweating, trembling, and stuttering were typical expressions of this emotional disturbance. One unexpected sign of tension—yet to be explained—was the regular occurrence of nervous laughter, which in some Ss developed into uncontrollable seizures.[34]

In the Willowbrook study, the subjects were children with mental disabilities. In the Tuskeegee study, the subjects were rural Alabama African-American males. The subjects in the Tearoom Trade experiment were males, some of sexual minorities. Milgram's subjects were college students. In the studies in which Beecher identifies the subjects they include: teens, youth, toddlers, infants, the elderly, military servicemen, charity patients, "mental defectives and juvenile delinquents who were inmates of a children's center," and hospital patients. In some instances "normal" persons were subjected to the injection of pathogens, cancer cells, and more. The patterns that emerge include the use of vulnerable persons or "status individuals" and the complete absence of consent. In addition, many of the experiments were of questionable scientific value and some were life-threatening.[35]

The United States is not alone in this. Pappworth published an article listing research projects in the United Kingdom that were, like Beecher's list, conducted at reputable institutions, published by prestigious journals, and involved signal and egregious ethical violations.[36, 37] There was also a study conducted at the National Women's Hospital in Auckland, New Zealand. Dr. Herbert Green, head of OB/GYN followed 948 patients with carcinoma in situ. Beginning in 1966, Green sought to prove that carcinoma in situ never progresses into invasive cervical cancer, is not premalignant, and need not be treated with the then standard eradication by conization.[38]

Green enrolled women in the study without their knowledge or consent. Three of Green's colleagues at Auckland University…tried to put a halt to the experiment for years, but they were ignored until they published a 1984 article in *Obstetrics and Gynecology* showing that the untreated women were 25 times more likely to develop invasive cancer. According to the…governmental commission set up to investigate the scandal, this amounted to a total of approximately 40 women developing invasive cancer, many of whom died.[39]

The current Department of Health and Human Services' (DHHS) regulations governing the use of human participants in research have been in place since 1991. There is currently a process underway to enhance these regulations.[40] The full text of the current regulations is available online and includes separate sections for pregnant women, neonates, fetuses, prisoners, and children as human subjects in research.[41] As a useful tool, the DHHS has compiled a table with links to the research requirements of 104 nations.[42] The 2015 revision of the Code requires nurses to be in compliance with national and international standards for research; the ANA website contains links to training in human subjects protection.[43]

When research is completed and the results analyzed and findings determined, the nurse researcher has an obligation to disseminate the results of the research. Dissemination customarily takes the form of publication, but also includes conference presentations. Once research is completed, it is tempting to move on to the next research proposal, bypassing the step of dissemination. However, doing so fails to show respect for the human participants. Nursing practice and nursing research operate within a donative economy. Donative means "gift." Recipients of nursing care and participants in nursing research freely and often without question gift nursing with their trust, willingness, time, and much more. Many nurses can recall the first patient to whom they gave an injection as a trembling student. That patient freely placed herself or himself in the student's care. It was a gift. The failure to disseminate research results is a failure to show respect for the participants who willingly participated in the study and is a measure of ingratitude.

Not all nurses conduct research. Some nurses nonetheless participate in research that is taking place in their clinical setting during customary clinical care. Whether the nurse is a researcher, or a data collector, or one who renders care in a research setting, the nurse's primary allegiance is always first and foremost to the patient: "The Patients'/Participants' welfare may never be sacrificed for research ends."[44]

There are many elements that comprise nursing. Research for knowledge development is but one. Research is not conducted for its own sake but rather to test theory and help develop theory, so that all the settings and roles of nursing practice might be informed, developed, and advanced.

7.2 Contributions through Developing, Maintaining, and Implementing Professional Practice Standards

Like the ANA Code, the ANA work *Nursing: Scope and Standards of Practice* is a foundational document. A profession is responsible for developing and overseeing its standards and for communicating those standards to the public. The public in turn has a right to demand that the profession adhere to those standards. But what are standards?

> The Standards of Professional Nursing Practice are authoritative statements of the duties that all registered nurses, regardless of role, population, or specialty are expected to perform competently. ...[they] serve as evidence for the standard of care...are subject to change with the dynamics of the nursing profession, as new patterns of professional practice are developed and accepted by the nursing profession and the public. ...the competencies that accompany each standard may be evidence of compliance with the corresponding standard.[45]

These standards interface with state nurse practice acts and federal laws governing nursing. Standards of practice are not limited to entry-level practice. As nursing's leading professional association, the ANA works with specialty organizations to develop and maintain standards for specialty nursing practice such as addictions nursing, correctional nursing, faith community nursing, forensic nursing, gerontological nursing, nursing administration, neonatal nursing, palliative care nursing, and many more. Currently there are standards for 22 nursing specialties, and as the profession continues to grow and develop and new specialties arise, additional standards will be developed.[46] Such standards contribute to the integrity, rigor, and advance of the profession. All those who would become nurses are obliged to know and uphold these standards of practice and the Code as a part of what it means to "practice nursing."

7.3 Contributions through Nursing and Health Policy Development

Policies are linked to problems or issues and contain strategies to address or resolve them. Policy functions at all levels of nursing practice from those in a single, unique hospital unit, to those issued by the DHHS, or those that govern international health matters. Depending upon the level at which they function, they may contain principles, guidelines, procedures, protocols, or algorithms that guide action. Nurses are, can, and should be involved in policy at any and all of these levels. In some instances, policy work is accomplished through professional associations; this will be addressed in the chapter on Provision 9. Here we focus on the policy involvement of the individual nurse. Most likely this policy involvement takes place within the nurse's work setting or perhaps the county or region, or state. If the work setting is part of a larger system or network, policy generated within one institution may ultimately affect the whole system. However, most nurses as individuals will be involved in institutional or local policy. With the range of ways in which nurses can be involved in policy, there is something for everyone. Involvement may take the form of participation on an institutional policy committee, or supporting nurse legislators or nurses involved in political action—such as through the ANA Political Action Committee (PAC).

At the most immediate level nurses can be involved in institutional policy in a variety of ways, as best suits their particular preference, knowledge and skill. There is an inter-relationship of quality and safety of care, nursing research, and standards of care. This is hinted at in the National Database of Nursing Quality Indicators (NDNQI®) statement:

> There are some patient quality and safety measures which have been shown through research to be significantly affected by nursing care or "nurse-sensitive" measures. These are collected through a combination of medical record review and administrative data, according to common definitions. The National Database of Nursing Quality Indicators is a leading voluntary system for collection and analysis of these data.[47]

Institutional policy can be formulated to support any of these interactive elements. Research utilization, incorporation of quality standards in planning, and quality initiatives all contribute to the improvement or development of nursing interventions for better patient care. Here, nurses can participate in or even lead research that investigates outcomes of specific care practices in order to establish new standards of care and even "best practices" on a unit or within an institution, agency, or clinic.[48] Evidence-informed practice includes but goes beyond research data alone. The emerging language is that of *evidence informed* over *evidence based* practice. The term *evidence based practice* has tended to over-emphasize research findings, to the exclusion of other forms of knowledge. Thorne and Sawatzky note that the following:

> Different aspects of the complex set of knowledge and skill we know as nursing practice are necessarily informed by distinctly different forms of knowledge. Some forms of knowledge come with a degree of certainty and generalizability, while other forms of knowledge pertain more explicitly to the individual case without having generalizable implications. It is therefore essential that we expand our collective disciplinary conversation so as to ensure that we maintain a strong grasp on the nature of knowledge needed in relation to particular aspects of nursing practice.[49]

The ICN document *Closing the Gap: From Evidence to Action* (2012) clearly acknowledges that practice is based on more than research:

> what the EBP [Evidence Based Practice] approach has always acknowledged is that decisions are rarely based on evidence alone; judgments, values and individual factors always play a role. However what is also clear is that if nurses use an evidence-based approach to their practice they are more able to ask good questions about how and when they should change their practice, demonstrate that they are using good information on which to base their decisions, evaluate their practice and know that the outcomes they are being measured on are appropriate and agreed in advance.[50]

Evidence-informed practice, then, utilizes a diversity of forms of knowledge including clinical expertise; ethical understanding; patient and family values, beliefs, and preferences; theories, healthcare resources and practice environments; and even nurse practice or DHHS regulations. While it includes evidence-based practice, *evidence informed practice* is a more encompassing term.

Evidence-informed practice is not simply a matter of improving direct patient care. Evidence-informed approaches ultimately affect health systems world-wide, work to reduce inequalities in care, and challenge policy-makers toward the improvement of health systems. Again, the ICN notes this:

> In our quest for quality and access to health care, we must constantly strive to use evidence-based approaches to nursing services. Today, health systems throughout the world are being challenged by inequities in quality and quantity of services and by reduced financial resources. Poorly informed decision making is one of the reasons services can fail to be delivered in an optimal way. It can also result in less efficient, ineffective and inequitable availability of health services. The use of evidence to inform our actions is a critical and achievable way to improve health system performance.[51]

Evidence informed practice, then, is a matter of justice. Justice begins at home with every nurse committed to evidence-informed practice, support of nursing research, implementation and development of patient care quality and safety standards, and institutional or agency policies that support all of these.

Influencing nursing and health policy beyond the confines of one's own institution begins with utilizing nursing knowledge to evaluate ballot initiatives or propositions, engaging in local legislative and governmental conversations, informed voting, and communication with legislators at every level. Nurses have much to offer as experts who testify at legislative hearings, as public educators who can offer commentary on local or regional radio or television programs, by serving on town councils or school boards, by involvement in environmental issues, by volunteer service in community or state programs that are health related (e.g., Special Olympics, food pantries, Ciclovia [paths freed from motorized traffic to promote cycling, skating, and walking], Habitat for Humanity, community sponsored agriculture, Bread for the World, Avodah [the Jewish service corps], Red Cross, Humane Societies) and by representing the values of nursing to the public. The health of the nation, and of the globe, necessitates nursing involvement at every level of program and policy; it cannot improve without us.

Cases

Case 1

Raj Kaushik has been a clinical nurse in a busy neurology unit for the past eight years. His hospital is one of seven in a larger regional healthcare system. He is dedicated to his work and has developed especially good skills in working with families. He is now working on his PhD in nursing and is interested in ethics, law, and policy surrounding neurotrauma. He is active in the regional chapter of a neurology nurse specialty organization. Raj has already extended his leadership into the health policy arena by giving expert testimony before the state legislature.

The nurse manager recognizes Raj's expertise and passion and asks Raj what he might do improve care for neurology patients both on his unit and perhaps throughout the system. However, he has been invited to sit on the Institutional Ethics Committee and is eager to do so, though it would take him away from the unit. However, the nurse manager says "no," that he is only a staff nurse and that it would be better for him to focus his concern on the unit.

Case 2

After completing her PhD, Dr. Brincar was recently hired as a nursing instructor. This is her first teaching position and she has seven years in which to become tenured. The tenure process requires excellence in teaching, some professional service, and research, research, research, and publications from that research. She is about to embark upon her first post-doctoral research. Her topic is post-operative shivering and body heat loss. She had prepared her research proposal for the IRB and submitted it for their review four months ago; they meet only every other month. The committee indicated that they would approve the proposal but that it was being returned because of budget issues. They directed her to address these issues and re-submit her proposal for final review the next time that they would meet (in seven weeks). In the meantime, because the committee had indicated that they would approve the proposal after revision, and because budget issues were not scientific issues, Dr. Brincar proceeded to initiate the study and began data collection without final approval of the IRB.

ENDNOTES

1. American Nurses Association, *Interpretation of the Statements of the Code for Professional Nurses* (New York: ANA, 1960), 15.

2. Ibid., 16.

3. ANA, *A Code for Professional Nurses* (Kansas City, MO: ANA, 1968), 7.

4. American Nurses Association. *The Nurse in Research: ANA Guidelines on Ethical Values. American Journal of Nursing.* 1968 Jul (7): 1504-7.

5. Ibid., 7.

6. *Code of Federal Regulations*, Department of Health and Human Services, title 45, part 46: "Protection of Human Subjects," 2009. Available at http://www.hhs.gov/ohrp/policy/ohrpregulations.pdf

7. ANA, *Code for Nurses with Interpretive Statements* (Kansas City, MO: ANA, 1976), 14.

8. Ibid.

9. ANA Commission on Nursing Research, *Human Rights Guidelines for Nurses in Clinical and Other Research* (Kansas City, MO: ANA, 1974).

10. Ibid., 14–15.

11. ANA, *Code of Ethics for Nurses with Interpretive Statements* (Kansas City, MO: ANA, 1985), 12.

12. ANA, *Code of Ethics for Nurses with Interpretive Statements* (Washington, D.C.: ANA, 2001), 27.

13. Ibid.

14. Ibid., 28.

15. Ibid.

16. W. H. Newton-Smith, *The Rationality of Science* (London: Routledge & Kegan Paul, 1981).

17. "About NEH," National Endowment for the Humanities, http://www.neh.gov/about

18. E. Garfield and A. I. Pudovkin, "From Materials Science to Nano-Ceramics – Citation Analysis Identifies the Key Journals and Players," (conference paper presented at the 2003 International Nano Ceramic/Crystal Forum and International Symposium on Intermaterials, Hanyang University, Seoul, September 26, 2003), http://garfield.library.upenn.edu/papers/korea2003.pdf

19. Denise Gehring, Reference librarian, personal communication, October 22, 2014. Reference Amy Shuba, at Tompson Reuters Technical Support, Case #TS-01856884:updated:ref:_00D30 un._50070pM6HK:ref

20. Patricia Benner, Molly Sutphen, Victoria Leonard, and Lisa Day, *Educating Nurses: A Call for Radical Transformation* (New York: JosseyBass/Carnegie Foundation for the Advancement of Teaching, 2009), 4.

21. A. Jameton and M. D. Fowler, "Ethical Inquiry and the Concept of Research," *Advances in Nursing Science* 11, no. 3 (1989): 11–24.

22. American Nurses Association, *Code of Ethics for Nurses with Interpretive Statements* (Silver Spring, MD: ANA, 2015), 27.

23. *Oxford English Dictionary* s.v., "Equiponderate," accessed 2012, http://0-www.oed.com.patris.apu.edu/view/Entry/63809?rskey=1d8c35&result=2#

24. Chad Cook and Charles Sheets, "Clinical Equipoise and Personal Equipoise: Two Necessary Ingredients for Reducing Bias in Manual Therapy Trials," *Journal of Manual and Manipulative Therapy* 19, no. 1 (2011): 55.

[25] World Health Organization, *Standards and Operational Guidance for Ethics Review of Health-Related Research with Human Participants* (Geneva: WHO, 2011), 1–44.

[26] National Research Council (US) Committee to Update Science, Medicine, and Animals, *Science, Medicine, and Animals* (Washington, DC: National Academies Press, 2004).

[27] "The Nuremberg Code," Department of Health and Human Services, http://www.hhs.gov/ohrp/archive/nurcode.html

[28] Ibid.

[29] "WMA Declaration of Helsinki - Ethical Principles for Medical Research Involving Human Subjects" (6th ed.), World Medical Association, last modified October 2013, http://www.wma.net/en/30publications/10policies/b3/index.html

[30] H. K. Beecher, "Ethics and Clinical Research," *New England Journal of Medicine* 274, no. 24 (June, 1966): 1354–60

[31] "Willowbrook Hepatitis Experiments," National Institutes of Health, Office of Science Education http://science.education.nih.gov/supplements/nih9/bioethics/guide/pdf/Master_5-4.pdf

[32] "The Tuskegee Timeline," Centers for Disease Control and Prevention, last modified September 24, 2013, http://www.cdc.gov/tuskegee/timeline.htm

[33] Laud Humphreys, *Tearoom Trade: Impersonal Sex in Public Places* (London: Gerald Duckworth, 1970).

[34] S. Milgram, "Behavioral study of obedience," *Journal of Abnormal and Social Psychology* 67 (1963): 371.

[35] Beecher, "Ethics and Clinical Research."

[36] M. H. Pappworth, *Human Guinea Pigs: Experimentation on Man* (London: Routledge & Keagan, 1967).

[37] M. H. Pappworth, "'Human Guinea Pigs'—a history," *British Medical Journal* 301 (December 1990): 1456–60.

[38] Alastair Campbell, "A Report from New Zealand: An 'Unfortunate Experiment'," *Bioethics* 3, no. 1 (January 1989): 59–66.

[39] Carl Elliott, "'Unfortunate experiments' in New Zealand and Minnesota," Mad In America, last modified July, 2012, http://www.madinamerica.com/2012/07/unfortunate-experiments-in-new-zealand-and-minnesota/

[40] "Office for Human Research Protections (OHRP)," U.S. Department of Health and Human Service, http://www.hhs.gov/ohrp/

[41] *Code of Federal Regulations*, Department of Health and Human Services, title 45, part 46: "Protection of Human Subjects," 2009, http://www.hhs.gov/ohrp/policy/ohrpregulations.pdf

[42] U.S. Department of Health and Human Services Office for Human Research Protections, *International Compilation of Human Research Standards* (2014 ed.) http://www.hhs.gov/ohrp/international/intlcompilation/2014intlcomp.pdf.pdf

[43] "Human Subjects Protection," NursingWorld, http://nursingworld.org/MainMenuCategories/ThePracticeofProfessionalNursing/Improving-Your-Practice/Research-Toolkit/Human-Subjects-Protection

[44] ANA, *Code of Ethics for Nurses with Interpretive Statements* (Silver Spring, MD: ANA, 2015), 27–28.

[45] American Nurses Association, *Nursing: Scope and Standards of Practice* (2nd ed.) (Silver Spring, MD: ANA, 2010), 2.

[46] "ANA Standards O–Z," Nursesbooks.org, http://www.nursesbooks.org/Main-Menu/Standards/O–Z. aspx

[47] Isis Montalvo, American Nurses Association, "Nursing Sensitive Measures: National Database of Nursing Quality Indicators (NDNQI®)." (2007). http://www.ncvhs.hhs.gov/wp-content/uploads/2014/05/070619p8.pdf

[48] "National Database of Nursing Quality Indicators (NDNQI)," NursingWorld, http://www.nursingworld.org/research-toolkit/ndnqi; "NDNQI: Transforming Data into Quality Care," NursingWorld. http://www.nursingworld.org/MainMenuCategories/ThePracticeofProfessionalNursing/PatientSafetyQuality/Research-Measurement/Data-Access/NDNQIBrochure.pdf

[49] Sally Thorne and Richard Sawatzky, "Particularizing the General: Sustaining Theoretical Integrity in the Context of an Evidence-Based Practice Agenda," *Advances in Nursing Science* 37, no. 1 (January/March 2014): 14.

[50] International Council of Nurses, *Closing the Gap: From Evidence to Action* (Geneva, Switzerland: ICN, 2012), 5.

[51] Ibid., 1.

Provision 8
The nurse collaborates with other health professionals and the public to protect human rights, promote health diplomacy, and reduce health disparities.

Provision 8. Collaboration to Reach for Greater Ends

Introduction

The first seven provisions and interpretive statements received modest though significant revision. Provisions 8 and 9 and their interpretive statements were more thoroughly revised. Provision 9 continues to focus on collaboration but the reach of that collaboration is extended.

In some respects, Provision 8 is one of the oldest continuing provisions in the Code. However, its foundation, found in both the Nightingale Pledge as well as in the earliest codes, has become obscured over the years as the provision has been reshaped. It begins in the relational nexus of nursing's ethics from the late 1800s, dividing nurses' ethical duties into seven fundamental classes: those owed to the patient; those owed to the physician; those owed to the patient's family, friends, and servants; those owed to herself [oneself]; those owed to her [the nurse's] friends; those owed to her [the nurse's] own hospital or school; those owed to other nurses.[1] This provision originally arose from the "duties owed to the physician," that is, from moral concerns regarding the nurse–physician relationship.

That relationship itself has evolved over the years from "handmaiden to the doctor," to the "doctor–nurse game,"[2] to a more collaborative relationship. Collaboration can be defined in a number of ways but at heart, it is a nonhierarchical, interactive process between or among people or small groups working toward a common purpose or common good. It is marked by parity between and amongst individuals and by voluntary participation.[3] Collaboration intrinsically requires respect, trust, and equality within the work group.

The evolution of the provision is interesting in the disappearance of the physician over the decades. The Nightingale Pledge (1893) states: "with loyalty will I endeavor to aid the physician in his work."[4] *A Suggested Code*

(1926) contains a section titled "The Relation of the Nurse to the Medical Profession." There is a subtle shift here from the "physician" specifically to the "medical profession." It states, in part:

> The term "medicine" should be understood to refer to *scientific* medicine and the desirable relationship between the two should be one of mutual respect. The nurse should be fully informed on the provisions of the medical practice act of her own state in order that she may not unconsciously support quackery and actual infringements of the law...she should endeavor to give such intelligent and skilled nursing service that she will be looked upon as a co-worker of the doctor in the whole field of health.[5]

A Tentative Code (1940) picks up the language of *A Suggested Code* (1926) verbatim and then adds this:

> Loyalty to the physician demands that the nurse conscientiously follow his instructions and that she build up the confidence of the patient in him. At the same time she will exercise reason and diligence in carrying out orders. She is to avoid criticism of him to anyone but himself, and, if necessary, to the proper administrative officers in the institution or agency where both may be working, or to the local medical professional society.[6]

The first officially adopted *Code for Professional Nurses*, in 1950 (and 1957), states that:

> Provision 7: The nurse is obligated to carry out the physician's orders intelligently.

> Provision 8: The nurse sustains confidence in the physician and other members of the health team.

> Provision 16: A nurse should participate and share responsibility with other citizens and health professionals in promoting efforts to meet the health needs of the public — local, state, national, and international.[7]

There is a subtle shift here. Obligations to the physician are retained but the notion that nurses are to participate and share responsibility with other health professionals in meeting health needs is new to the Code. By 1960, the nurse works "with other citizens and health professions in promoting efforts to meet health needs of the public."[8] In addition, Provision 16 states that the "nurse works harmoniously with, and sustains confidence in, nursing associates, the physician, and other members of the health team."[9] The physician is beginning to disappear from the Code to be replaced by "other health professionals," as nursing roles begin to specialize. By the 1968 revision of the Code, the male pronoun is gone completely and the focus shifts to working with the public ("citizens") and other health professionals to meet the health needs of the public.[10] This provision begins as a statement on obligations to the physician but is eventually supplanted by an obligation to work with other health professionals to meet health needs. The vocabulary of this obligation is today far more collaborative in nature and contains the implicit expectation that the nurse is one among equals in collaboration. As noted above, as early as 1950, there was a sense that collaborative effort to meet health needs was to extend to include local, state, national, and international health.[11]

8.1 Health is a Universal Right

While a commitment to health as a universal right is not new to nursing or its position statements, it has not previously been stated so directly in the Code. The preamble of the 1946 Constitution of the World Health Organization (WHO) defines health as "a state of complete physical, mental and social well-being and not merely the absence of disease or infirmity."[12] The WHO Constitution itself states that: "The enjoyment of the highest attainable standard of health is one of the fundamental rights of every human being without distinction of race, religion, political belief, economic or social condition."[13] The Constitution of the WHO "marks the first formal demarcation of a right to health in international law." [14,15] ANA's *Health System Reform Agenda* (2008) declares that in its reform agenda for American health care, "ANA remains committed to the principle that health care is a human right and that all persons are entitled to ready access to affordable, high-quality health care services."[16]

But what precisely does this right entail? The Code of 2015 includes those elements that are detailed in the *Declaration of Alma-Ata*[17] adopted in Almatay (formerly Alma-Ata), Kazakhstan in 1978. It states:

> An acceptable level of health for all the people of the world by the year 2000 can be attained through a fuller and better use of the world's resources, a considerable part of which is now spent on armaments and military conflicts.[18]

The Declaration sought to promote health for all through primary health care that:

> includes at least: education concerning prevailing health problems and the methods of preventing and controlling them; promotion of food supply and proper nutrition; an adequate supply of safe water and basic sanitation; maternal and child health care, including family planning; immunization against the major infectious diseases; prevention and control of locally endemic diseases; appropriate treatment of common diseases and injuries; and provision of essential drugs.[19]

These then are the foundational expectations for primary health essential to the attainment of the goal of health for all. The specific goal of "health for All by 2000" derives from the Alma-Ata conference declaration. But health for all was not achieved by 2000. Subsequently, in 2000, the UN established the Millennium Development Goals (MDGs). In brief, the goals were:

- To halve the number of undernourished people
- To achieve universal primary education
- To promote gender equality and empower women
- To reduce child mortality
- To improve maternal health
- To combat HIV/AIDS, malaria, and other diseases
- To ensure environmental sustainability
- To develop a global partnership for development[20]

Note that what is being targeted is what constitutes the social determinants of health in addition to specific diseases that have remained resistant to eradication. Today we would include Ebola with HIV/AIDS, malaria, M. tuberculosis, and childhood diseases such as measles.

8.2 Collaboration for Health, Human Rights, and Health Diplomacy

Health for all whether international, national, regional, or local cannot be achieved without wide and concerted collaboration, in which nursing plays a crucial and leadership role. The Code of 2015 states that the nursing commitment to advancing health, welfare, and safety "reflects the intent to achieve and sustain health as a means to the common good so that individuals and communities worldwide can develop to their fullest potential and live with dignity."[21] Thus *health* is a *good* in several senses—it serves the common good (that is, what is shared and of benefit to all or most members of a community or nation), it allows individuals and communities to flourish, it allows individuals and communities to live up to their potential, thus contributing to the well-being and welfare of the community and society, and it affirms human dignity.

Health is, as noted above, a universal human right. But what is a *human right?* And what is a *right?*[22] The United Nations' *Universal Declaration of Human Rights* specifies basic human rights, phrased both positively and negatively. It declares that universal human rights include a right to life, liberty, and security of person; a right not to be enslaved, subject to torture or to cruel, inhuman or degrading treatment or punishment; to recognition as a person under the law; to equality before the law; to protection from arbitrary arrest, detention or exile; to fair and impartial judgment under the law; to freedom from arbitrary interference with privacy, to freedom of movement within the State, a right to a nationality, and more.[23] These rights and more are regarded, internationally, as fundamental *human rights* to which all persons have a moral and legal claim. That is, *rights* give rise to legitimate *claims* that can be made upon the state that then become *civil rights* when codified in the law of the nation. While there are a number of views of the ultimate sources of rights, today it is generally held that human rights are tied to human dignity and are universal, and that civil rights derive from the state and are created by law. For example, in the United States, a general legal right to protection from arbitrary interference with one's privacy gives rise to a claim against the State seizing and searching one's phone or computer—or a hospital gathering data not related to care.

Under the law, a *right* is a *claim* possessed by a particular person and supported by the law. An example of a claim is an individual's right not to be given treatment by a physician that is unwanted.[24] Every right has a *correlative duty*. That is, for each right that an individual possesses, there is a corresponding duty imposed upon another. Using the same example, the physician has an obligation not to treat an unwilling patient and a duty to respect the patient's autonomous refusal of treatment. Additionally, a patient has a right to safe nursing care while in the hospital and the nurses employed by the hospital have a corresponding legal and moral obligation to provide safe care. If health care is a right then there is an obligation on the part of another (e.g., the government, the state) to provide it.

In 1952, the President's Commission on the Health Needs of the Nation wrote that "access to the means for the attainment and preservation of health is a basic human right."[25] The President's Commission for the Study of Ethical Problems in Medicine and Biomedical and Behavioral Research (replaced by a series of councils under successive presidents), working from 1978 through 1983, was tasked with the responsibility of examining several major bioethical issues, one of which was securing access to health care. Their report identified six fundamental ethical obligations regarding securing access to care. They are:[26]

- That society has an ethical obligation to ensure equitable access to health care for all.
- The societal obligation is balanced by individual obligations.
- Equitable access to health care requires that all citizens be able to secure an adequate level of care without excessive burdens.
- When equity occurs through the operation of private forces, there is no need for government involvement, but the ultimate responsibility for ensuring that society's obligation is met, through a combination of public and private sector arrangements, rests with the Federal government.

- The cost of achieving equitable access to health care ought to be shared fairly.
- Efforts to contain rising health care costs are important but should not focus on limiting the attainment of equitable access for the least well served portion of the public.

These are rights that the commission chose to frame as ethical obligations. Under the current healthcare reform, the ANA has affirmed that:

> ANA believes that health care is a basic human right, and supports the World Health Organization's challenge – originally articulated in 1978, and reaffirmed as late as 2007 – for all nations to provide a basic level of health care to their citizens. The U.S. is the only industrialized country that does not explicitly express a commitment to its people to take care of at least their basic health needs.[27]

In addition, the ANA House of Delegates in 2010 made the following resolutions that would seek to extend access to health care beyond citizens:

> Resolved, that the American Nurses Association will reaffirm its position that all individuals living in the U.S., including documented and undocumented immigrants, have access to health care; and

> Resolved, that the American Nurses Association will educate nurses regarding the wide-ranging social, economic and political ramifications of undocumented immigrants' lack of access to healthcare services.[28]

The Constitution of the United States sets forth what people may generally expect from the federal government, its purposes and functions, the relationship with state governments, and what individuals must give up in order to preserve the interests and safety of all. Constitutional amendments speak more distinctly to rights. While constitutional amendments provide citizens with a very broad sweep of rights, there is no constitutional amendment specific to health or health care.

In asserting certain rights in health care, one should recognize that this is only one way of placing issues within an ethical framework. Framing an issue solely in terms of rights, with no consideration of corresponding obligations or responsibilities, often leads to adversarial confrontations rather than resolution. For the purposes of this chapter, the concept of *rights* will be used to indicate some legitimate expectations of persons in an identified society at a given time. It may be more useful to think of *claims* about rights not as things to be discovered as true or false but as language used to promote change and social legislative reform. Rights do not assert anything about the moral order per se, but the idea that jeopardizing human rights is an affront to justice is compelling. Many would agree that human rights include a right to health care as a necessary means to carrying on one's life and to contribution to the common good. If this is the case, the fact that not all people have access to health care is ethically unacceptable.

If there is a right to health care, then a claim to health care can be made. But to whom does one present this claim? Part of the problem in responding to such a claim lies in our definitions of health itself.

Health is a vague term, even when one thinks of it as absence of illness or the ability to carry on daily activities. The World Health Organization's (WHO) concept is that health is a "state of complete physical, mental and social well-being and not merely the absence of disease or infirmity."[29] This definition does not give much direction when considered in the light of rights claims, development and implementation of organizational and public policies, and the limitless economic burdens that an attempt at its realization would entail for society. It provides no boundaries within which to consider moral or legal obligations to provide health care. Health is not always a top social priority, even as the means to other ends. The concept of a right to health care also runs into difficulty when one starts talking about individual choices and responsibility for one's health, especially when those choices involve identified health risk factors and unhealthy lifestyles or choices. [30]

The 1980s saw a shift to a focus on obligations in health care as illustrated in the important report entitled *Securing Access to Health Care*.[31] This report concludes that society as a whole has an ethical obligation to ensure equitable access to health care. Equitable access, as discussed in the report, refers to everyone having access to some level of health care, that is, "enough care to achieve sufficient welfare, opportunity, information, and evidence of interpersonal concern to facilitate a reasonably full and satisfying life."[32] Inherent in these societal obligations is the notion of the special importance of health care in relieving suffering and in demonstrating mutual empathy and compassion for all persons residing within a nation. Achieving health for all and a right to health will require a heightened emphasis on *health diplomacy*. WHO states that:

> Global health diplomacy brings together the disciplines of public health, international affairs, management, law and economics and focuses on negotiations that shape and manage the global policy environment for health. The relationship between health, foreign policy and trade is at the cutting edge of global health diplomacy.[33]

The WHO unit on Trade, Foreign Policy, Diplomacy and Health (TFD) in the Department of Ethics, Equity, Trade and Human Rights (ETH)

> works to catalyze, facilitate and coordinate actions towards greater policy coherence between the promotion and protection of health and other government policies such as trade and foreign policy. Key external partners include the World Trade Organization and UNCTAD [United Nations Conference on Trade and Development].[34]

On the surface it seems odd to combine a concern for health with issues of global trade and economics, but they are profoundly intertwined. Take for example the Structural Adjustment Programmes (SAPs). SAPs

> are economic policies for developing countries that have been promoted by the World Bank and International Monetary Fund (IMF) since the early 1980s by the provision of loans [to low income nations] conditional on the adoption of ...policies...designed to encourage the structural adjustment of an economy by, for example, removing "excess" government controls and promoting market competition.... One important criticism of SAPs, which emerged shortly after they were first adopted and has continued since, concerns their impact on the social sector. In health, SAPs affect both the supply of health services (by insisting on cuts in health spending) and the demand for health services (by reducing household income, thus leaving people with less money for health). Studies have shown that SAPs policies have slowed down improvements in, or worsened, the health status of people in countries implementing them. The results reported include worse nutritional status of children, increased incidence of infectious diseases, and higher infant and maternal mortality rates.[35]

Global economics and trade can have a profound impact upon the social safety net of poorer nations, damaging health, education and other sectors of society in those nations. The objectives of the WHO TFD unit are: [36]

1. To support countries in understanding and responding to the implications of international trade and trade agreements for health

2. To support efforts to ensure that health is promoted and protected in the context of foreign policy

3. To build the capacity of countries to negotiate in support of collective action to address global health challenges

When on the international stage, health has to compete with commerce, military support, and other expenditures, health stands to lose. Health diplomacy seeks to raise health concerns to parity with other, competing concerns. For the purposes of nursing, a more useful definition of global health diplomacy is found in the article by members of the American Academy of Nursing's Expert Panel on Global Nursing and Health. They adopt Novotny and Adams' well-recognized definition:

> Novotny and Adams defined global health diplomacy as "a political change activity that meets the dual goals of improving global health while maintaining and strengthening international relations abroad, particularly in conflict areas and resource-poor environments [and that] health diplomacy is not only the job of diplomats or health leaders in government structures, it is a professional practice that should inform any group or individual with responsibility to conduct research, service, programs, or direct international health assistance between donor and recipient institutions." [37]

Developing this definition the Expert Panel cites Koplan:

> The term global health refers to "an area for study, research, and practice that places a priority on improving health and achieving equity in health for all people worldwide. Global health emphasizes trans-national health issues, determinants, and solutions; involves many disciplines within and beyond the health sciences and promotes interdisciplinary collaboration; and [it] is a synthesis of population based prevention with individual-level clinical care." [38]

Global Health Diplomacy is an as yet underdeveloped—but emerging and intriguing—domain of nursing involvement (and curriculum).

8.3 Obligation to Advance Health and Human Rights and Reduce Disparities

While this provision's interpretive statements take off from an international destination, they land at home. It emphasizes health disparities, unjust social structures and processes, and social and institutional inequalities within the United States. Nurses are specifically called upon to address "barriers to health, such as poverty, homelessness, unsafe living conditions, abuse and violence and lack of access" to health care. This is complicated by the growing provision of health care to increasingly culturally diverse populations. Again, the emphasis of this provision is upon collaboration to meet the health needs of individuals, communities, and the public and to reduce health disparities.

The Centers for Disease Control and Prevention (CDC) is crystal clear in indicating the problem of health disparities in the US healthcare system. In its 2013 report it declares that the United States lags behind many other nations in life expectancy and that the upward trend in life expectancy is neither as rapid as it should be nor is it uniformly experienced. It states that

> these two shortcomings of our health system are distinct but related. Our overall health status does not achieve our potential. An important part of this — even though preventable illness, injury, disability, and death affect all segments of society — is that life expectancy and other key health outcomes vary greatly by race, sex, socioeconomic status, and geographic location. In the United States, whites have a longer healthy life expectancy than blacks, and women live longer than men. There are also marked regional differences, with much lower life expectancy among both white and black Americans who live in the Southeast.[39]

The report cites a statement made by Martin Luther King Jr. in 1966: "Of all the forms of inequality, injustice in health care is the most shocking and inhumane."[40] The report makes it clear that the majority of health disparities redound to the least well off in society and to social minority groups, especially to racial and ethnic minorities. It notes that eliminating health disparities is not easy but it is possible and it cites the Vaccines for Children program of 20 years ago as a resounding success. This program helped to "virtually eliminate disparities in childhood vaccination rates."[41] Admittedly, childhood vaccination may be a less difficult issue to tackle than complex diseases of adults that disproportionately affect minority persons. The report highlights four findings in particular:

> Four findings bring home the enormous personal tragedy of health disparities:
>
> • Cardiovascular disease is the leading cause of death in the United States. Non-Hispanic black adults are at least 50% more likely to die of heart disease or stroke prematurely (i.e., before age 75 years) than their non-Hispanic white counterparts.
> • The prevalence of adult diabetes is higher among Hispanics, non-Hispanic blacks, and those of other or mixed races than among Asians and non-Hispanic whites. Prevalence is also higher among adults without college degrees and those with lower household incomes.
> • The infant mortality rate for non-Hispanic blacks is more than double the rate for non-Hispanic whites. Rates also vary geographically, with higher rates in the South and Midwest than in other parts of the country.

- Men are far more likely to commit suicide than women, regardless of age or race/ethnicity, with overall rates nearly four times those of women. For both men and women, suicide rates are highest among American Indians/Alaska Natives and non-Hispanic whites.[42]

The implications that these findings have for nursing are profound. They indicate areas for nursing education, practice, research, and policy—and the continued need to recruit social minority faculty for nursing schools and students into nursing. And, as is emphasized by this provision, nurses need to collaborate with other health professionals, groups and organization to work toward ameliorating health disparities. Further, "nurses should collaborate to create a moral milieu that is sensitive to diverse cultural values and practices."[43]

In 2010, the Department of Health and Human Services initiated the project "Healthy People 2020." The program categorized the determinants of health into five categories that the project addresses: policymaking, social factors, health services, individual behavior, and biology and genetics. Policymaking includes an enormous range of concerns such as tobacco taxes, seatbelt laws, helmet laws for motorcyclists and bicyclists, bike lanes on city streets, restaurant kitchen grading, infant and child car seat laws, and regulations requiring sidewalk curb cuts and wheelchair ramps. Social determinants of health include, for example, social norms and discrimination, the quality of schools, availability of transportation, presence of grocery stores, employment opportunities, neighborhood exposure to toxic elements, and exposure to violence or crime. The health services category is concerned with barriers to care, such as cost, availability, access, insurance, and language/translation access. The category of individual behaviors with which the project is concerned includes all of the usual suspects—smoking, substance use or abuse, diet, obesity, health behaviors such as hand washing and tooth brushing, and exercise. The category of biological and genetic determinants looks at those factors that predispose to illness, such as ancestral genes (e.g., sickle cell anemia, Tay-Sachs' gene, BRCA 1 or 2), family history, age, sex, and serostatus for HIV.[44] The Healthy People 2020 project encompasses 42 topic areas and more than 1,200 objectives with 26 leading health indicators that indicate high priority areas and are periodically updated about their progress.[45] There is a very long way to go to meet these 1,200 objectives but to date, four of the 2020 targets have been met. These are: improvement in air quality, reduction of children exposed to secondhand smoke, reduction of homicides, and adult increase in aerobic exercise and physical strengthening.[46] Note that the goals have been met for the 2020 target, which does not necessarily mean that the problem has been fully resolved.

The four general goals of the Healthy People 2020 Project are:

- Attain high-quality, longer lives free of preventable disease, disability, injury, and premature death;
- Achieve health equity, eliminate disparities, and improve the health of all groups;
- Create social and physical environments that promote good health for all; and
- Promote quality of life, healthy development, and healthy behaviors across all life stages.[47]

These goals are clearly within the domain of nursing practice and research, and more specifically, they are particularly amenable to nursing collaboration with other health professions in efforts to resolve health disparities and move the nation toward greater health.[48]

8.4 Collaboration for Human Rights in Complex, Extreme, or Extraordinary Practice Settings

Natural disasters and warfare or regional conflict become incubators for human rights violations. Such violations can take a number of forms including but not limited to:

> Unequal access to assistance, discrimination in aid provision, enforced relocation, sexual and gender-based violence, loss of documentation, recruitment of children into fighting forces, unsafe or involuntary return or resettlement, and issues of property restitution are just some of the problems that are often encountered by those affected by the consequences of natural disasters. In addition, a high number of persons also become internally displaced when volcanic eruptions, tsunamis, floods, drought, landslides, or earthquakes destroy houses and shelter, forcing affected populations to leave their homes or places of residence. Experience has shown that the longer the displacement lasts, the greater the risk of human rights violations. In particular, discrimination and violations of economic, social and cultural rights tend to become more systemic over time. [49]

Mass casualty events, one type of extraordinary practice setting, place thousands of human lives at risk of morbidity and mortality. These events may be natural or human-made and may or may not be accompanied by extensive environmental destruction. Mass casualty events can include bioterrorism, epidemics or pandemics, warfare or genocide, hurricanes, tsunamis, uncontained wildfires, volcanic eruptions, and chemical or radiation emergencies. These events typically compromise or overwhelm regional or even national ability to respond effectively or to respond in a manner that is consistent with customary standards of care under conditions of normalcy. While it

> is that the goal of the health and medical response to a mass casualty event is to save as many lives as possible. There is consensus that, to achieve this goal, health and medical care will have to be delivered in a manner that differs from the standards of care that apply under normal circumstances.[50]

Allswede identifies four levels by which health or medical care standards might have to be modified in mass casualty events. They are:

- Normal medical care standards
- Near normal medical care standards: alternate sites of care, use of atypical devices, expanded scope of practice
- Focus on key lifesaving events: cannot offer everyone highest level of care but can offer key lifesaving care
- Total system/standards alteration: questions asked about who gets access to what resources[51]

The DHHS document *Bioterrorism and Other Public Health Emergencies: Altered Standards of Care in Mass Casualty Events* (2005) was prepared subsequent to the September 11, 2001, terrorist attacks and the anthrax attacks in 2001. In 2004, a meeting was convened to address the question of health system preparedness for mass casualty. The participants included experts in bioethics, emergency medicine, emergency management, health law, health policy, public health, and health administration, as well as representatives of the Department of Health and Human Services Agency for Healthcare Research and Quality, and the Office of the Assistant Secretary for Public Health Emergency Preparedness. The key findings of the meeting are detailed in this document. A number of potential changes in standards of care may occur in mass casualty including that the "usual scope of practice standards that will not apply. Nurses may function as physicians, and physicians may function outside their specialties. Credentialing of providers may be granted on an emergency or temporary basis."[52]

Five guiding principles for altered standards of care during mass casualty events were developed. They are:

Principle 1. In planning for a mass casualty event, the aim should be to keep the health care system functioning and to deliver acceptable quality of care to preserve as many lives as possible.

Principle 2. Planning a health and medical response to a mass casualty event must be comprehensive, community-based, and coordinated at the regional level.

Principle 3. There must be an adequate legal framework for providing health and medical care in a mass casualty event.

Principle 4. The rights of individuals must be protected to the extent possible and reasonable under the circumstances.

Principle 5. Clear communication with the public is essential before, during, and after a mass casualty event. [53]

Principle 4, on individuals' rights, is concerned about the legal framework for constraining rights, the basis for allocation of care decisions, limitations to freedom due to quarantine or isolation, and issues of privacy and confidentiality. This is the limit of the consideration that the document gives to rights; nowhere is a broader concern human rights addressed. In addition, the document fails to address or even acknowledge disparities that often exist in mass casualty events, specifically natural disasters, in terms of vulnerability, response, and recovery phases.[54,55] In terms of response, such disparities can exist within as well as between disasters.[56]

The ANA policy *Adapting Standards of Care Under Extreme Conditions: Guidance for Professionals During Disasters, Pandemics, and Other Extreme Emergencies*[57] adopts 15 ethical guidelines from the University of Toronto Joint Centre for Bioethics for a Canadian Discussion of Pandemic Influenza Planning 2005 report *Stand on Guard for Thee*.[58] The 15 ethical principles are: the values of individual liberty, protection of the public from harm, proportionality, privacy, duty to provide care, reciprocity, equity, trust, solidarity, stewardship, and procedures that are reasonable, open and transparent, inclusive, responsive, and accountable.[59] While human rights are not specifically mentioned, some of these principles (such as equity care and transparency) get at the concerns for human rights. The Toronto paper does specifically enjoin decision makers to

turn for guidance to documents such as charters of rights and freedoms and human rights legislation. They can look to the United Nations' Siracusa Principles, which are based upon human rights documents. The principles stipulate the extent to which state powers should be exercised in times of public health emergencies. The principles hold that public health may be invoked as grounds for limiting certain rights in order to manage a serious threat to the health of individuals or a population. These measures must be specifically aimed at preventing disease or injury, or providing care for the sick and injured. The actions taken must be legal, necessary, and proportional to the threat.[60]

The UN Siracusa Principles deal with the derogation (relaxation of or exemption from) of civil and political rights "when a public emergency threatens the life of the nation."[61] Corroborating the DHHS document, the ANA *Adapting Standards of Care Under Extreme Conditions*

shifts ethical standards to a utilitarian framework in which the clinical goal is the greatest good for the greatest number of individuals. As a result, not everyone may receive the optimal services that might be available at other times or places. This means that care decisions are not about "the most that can be done" or "the best that can be done under perfect conditions" but about what is sufficient given the specific conditions at the time. This might include expanding the role of family members in monitoring patient status, or outpatient care for a condition that might otherwise be treated in an inpatient setting.[62]

Extraordinary circumstances or extraordinary settings may not be extreme settings and may not risk mass casualties. Examples might include mountain search and rescue, plane crashes or major freeway collisions, industrial explosions, some rural settings, or military detention centers. Some natural disasters might be included, such as an earthquake or tornado where there is major property damage but few lives put at risk. Extraordinary care settings still require the preservation of human rights. For example, in military health care, the nurses' primary obligation remains to the patient; this is true of the entire military health system. Yet it is possible that nurses may be expected to care for an enemy combatant. In her work on nursing ethics in the military, Southby writes that

[p]risoners and detainees are entitled to healthcare, humane treatment, and the right to refuse these offers and to die with dignity in a peaceful manner. Nurses are often the first to suspect or detect ill treatment of these persons and must take appropriate actions to safeguard their rights. This is an awesome responsibility.[63]

The International Council of Nurses' position paper *Nurses' Role in the Care of Detainees and Prisoners* is resolute about the nurse's role in preserving the human rights of detainees and prisoners. Its position paper states:

> The International Council of Nurses (ICN) endorses the UN *Universal Declaration of Human Rights* (1948), the Geneva Convention of 1949 and the additional protocols and the United Nations Basic Principles for the Treatment of Prisoners and therefore asserts that:
>
> - Prisoners and detainees have the right to health care and humane treatment regardless of their legal status.
> - Interrogation procedures and any act or behaviour harmful to mental and physical health, including denial of treatment and care during detention must be condemned.
> - Prisoners and detainees, including those on hunger strike have a right to clear and sufficient information; to consent for or refusal of treatment or diagnostic procedures; and to a dignified and peaceful death.
> - Nurses have a role in making sure informed consent and capacity to consent is established, particularly for vulnerable groups and those with mental health problems or learning disabilities.
> - Nurses' primary responsibility is to those people who require nursing care. In caring for detainees and prisoners nurses are expected to adhere to human rights and ethical principles.[64]

In the recent case of military nurses who refused to force-feed detainees on a hunger strike at the United States Guantanamo Bay detention facility, these nurses' conscientious objection to participate falls within the guidelines of the 2015 Code as well as the ICN guidelines. Their refusal also falls within the thoughtful moral reflection characteristic of the tradition of military nursing in the United States.

Extreme and extraordinary settings and circumstances demand the best that nursing has to offer, as nurses collaborate with other health professions and disciplines to meet the needs of individuals, the public and populations. Only by collaborative and concerted effort can there be hope under the terrible circumstances that natural and human-made disasters can create.

Cases

Case 1

Maridell Kitchen, RN, works in the orthopedic clinic. Her first patient is Juan Santos, a 19-year-old man from Honduras, who is being seen for a cast check on his broken arm. Another man is with him and he explains that he is a friend, there to help with the appointment since the patient doesn't speak much English. As she does her assessment it seems as if the friend is answering questions without consulting the patient. The clinic has a translation service, so Maridell calls for a translator. Maridell asks the friend to wait in the waiting room.

When the translator arrives, Mr. Santos doesn't make eye contact but looks at the floor and speaks softly. Even simple questions are hard for him to answer. He cannot give an address for where he lives nor can he say long he has been in the city. When asked what kind of work he does, he just says that he works at a motel cleaning rooms, does some odd jobs, and whatever else he is told to do. The translator lets Maridell know that the patient is afraid to answer her questions and that he refers to the "friend" as his boss. He does not want his boss to hear him. Issues of human trafficking have been in the local news the past six months, and last month Maridell had attended an interdisciplinary in-service on human trafficking. She suspects that Juan is a human trafficked laborer.

She calls the national help line at 1(888) 373-7888. The helpline staff agree that Mr. Santos' situation is consistent with being a human-trafficked laborer, so they give her instructions on what to do next. In addition, Maridell is concerned that the department as a whole be alerted so that additional patients who might be trafficked are quickly recognized. She and a physician colleague want the department to be as effective as possible in assisting persons who might be human trafficked laborers, so they plan to work together to develop a departmental strategy and to enhance departmental preparation.

Case 2

The Diabetes Care Management program at South East Community Clinic has been very successful during the last year in identifying patients with diabetes. Recently, there have been more Cambodian immigrants seen for foot problems in the clinic.

To address this problem, the nurse manager brought this up at the strategic planning meeting. Since the clinic has great success with reducing the foot problems among the Latino patients, they decide to develop a similar program for the Cambodians. All agree to offer bilingual (Khmer–English) diabetes education classes, to expand the outreach program for follow-up visits, and to hire a coach or navigator for this population, especially to discern the cultural differences that may have implications for differences in the two programs. To effectively address the unique cultural challenges, they partner with the local university healthcare sciences faculty and the public health team. The budget is modest, but the clinic funds are rumored to be cut back for the next year. The clinic staff has to figure out how to convince the Board of Directors to fund their efforts.

Case 3

The student nurses in the DNP midwifery program at Kentwick College are discussing human rights in complex, extreme, or extraordinary practice settings. Two have previously served as short-term volunteer nurses, one in a conflict zone, and one in a disaster zone, though neither in obstetrics. Their assignment is to write an orientation/preparation list to use when they volunteer to respond to an emergency or disaster abroad. Questions they have to address include:

- What is the vocabulary used by the local healthcare providers for OB care?
- What is the role of a midwife in that country?
- Are midwives nurses or lay persons?
- What are the education and roles of other nurses?
- How will the nurses and midwives coordinate as a team?
- Will obstetricians be available, or will they be seconded to triage and general trauma care?
- What materials, drugs, and resources will be available?
- What level of case complications will be able to be handled?
- What will OB triage look like?
- Will it be a safe, secure environment for patients?
- Will it be a safe, secure environment for healthcare workers?

Their professor, who has served with Doctors Without Borders (Médecins sans Frontières; MSF) International for over a decade, agrees they have made a good start but encourages them to delve further into the possibilities.

ENDNOTES

1   H. C. C., "Ethics in nursing: A nurse's duty to herself: Talks of a superintendent with her graduating class," *The Trained Nurse and Hospital Review* 2, no. 5 (May 1889): 179. (H. C. C. is an unidentified superintendent of a hospital nursing school in Brooklyn.)

2   L. Stein, "The doctor–nurse game," *Archives of General Psychiatry* 16 (1967): 699–703. See also: L. Stein, D. T. Watts, and T. Howell, "The doctor–nurse game revisited," *New England Journal of Medicine* 322 (1990): 546–49.

3   E. F. Barkley, K. P. Cross, and C. H. Major, *Collaborative learning techniques: A handbook for college faculty* (San Francisco, CA: Jossey-Bass, 2005). See also: P. Dettmer et al., *Collaboration, consultation, and teamwork for students with special needs* (6th ed.) (Columbus, OH: Pearson, 2009).

4   Lystra Gretter, *The Florence Nightingale Pledge* (Detroit, MI: Farrand Training School for Nurses, 1893). Photocopy of autograph manuscript.

5   American Nurses Association, "A Suggested Code," *American Journal of Nursing* 26, no. 8 (August 1926), 599–601.

6   ANA, "A Tentative Code," *American Journal of Nursing* 40, no. 9 (1940).

7   ANA, *A Code for Professional Nurses* (New York: ANA, 1950).

8   ANA, *A Code for Professional Nurses* (New York: ANA, 1960).

9   Ibid.

10   American Nurses Association, *A Code for Professional Nurses* (Kansas City, MO: ANA, 1968).

11   There are discourses within nursing that maintain that "collaboration" is still, itself, a continuation of the doctor–nurse game and falls within the parameters set by patriarchy. See: D. D. Holyoake, "Is the doctor-nurse game still being played?" *Nursing Times* 107, no. 43 (2011): 12–14; S. J. Closs, "Interdisciplinary research and the doctor–nurse game," *Clinical Effectiveness in Nursing* 5 (2001): 101–03; Barbara Keddy, Margaret Jones Gillis, Pat Jacobs, Heather Burton, and Maureen Rogers, "The doctor–nurse relationship: an historical perspective," *Journal of Advanced Nursing* 11, no. 6 (1986): 745–53; S. Sweet and I. Norman, "The nurse–doctor relationship: A selective literature review," *Journal of Advanced Nursing* 22 (1995): 165–70.

12   Frank P. Grad, "The Preamble of the Constitution of the World Health Organization," *Bulletin of the World Health Organization* 80, no. 12 (January 2002): 981.

13   Ibid.

14   Ibid.

15   Ibid.

16   American Nurses Association, *Health System Reform Agenda* (Silver Spring, MD: ANA, 2008), 2. See also: American Nurses Association, *Health care as a basic human right* (Washington, D.C.: Author, 1989); American Nurses Association, *Nursing's agenda for health care reform* [Brochure] (Washington, D.C.: Author, 1991).

17   International Conference on Primary Health Care, *Declaration of Alma-Ata* (Alma-Ata, USSR, September 1978).

18   Ibid., §X.

[19] Ibid., §VII.3.

[20] "Millennium Development Goals: 2013 Progress Chart," United Nations. http://www.un.org/millenniumgoals/pdf/report-2013/2013_progress_english.pdf

[21] ANA, *Code of Ethics for Nurses with Interpretive Statements* (Silver Spring, MD: ANA, 2015) 31.

[22] The following section on rights is modified and adapted from: Marsha Fowler, "Rights, Obligations, and Health Care," in Davis, Anne, Fowler, Marsha and Aroskar, Mila, in *Ethical Dilemmas and Nursing Practice.* 5th ed. (Upper Saddle River, NJ: Prentice Hall, 2009), 59-76.

[23] Ibid.

[24] William J. Curran, "Health Law and Policy," (lecture, Harvard School of Public Health, Boston, MA, October 5, 1976).

[25] President's Commission on the Health Needs of the Nation. Building America's Health. USGPO: Washington D.C., 1953, 3, http://babel.hathitrust.org/cgi/pt?id=uc1.b4211157;view=1up;seq=1

[26] President's Commission for the Study of Ethical Problems in Medicine and Biomedical and Behavioral Research, *Securing Access to Health Care: The Ethical Implications of Differences in the Availability of Health Services* (Volume One: Report) (Washington, D.C.: USGPO, March 1983), 4–5.

[27] "Health Care Reform: Expanding Access," American Nurses Association, http://www.nursingworld.org/MainMenuCategories/Policy-Advocacy/HealthSystemReform/HealthCareReformResources/Health-Care-Reform-Backgrounders/Expanding-Access.pdf

[28] "Nursing Beyond Borders: Access to Health Care for Documented and Undocumented Immigrants Living in the US," ANA Issue Brief accessed on Month day, year, http://www.nursingworld.org/MainMenuCategories/Policy-Advocacy/Positions-and-Resolutions/Issue-Briefs/Access-to-care-for-immigrants.pdf

[29] World Health Organization, *Preamble to the Constitution of the World Health Organization* as adopted by the International Health Conference, New York, June 19–22 1946; signed on July 22, 1946, by the representatives of 61 states (Official Records of the World Health Organization, no. 2, 100) and entered into force on April 7, 1948.

[30] President's Commission, *Securing Access.*

[31] Ibid.

[32] Ibid., 20.

[33] "Global Health Diplomacy," WHO, http://www.who.int/trade/diplomacy/en/ See also: Ilona Kickbusch, Thomas E. Novotny, Nico Drager, Gaudenz Silberschmidt, and Santiago Alcazar, "Global health diplomacy: training across disciplines," *Bulletin of the World Health Organization* 85, no. 12 (December 2007), http://www.who.int/bulletin/volumes/85/12/07-045856/en/

[34] WHO unit on Trade, Foreign Policy, Diplomacy and Health, Department of Ethics, Equity, Trade and Human Rights http://www.who.int/trade/en/

[35] "Structural Adjustment Programmes," WHO, http://www.who.int/trade/glossary/story084/en/

[36] "Trade, Foreign Policy, Diplomacy and Health," WHO, accessed on Month day, year, http://www.who.int/trade/en/

[37] Anita Hunter, Lynda Wilson, Marcia Stanhope, Barbara Hatcher, Marianne Hattar, DeAnne K. Hillfinger Messias, and Dorothy Powell, "Global health diplomacy: An integrative review of the literature and implications for nursing," *Nursing Outlook* 61, no. 2 (2013): 85.

[38] Ibid., 86.

[39] Centers for Disease Control and Prevention, "CDC Health Disparities and Inequalities Report – United States, 2013," Morbidity and Mortality Weekly Report 62, suppl. 3 (November 2013): 1, http://www.cdc.gov/mmwr/pdf/other/su6203.pdf

[40] Ibid.

[41] Ibid.

[42] Ibid.

[43] ANA, *Code of Ethics for Nurses with Interpretive Statements* (2015), Interpretive Statment 8.3, 32.

[44] "Determinants of Health: Policymaking," HealthyPeople, http://www.healthypeople.gov/2020/about/DOHAbout.aspx#policymaking

[45] https://www.healthypeople.gov/2020/leading-health-indicators/Healthy-People-2020-Leading-Health-Indicators%3A-Progress-Update

[46] Healthy People 2020, *Leading Health Indicators: Progress Update* (Washington, DC: DHHS, March 2014), 3. See: http://www.healthypeople.gov/sites/default/files/LHI-ProgressReport-ExecSum_0.pdf; http://www.healthypeople.gov/2020/leading-health-indicators/Healthy-People-2020-Leading-Health-Indicators%3A-Progress-Update

[47] Centers For Disease Control and Prevention, "Healthy People 2020", http://www.cdc.gov/nchs/healthy_people/hp2020.htm

[48] P. Braveman and L. Gottleib, "The Social Determinants of Health: It's Time to Consider the Causes of the Causes," *Public Health Reports* (supplement) 129, no. 2 (2014): 19–31.

[49] Brookings-Bern Project on Internal Displacement, *Human Rights and Natural Disasters: Operational Guidelines and Field Manual on Human Rights Protection in Situations of Natural Disaster* (Washington, DC: Brookings Institute, March 2008), 1.

[50] Agency for Healthcare Research and Quality, *Altered Standards of Care in Mass Casualty Events* (pub. no. 05-0043), prepared by Health Systems Research Inc. (Rockville, MD: AHRQ, April 2005), 7.

[51] Michael Allswede, "Appendix G: Altered Standards of Care in Mass Casualty," in *Hospital Preparation for Bioterror*, ed. Joseph McIsaac (New York: Elsevier, 2006), 383–412.

[52] AHRQ, *Altered Standards*, 10.

[53] Ibid., 16–18.

[54] Jean Carmalt, "Prioritizing Health: A Human Rights Analysis of Disaster, Vulnerability, and Urbanization in New Orleans and Port-au-Prince," *Health & Human Rights: An International Journal 16*, no. 1 (June 2014): 41–53.

[55] Kathleen Tierney and Anthony Oliver-Smith, "Social Dimensions of Disaster Recovery," *International Journal of Mass Emergencies and Disasters* 30, no. 2 (August 2012): 123–46.

[56] T. Christie, G.A. Asrat, B. Jiwani, T. Maddix, and J.S. Montaner, "Exploring Disparities Between Global HIV/AIDS Funding and Recent Tsunami Relief Efforts: An Ethical Analysis," *Developing World Bioethics* 7, no. 1 (2007): 1–7.

[57] American Nurses Association, *Adapting Standards of Care under Extreme Conditions: Guidance for Professionals during Disasters, Pandemics, and other Extreme Emergencies*, (Silver Spring, MD: ANA, March 2008), 8, http://nursingworld.org/MainMenuCategories/WorkplaceSafety/Healthy-Work-Environment/DPR/TheLawEthicsofDisasterResponse/AdaptingStandardsofCare.pdf

[58] University of Toronto Joint Centre for Bioethics Pandemic Influenza Working Group, *Stand on Guard for Thee: Ethical Considerations in Preparedness Planning for Pandemic Influenza* (Toronto, Ontario: University of Toronto Joint Centre for Bioethics, 2005), 7–8.

[59] Ibid.

[60] Ibid., 14.

[61] U.N. Commission on Human Rights, *Siracusa Principles on the Limitation and Derogation Provisions in the International Covenant on Civil and Political Rights* (E/CN.4/1985/4, September 1985).

[62] ANA, *Adapting Standards of Care.*

[63] Janet Southby, "Nursing Ethics and the Military," in *Textbooks of Military Medicine, Military Medical Ethics* (vol. 2), eds. Dave Lounsbury and Ronald Bellamy (Washington DC: Office of the Surgeon General, 2003), 661–86, http://www.cs.amedd.army.mil/borden/Portlet.aspx?ID=d25c00de-8284-40bf-8448-72a775fb5110

[64] International Council of Nurses, *The Nurse's Role in the Care of Detainees and Prisoners*, adopted 1998; revised 2006, 2011, http://www.icn.ch/images/stories/documents/publications/position_statements/A13_Nurses_Role_Detainees_Prisoners.pdf

Provision 9

The profession of nursing, collectively through its professional organizations, must articulate nursing values, maintain the integrity of the profession, and integrate principles of social justice into nursing and health policy.

Provision 9. Social Justice: Reaching Out to a World in Need of Nursing

Introduction

The inclusion of a provision specifically directed toward the profession through its professional associations, rather than toward the individual nurse alone, was dramatically new to the 2001 Code and a source of considerable debate prior to the House of Delegates' adoption of it. Many of its elements were found scattered in previous versions of the Code, as will be shown shortly, but as a separate provision its focus on the profession and its social ethics was entirely distinctive and new. The focus of the provision is on the moral expectations for professional organizations in relation to issues of social criticism, social justice, and social change. In the development of the Code over the decades, the provisions of all previous codes were directed toward individual nurses, most often the nurse at the bedside. In the later revisions, some attention was given to nurse researchers, and then, in the most recent codes, to nurse educators as well. The 2001 Code expanded the compass of the Code to include all nurses in all nursing positions, as well as the profession itself. That expansion was a bit uneven and thus, the 2015 revision gives more even attention to nursing in all roles and settings. Earlier codes could not have foreseen the astonishing array of roles and settings in which nursing would eventually take place. For instance, early modern nursing after the Civil War took place in the home in the form of private duty nursing, in which nurses were hired by the families, usually through a registry operated by the school from which they had graduated. Private duty nursing dominated nursing practice until World War II, after which the majority of nursing shifted from homes to hospitals, that were often staffed by students. Nurses also became employees of the hospitals, all of this becoming known as general duty nursing. Prior to this shift, even into the 1970s, there was a remnant of private duty nursing, often called "specialing," that took place within hospitals. Private duty nursing within the hospital context rapidly disappeared after the late 1960s with the advent of the centralization of illness care, the inception of intensive care units, and the subsequent specialization and subspecialization within nursing.

Those nurses now retiring came into nursing at a time when intensive care units were experimental, and are leaving at a time when nurse practitioners are operating nursing clinics in retail venues, nurses specializing in global health hold office in the World Health Organization, and the Institute of Medicine (IOM) calls upon nurses to participate in policy-making at both the organizational and governmental level. More specifically the IOM report on the future of nursing states:

> Being a full partner translates more broadly to the health policy arena. To be effective in reconceptualized roles, nurses must see policy as something they can shape rather than something that happens to them. [...] Nurses should have a voice in health policy decision making, as well as being engaged in implementation efforts related to health care reform. Nurses also should serve actively on advisory committees, commissions, and boards where policy decisions are made to advance health systems and to improve patient care.[1]

Nurses graduating in the 1950s and 1960s might never have believed what lay in nursing's future, even within their lifetime.

The effect that nursing's location in the home had upon early codes of ethics was that the codes' guidelines were written for (female) nurses who did not receive direct supervision and who had to make clinical and moral decisions on her own. *Confidentiality* received particularly heavy emphasis as a nurse was privy to the goings-on within a family home. In this early period, many nursing educators were physicians, not nurses, though a nurse was often the superintendent of a given nursing school. The shift toward nurses as nurse educators was slow in coming, accelerating after WWII, and reaching completion by the 1970s. As for research, the role of a nurse researcher did not arise until well after the 1950s. Thus, early codes would not have needed to address nurse educators or nurse researchers, or, of course, clinical nurse specialists, nurse practitioners, or nurses in evolved roles or settings. This current Code, then, deepens the intent to apply the Code to all nurses in all nursing positions individually and to all nurses collectively through nursing associations and organizations. This provision goes significantly farther than did its corollary provision in 2001, and specifically focuses on the role of professional associations in social ethics and issues of social justice.

Social ethics is fundamentally about the application of ethics to large, even global, social problems and issues with an emphasis on the sociopolitical conditions and structures that foster injustice. Social ethics may be defined as the domain of ethics that deals with "issues of social order—the good, right, and ought in the organization of human communities and the shaping of social policies. Hence the subject matter of social ethics is moral rightness and goodness in the shaping of human society."[2] Social ethics engages in social criticism, applying a range of ethical and critical theories that can frame the discussion and move toward policies that will help to redress unjust conditions such as the social determinants of illness, poverty, hunger, illiteracy, and so forth.

There are three fundamental functions of social ethics, all of which fall within the legitimate, if not essential, sphere of professional nursing associations: reform of the profession, epideictic discourse (which is a type of public values-based speaking), and social reform.[3] The first function of social ethics—reform of the profession—assures that the profession itself lives up to its own values. Reform seeks to bring the profession and its practice, goals, and aspirations into conformity with the values that it cherishes. At times, this necessitates change within the professional community itself, seeking to move the profession toward an envisioned ideal, to bring the "ought" into conformity with the reality of the profession's lived expression. This aspect of social ethics demands an intentional, ongoing, critical self-reflection and self-evaluation of the profession based on a range of critical theories that can assist in an incisive, rigorous, self-assessment of the profession.

Epideictic discourse, the second function of social ethics, refers to a form of communication that takes place within and for the group. Unfortunately, *epideictic* has no exact translation in the English language. The term refers to that kind of speech that reaffirms and reinforces the values that the community itself embraces, especially when confronted with competing values. It "sets out to increase the intensity of adherence to certain values, which might not be contested when considered on their own but may nevertheless not prevail against other values that might come into conflict with them."[4] Epideictic discourse is essentially a rallying cry that reinforces the group's values to and for the group. It strengthens the values that are held in common by the group and the speaker, thus "making use of dispositions already present in the audience."[5] Epideictic discourse galvanizes the group to employ the group's cherished values in order both to bring about the changes elicited by the first function of social ethics, and to move the group into the third function of social ethics—speaking the values of the group into society at large to help bring about social change that is congruent with the group's values. Examples of epideictic speech in public address abound. A few examples include: Martin Luther King's "I Have a Dream"; John Kennedy's "Ich bin ein Berliner"; Franklin Roosevelt's Pearl Harbor address to the nation; Douglas MacArthur's farewell address to Congress; Patrick Henry's "Give Me Liberty or Give Me Death." Epideictic discourse is not solely the domain of famous men. These women's speeches are excellent examples as well: Jane Addams' "The

Subjective Necessity for Social Settlements"; Susan Anthony's "On Women's Right to Vote"; Eleanor Roosevelt's "The Struggle for Human Rights"; Sojourner Truth's "Ain't I a Woman?"; Margaret Sanger's "The Children's Era"; Maya Angelou's "On the Pulse of Morning"; and Ursula Le Guin's "A Left-Handed Commencement Address."

The third function of social ethics is that of activism in social reform. In this, the profession critiques society and attempts to bring about social change that is consistent with the values of the group. For instance, if the nursing profession affirms that health is a universal right and that affordable, accessible health care for all is also a right, it would assess the current state of the healthcare system for the following: cost, distribution, and fairness of costs; access and ease of access by all sectors of society, including those with limitations such as mobility, age, literacy, etc., and including ethnic and minority constituencies; and openness of the system to all, including resident noncitizens, tourists, and others. In addition, nursing's affirmation of health as a universal right would lead nursing organizations to look at social structures for marks of structural injustice that mitigate against health, that is, the "social determinants of health"—and illness. The United Nations notes that

> the bulk of the global burden of disease and the major causes of health inequities, which are found in all countries, arise from the conditions in which people are born, grow, live, work and age. These conditions are referred to as social determinants of health, a term used as shorthand to encompass the social, economic, political, cultural and environmental determinants of health.[6,7]

Where nursing would become involved in seeking to ameliorate structurally caused inequities in health, it would require nursing research, scholarship, policy, and activism in social, economic, political, cultural, and environmental spheres. Social ethics is, therefore, intrinsically political and a work of nursing professional associations, in part through their political action committees. This provision is the foundation of that involvement.

It is expected that all nurses will be involved in some way in this aspect of the profession's social ethics. This involvement requires acquiring knowledge about social conditions, informed voting, and participation in legislative processes through local and national representatives. For some it will involve research or policy formation. While some charismatic nursing leaders are able to bring about social change as individuals, the actual implementation of social criticism and social change generally depends upon collective action, usually through a professional association. In order to engage in social criticism and to bring about social change, the profession must have knowledge based in critical theories that can guide and deepen social analysis and critique. Critical theories have different perspectives but hold in common that they are explanatory, practical, and normative (ethical). Here we often see postcolonial, feminist, liberation, Marxist, critical race theory, or other critical social theories employed, both to assess and critique society as well as the profession itself. The goal of these theories is to uncover, explain, and transform social conditions "to liberate human beings from the circumstances that enslave them."[8] In order to bring about social change that liberates, these theories and a knowledge of political and policy processes becomes essential. The resources of the professional association, including its political action committees, would then be drawn upon to support action for social change. It is important for this function of the profession's social ethics that nurse educators include in nursing curricula content on social ethics relating to issues of justice, social theories, nursing history related to social involvement of nursing and nurses, health policy formulation, and the state and federal political processes. These areas of curricular content are noted in a newly added section of this provision. All three functions of social ethics— reform within, epideictic discourse, and social reform—are incorporated into the first of the interpretive statements for this provision.

Interpretive Statement 9.1 Articulation and Assertion of Values

The nursing profession affirms core values such as respect, dignity, worth, well-being, health, and caring, to name a few. These values can be challenged or come into conflict when confronted by other values operative within the healthcare system, values such as profit, efficiency, risk reduction, expedience, and compliance. Here the system, of which individual institutions and agencies are a part, must be challenged. The scattered voices of individual nurses are amplified when nurses speak together through professional associations. Nurses, united nationally and globally, can be an imposing and effective force for re-creating social, economic, political, and cultural conditions to bring about health for all.

Interpretive Statement 9.2 Integrity of the Profession

This second of the provision's interpretive statements alludes to the fact that nursing like all social structures is comprised of two kinds of structures that are important to ethics: *meaning and value structures*, as well as *power structures*. The values of a profession are articulated by its representatives, associations, societies and organizations in part through their documents, structures, decisions, and actions that embody the ideals, values, and ethics of the profession and comprise its meaning and value structures. This would include not only the Code of Ethics, the Social Policy Statement, and Position Statements of the American Nurses Association (ANA), but also structures such as the ANA Center for Ethics and Human Rights, ethics committees, Professional Issues Panels, and so on. Meaning and value structures articulate the values, moral ideals, and moral requirements of a group, and also serve to inform and guide, critique—and sometimes to correct—the goals, practices, or activities of a profession and its organizations. Meaning and value structures are juxtaposed against power structures. Power structures are those social structures that embody, utilize, or direct power in any of its forms. Power comes in many forms, including political power, economic power, social prestige and trust, honor, respect, expertise, and authority. Without power structures, meaning and values structures are dead in the water. Power structures enable a group to achieve its goals; without adequate meaning and value structures, power structures can exercise runaway self-interest. Meaning and value structures must work reciprocally with power structures to advance the goals of a group in accord with its ideals.[9] Nursing's own power structures must be informed by and serve its meaning and value structures. It is through the exercise and strength of nursing's meaning and values structures that nursing works to preserve the integrity of the profession and to enact its values, its broad social vision, both within the profession and in society.

The *Tentative Code* of 1940 states that "a truly professional nurse with broad social vision will have a sympathetic understanding of different creeds, nationalities, and races and in any case she will not permit her personal attitude toward these various groups to interfere with her function as a nurse."[10] This early proposed Code tackles the issue of unjust discrimination. In the adopted 1950 Code, it states in the preamble that: "Need for nursing is universal. Professional service is therefore unrestricted by considerations of nationality, race, creed, or color."[11] Successive Codes reiterate this basic position and even expand it to encompass a wide range of other forms of social disadvantage, stigma, prejudice, and oppression. The current Code extends respect for persons and exclusion of unjust discrimination beyond patients to include colleagues, students, and all with whom the nurse comes into contact.

In the 1800s and early 1900s, when the United States engaged in the legal enslavement of racial minorities, women were legally defined as chattel and denied suffrage, and gender-based social roles were rigidly defined with the legal exclusion of women from some roles (e.g., physician), there were laws against teaching about or possessing contraceptives, little or no protection of children in sweat shops under labor laws, and no laws against domestic violence or animal cruelty. Eventually, American society came to address these ills and some progress, in varying degrees, has been made. The nursing association that formed 120 years ago has worked steadily for the correction of some of these ills including that of unjust discrimination.

Not all discrimination is unjust: not allowing a 10-year-old to drive a motor vehicle is discriminatory, but not unjust. When prejudice enters in, however, discrimination becomes unjust. Nursing as a profession has long espoused a principle of egalitarianism, even when society openly permitted or even authorized a wide range of prejudicial "-isms": racism, sexism, ageism, sectarianism, etc. This equalitarian stance flew in the face of the societal reality of dramatic social inequalities. In a profession that has remained predominantly Anglo, Christian, and female, this persistent egalitarianism is somewhat unexpected. And yet, it is interesting to speculate and to propose for research that because nursing has remained female-dominant, it identifies with social groups that, like women, have been socially disadvantaged.

In the 1950s, the anti-discrimination statements in the Code were not in alignment with the current situation of society, which still permitted and sometimes legally authorized various organized social manifestations of prejudice. However, at that time, the professional association operated on a federated model where the parent organization did not have members; rather, nurses were members of state nurses associations (SNAs), which simultaneously conferred membership in the American Nurses Association (ANA). States established their own criteria for membership. Some of these constituent states denied membership in the organization to those who, although otherwise fully qualified, were of African descent (in whole or in part). The Association could not control the state associations' criteria for membership. With its commitment to egalitarianism, there was a painful moral quandary for the ANA when some SNAs barred fully qualified black nurses from state membership, thereby denying them ANA membership in the federated model. What was the Association to do? Alternatives were for the Association to ignore the situation and proceed as usual, change the organizational structure (a massive undertaking), revise the current Code, or adjust the requirements for membership.

To be true to the first and second functions of social ethics. and as a precursor to the third, ANA chose the latter. In 1948, ANA made provisions for black nurses to have direct membership in ANA, without SNA membership. If an association proclaims that nurses should not discriminate on prejudicial grounds against those not of the dominant race, creed, color, or religion, it cannot sanction such discrimination within its own organization. The first function of social ethics is to clean one's own house or reform from within, which is what the ANA did. The action of the ANA in 1948 exemplified the values expressed in this provision, even though there was no such provision in the first *Code for Professional Nurses* in 1950.

Preserving the integrity of the profession requires that it maintain its standards consistent with the profession's covenant with society. To encourage the profession and its organizations and associations to function in accord with its values, the professional association is to create and promote adherence to the Code. Awareness of the Code begins, properly, in early nursing education. Awareness is furthered by distribution of Code bookmarks, posters, e-copies and other Code-related materials, by conferences, webinars and continuing education offerings, and by posting the full text of the *Code of Ethics for Nurses with Interpretive Statements* on the ANA website.[12]

Promoting adherence to the Code has taken a number of forms. In the 1960s, the ANA actually formulated a document, process, and guidelines for reporting what were thought to be violations of the Code.[13] The *Suggested Guidelines for Handling Alleged Violations of the Code for Professional Nurses* opens with these words: "Unfortunately, there are always those whose ethical practice is far less than acceptable. Yet a profession must assume responsibility for guaranteeing to the public that all services rendered by its members are of high quality."[14] Subsequently, this document was not revised and fell out of print. Today, adherence to the Code is generally fostered by moral suasion; that is, by persuasion and pressure for adherence to moral standards, which cannot be compelled or forced. The consequences of a proven violation of the Code are reprimand or censure by the organization or expulsion from membership. This does not necessarily affect a nurse's day-to-day employment world as the consequences are limited to the nurse's relationship with the professional association. However, moral violations will affect one's stature, respect, and honor among peers, and can affect self-respect.

The integrity of the profession is also fostered and furthered by rigorous education and requirements for entry into nursing programs and practice at all levels; development of nursing theory, research and scholarship; dissemination of nursing scholarship; creation and maintenance of standards of practice, certification and licensure for advanced practice, and a commitment to evidence-informed practice. All of this is required in order for nursing to provide society with safe, caring, and excellent nursing practice in the promotion or restoration of health, prevention of illness and injury, the alleviation of pain and suffering, and the promulgation of nursing and health policies that will further the health of society and may become a matter of law in those states that incorporate the Code in the nurse practice act.

The 2001 interpretive statement states that "[t]hrough critical self-reflection and self-evaluation, associations must foster change within themselves, seeking to move the professional community toward its stated ideals."[15]

The 2015 interpretive statement carries this further by declaring that:

> Balanced policies and practices regarding access to nursing education, workforce sustainability, nurse migration, and utilization are requisite to achieving these ends. Together, nurses must bring about the improvement of all facets of nursing fostering and assisting in the education of professional nurses in developing regions across the globe.[16]

Maintaining the integrity of the profession extends beyond our national borders, and presents us with an affirmative duty to seek excellence and justice in nursing globally.

Interpretive Statement 9.3 Integrating Social Justice

Nursing ethics in the United States has always been intimately concerned with the shape of society and its affect upon health and illness, that is, with social ethics. Though not its sole concern, *social justice* is a primary concern of social ethics. The profession's historical and continuing involvement with working for the health of all is remarkable and it is the stuff of pride of profession. This abiding concern for social ethics is reflected in early nursing ethics curricula. In 1917, the National League for Nursing Education (NLNE) established curricular requirements for ethics in nursing education within its Standard Curriculum for Schools of Nursing. The standard called for 10 hours of ethics instruction in the second year, a number of hours equal to that of other major topics such as medical nursing. The basic lectures were to include content on ethical theory, personal ethics, professional ethics, clinically applied ethics, and social ethics.[17] Topics to be covered in the social ethics section included the social virtues and ethical principles as applied to community life. State boards of registered nursing also specified curricular requirements for social ethics. The California State Board of Health's Bureau of Registration of Nurses 1916 curricular requirements in social ethics included: "democracy and social ethics," "modern industry," "housing reform," and "the spirit of youth and the city streets."[18,19]

These topics evidence nursing's social leadership. Nursing has lead in establishing the domain of public health care, has always given care in military and battlefield contexts, has been concerned for the social welfare of children and much more. In short, nursing's ethics has always been a social ethics which, with the rise of bioethics in the mid-1960s, was eclipsed by concerns for individual ethical decision-making by nurses, especially those in clinical practice.[20] In the 2001 Code, the social activism in evidence in nursing's history is reclaimed with the addition of this provision. Now, in 2015, with the rise of concern for the social determinants of health both in the United States and globally, it is time for nursing to restore and fully develop its social ethics, including heightening the emphasis in nursing curricula and research.

Yet, social ethics, and the development of the tools necessary to participate in social criticism and social change, currently find little expression in nursing curricula, whether that change is directed toward a particular institution or the larger healthcare system. Among its many recommendations for nursing education, the Carnegie Report, *Educating Nurses: A Call for Radical Transformation,* notes:

> Tools for influencing organizational and policy changes are essential, given the current state of health care institutions. Nurses are the ones most present and in a position closest to patients, and their advocacy for improving patient care can be powerful indeed. However, such positive change depends on knowledge and skills to redesign dangerous and outmoded systems and a unified effort to reduce communication barriers in hierarchical health care systems to create the level of change needed, partnerships between nurse educators and students in schools of nursing and nursing staff and administrators in service settings are essential.[21]

Having the tools for social criticism and social change alone is not enough. It must be supported by curriculum that addresses issues of justice and injustice, including the social construction of health disparities, unequal disaster response, racialization, classism, genderization, devaluation of care practices, and more, at all levels of nursing education appropriate to the student's curricular level.

Interpretive Statement 9.4 Social Justice in Nursing and Health Policy

Nursing's history is rich with examples of nurses who have individually brought about social–moral change. Many of the early women, and some men, who are counted as nurses, actually preceded the establishment of nursing schools in the United States. Even so, their achievements are credited to nursing. These include Dorothea Lynde Dix, Walt Whitman, Clara Harlowe Barton, Araminta (Harriet) Ross Tubman, Captain Sally Tompkins, and Mary Ann Ball Bickerdyke, among others. Of the women who received formal nursing education, four historic figures will serve as examples of individuals who, by themselves, wrought social change.

Margaret Higgins Sanger Slee studied nursing at White Plains Hospital, though when she married she could not complete her nursing education. She was shocked that women were unable to obtain accurate and effective birth control, which she believed was foundational to the freedom and independence of women. She challenged the 1873 Federal Comstock law that banned the dissemination of contraceptive information. She published a monthly paper, *The Woman Rebel*, in which she advocated for women's right to use contraception. She was indicted for violating postal obscenity laws, jumped bail, and escaped to England. Subsequently, she worked tirelessly in England and then again in the United States for women's rights to contraceptive information and contraceptives.[22]

Lillian D. Wald (originally Whal, then de Wald) graduated from New York Hospital Training School for Nurses. As a graduate she was asked to organize a nursing program to meet the needs of the impoverished immigrant population of Manhattan in the late 19th century. She observed the terrible conditions under which the city's poor survived. Wald was deeply moved and decided to dedicate her life to providing health and social services to the city's poor. In 1893, with Mary Brewster, she established The Henry Street Settlement, which eventually became the Visiting Nurse Service of New York City. Wald pioneered the creation of public health nursing, visiting nursing, and the social service system. By 1916, the Settlement had 250 nurses and offered health care, housing, education, employment assistance, and recreational activities to thousands of the city's poor families and individuals.[23]

Isabel Adams Hampton Robb, a graduate of Bellevue Hospital Training School for Nurses, (1860–1910), served as superintendent at the Illinois Training School in the Cook County Hospital, then became the first superintendent of the new nursing school at Johns Hopkins Hospital in Baltimore. After her marriage, she became a professor of gynecology at Case Western Reserve University. She brought about major changes in the process and curriculum of nursing education. Robb organized a nursing section at the International Congress of Charities, Corrections and Philanthropy of the World Columbian Exposition held in Chicago. The section became the first nursing organization, the Society of Superintendents of Training Schools (eventually the National League for Nursing Education and, then, the National League for Nursing). Robb became the first president of the Nurses Associated Alumnae of the United States and Canada (now the ANA), was a cofounder of the American Journal of Nursing Company, and was one of the founders of the International Council of Nurses. She helped nursing to become an organized profession at the turn of the last century.[24]

Mabel Keaton Staupers was born in 1890, in Barbados, West Indies. In 1903, she emigrated to the United States. She attended Freedmen's Hospital School of Nursing (later Howard University College of Nursing) in Washington, DC, graduating with honors in 1917. She worked as a private duty nurse until 1920, when joined two physician colleagues in establishing the Booker T. Washington Sanitarium in Harlem. It was the first sanitarium to treat African-

Americans with *M. tuberculosis*. She had a long and distinguished clinical career. However, she also had a passion for integration:

> Taking advantage of the high public awareness of the nursing profession during World War II, Staupers launched a campaign seeking the integration of black nurses into the Armed Forces Nurse Corps. By 1941 black nurses were admitted to the U.S. Army Nurse Corps, but a strict system of quotas hindered their full integration; the U.S. Navy continued its policy of exclusion. When the War Department began to consider a draft of nurses, Staupers enlisted the help of First Lady Eleanor Roosevelt and orchestrated a nationwide letter-writing campaign to convince President Franklin D. Roosevelt and other political leaders of the need to recognize black nurses. Overwhelming public support of desegregation persuaded the armed forces, both Army and Navy, to wholly accept black nurses by January 1945.[25,26]

In 1935 she met Mary McLeod Bethune, and they established the National Council of Negro Women. As noted above, in 1948, the ANA began to allow African-American nurses denied SNA membership to become direct members, even when the civil rights movement did not gain momentum until the mid-1950s.[27]

Individuals, like these named above and many more in nursing's history, can sometimes bring about social change, eventually gathering a like-minded group behind them. However, social change is also (more frequently) brought about by well-placed collective action that ultimately drives legislative and policy change.

From the early days of the Code, nurses were seen to have civic responsibilities as well as duties of citizenship, both of which received emphasis. Participatory citizenship by nurses has been a consistent and important thread through the various versions of the Code. By 1960, the Code became explicit with regard to nurses' duty to attend to legislative matters, individually and collectively:

> As a professional person, the nurse's special background enables her to have a greater understanding of the nature of health problems. This understanding poses a particular responsibility to interpret and speak out in regard to legislation affecting health. The resources of the professional association enables the nurse to work with colleagues in assessing current or pending health legislation and its effect upon the community and to determine the stand that should be taken in the interest of the greatest possible good. Sometimes this stand may lead to concerted action with other health groups. At other times, nurses may find it necessary to work alone to support principles that the profession believes will result in the greatest benefits to patient care.[28]

In its interpretive statement for Provision 9.4, the 2001 Code is both more direct and more succinct on the responsibility of the professional association in shaping healthcare policy and legislation, an example of the third function of social ethics. It embraces the emphasis on citizenship responsibilities of previous Codes, but is more incisive and aggressive about collective/professional association responsibility. It bears restatement:

> Nurses can work individually as citizens or collectively through political action to bring about social change. It is the responsibility of a professional nursing association to speak for nurses collectively in shaping and reshaping health care within our nation, specifically in areas of healthcare policy and legislation that affect accessibility, quality, and the cost of health care. Here the professional association maintains vigilance and takes action to influence legislators, reimbursement agencies, nursing organizations, and other health professions. In these activities, health is understood as being broader than delivery and reimbursement systems, but extending to health-related sociocultural issues such as violation of human rights, homelessness, hunger, violence, and the stigma of illness.[29]

While the 2001 Code does not precisely redefine health, it extends the vision of health and of working for the health of all to include both health broadly defined and, more specifically, the social causes of ill health: homelessness, hunger, violence, stigma, and the violation of human rights. A concern for poverty would be intrinsic to these concerns. The 2015 Code is even more vigorous. It states:

> Nurses must be vigilant and take action to influence leaders, legislators, governmental agencies, non-governmental organizations, and international bodies in all related health affairs for addressing the social determinants of health.

> The nursing profession must actively participate in solidarity with the global nursing community and health organizations to represent the collective voice of US nurses around the globe…. Global health, as well as the common good, are ideals that can be realized when all nurses unite their efforts and energies social justice extends to eco-justice….

> As nursing seeks to promote and restore health, prevent illness and injury, and alleviate pain and suffering, it does so within the holistic context of healing the world.[30]

Is this over-reaching? No, it's aspirational. Communication and collaboration among nurses is now possible worldwide and virtually instantaneous. As a consequence, global networks and collaborations for nursing research, scholarship, education, practice—and policy—have emerged. It is a much smaller world now than it was even in 2001.

A glance at the ANA website NursingWorld.org attests to the emergence of nursing's policy and action involvement in issues beyond those that affect national health alone, though that too is addressed. A look at the ANA Policy and Advocacy web page is instructive. At these web pages, there is access to the ANA legislative and regulatory agenda for the current session of Congress. There are issues analyses, legislative tracking, vote scorecards and information for all members of Congress, legislative updates, federal agency monitoring, a link to the *Federal Register*, a Nurses' Strategic Action Team, and an ANA Political Action Committee. In terms of state legislation regarding health care, the ANA State Relations webpage has links to a host of political resources, a means of identifying one's state and federal legislators, a list of nurse-legislators by state, information in each state's legislation from 1996 to the present, transcripts of ANA testimony before state legislators (and Congress), and more. Over the past two decades, ANA has become exceedingly well-organized for influencing the shape of legislation affecting health care, nursing practice, and education. This has been aided by the widespread use of the Internet that allows greater and more immediate communication with ANA members (and anyone who accesses the website) and legislators regarding legislative issues. The ANA has been active in giving testimony before legislators, in communicating with individual legislators, and in bringing the collective concern of nurses to bear upon health legislation. The Association is meeting its duty to be vigilant and to engage with the legislative process. But beyond a national agenda, the ANA's website, NursingWorld.org, has taken stands a variety of topics: "Global Climate Change and Human Health," "The 2003 SARS Outbreak: Global Challenges and Innovative Infection Control Measures," "Globalization of Higher Education in Nursing," "Nursing Leadership in Global and Domestic Tobacco Control," "Advocating Globally to Shape Policy and Strengthen Nursing's Influence." This level of global involvement by nursing and the ANA is emergent as the growing edge of nursing's collaboration and leadership.

So nursing's concern extends beyond national borders and beyond prior definitions of health by reaching into environmental concerns. Nightingale herself emphasized that the patient's environment could play a determinative role in a patient's recovery. But years after her work in the Crimea, after returning to England, Nightingale involved herself in larger environmental issues such as a statistical assessment of sanitation in India. She used statistics and graphs to communicate where potential sanitation reform could be implemented.[31] Thus environmental concerns, even global environmental concerns, are not new to nursing as they were present at the inception of modern nursing. The larger arena of environmental concern however has not kept pace and developed among nursing's concerns.

In 1995 the Institute of Medicine report: "Nursing, Health and the Environment" called upon nurses to be prepared to integrate environmental health into nursing practice, research, education, and advocacy. It defined *environmental health* as "freedom from illness or injury related to exposure to toxic agents and other environmental conditions that are potentially detrimental to human health."[32] The report calls upon nurses to develop an understanding of environmental health as a core function in all areas of nursing practice, to develop nursing curriculum for environmental health, to move to a population-based perspective, and to conduct nursing research in this domain.[33] The report calls upon nurses to engage in policy advocacy aimed at influencing social institutions:[34]

> Nurses who are knowledgeable about global environmental conditions, such as ozone depletion, can educate the public about measures to reduce or eliminate their exposure to such hazards, (e.g., by limiting direct exposure to the sun and through the use of sunglasses that limit transmission of ultraviolet radiation) and measures to limit further global changes that may have adverse effects on human health (e.g., by using public transportation or car-pooling when possible to reduce the production of greenhouse gases).[35]

While issues of environmental health are not co-extensive with the ecological sciences, environment and ecology are inseparable. The new Code calls upon nurses to be concerned for eco-justice, in part because of the interdependence of human health, the health of the environment, and ecology. However, the burden of environmental degradation often falls disproportionately upon the global poor. O'Neill et al. write:

> International attention is focusing increasingly on environmental concerns, from global warming and extreme weather to persistent chemical pollutants that affect our food supplies, health and well-being. These environmental exposures disproportionately affect the poor and those residing in developing countries, and may partly explain the persistent social gradients in health that exist within and between nations.[36]

Health disparities are related not only to poverty itself, but also to the uses of the environment in ways that detrimentally affect those who are already vulnerable.

Can issues of health disparities, social justice, and eco-justice be resolved? Not by nursing alone, but not without nursing. The duty is to be involved—not necessarily to succeed, though we do seek success. ANA is involved on behalf of nursing and nurses. As to whether ANA is successful in effecting change depends in part upon nurses' responsiveness and commitment to the state of the nation and the state of the world and through participation that enables the spokesorganization to act upon behalf of nurses.

Provision 9 of the 2015 Code incorporates concerns of earlier codes for participatory citizenship, for meeting civic responsibilities, and for speaking out both individually and collectively regarding health and nursing-related legislation. It also encompasses the historic activism of nurses in bringing about social change. However, this provision crystallizes the role of professional associations in social ethics on behalf of the profession to raise and address issues of social justice. This Code, finally, gives greater emphasis to what has historically been a preeminent concern of nursing: health disparities and vulnerable populations, unjust social structures that engender illness, the shape of society as it affects health, and the responsibility of nursing to participate in health policy and global health for the healing of the world.

Cases

Case 1

It is the annual meeting of the State Council of Deans and Directors of Schools of Nursing. One of the issues on the docket is the new State Board for Registered Nursing requirements for accreditation. The State Board is comprised of nine members: four public members who are not health professionals; three direct-care RNs, one RN educator, and one RN administrator. The executive officer of the board, Dr. Helen Nixon, is a political appointee and a nurse. She has been invited to the meeting to present the revised curricular requirements for accreditation.

As she goes through the requirements, the deans and directors are pleased that the state is increasing the requirements in the sciences. Requirements for content in communication skills related to cultural diversity were also increased. The nursing domains of content remained relatively unchanged except that, to the dismay of many present, content requirements for "legal, social and ethical aspects of nursing" were removed from the requirements category to a "recommended category." In the question and answer period, Dr. Nixon is challenged about moving this content to a recommended category with the concern that if it were not required, schools would drop content on ethics, patient advocacy, and social justice. She responded that she shared their concern but that the public members of the Board had thought the sciences more important and they prevailed in the vote when one of the nurse members voted with them.

Case 2

This case is taken from *Health Worker Shortages and Global Justice*, by Paula O'Brian and Lawrence Gostin NY: (New York: Milbank Memorial Fund, 2011), pp. 2–3:

"Developed countries…often rely significantly on foreign-trained health workers to staff their health systems. These developed countries do, or ought to, know that many workers come from countries that desperately need more health professionals themselves…. Second, the United States is a contributor to the global workforce shortage but also has the capacity to make a significant difference in addressing it. The United States has not demonstrated a commitment to pursue a policy of national self-sufficiency (or at least a high level of self-sufficiency) in the production of local health workers. Because of its failure to plan for the education of American health workers, the United States relies on large numbers of migrant health workers to keep its health system fully operational. The United States, as well as Western Europe and other highly developed regions, has become a magnet for foreign-educated physicians and nurses. …[d]ata suggest that all rich countries… must recognize their role in the shortage."

Case 3

A mixed group of mostly community health nurses, visiting nurses, and nursing educators attended a concurrent session at the annual meeting of your state nurses association. The session was on "Ecojustice: Economics, Environment, and Health Disparities." At the lunch break several of them began comparing notes on the young children from the Sobrante community, consisting largely of black and Latino families. This urban community suffers from significantly higher than expected rates of asthma, lead poisoning, obesity, and nutrition-related diseases. These families live in moderate to impoverished economic conditions close to industrial factories and incinerators and the freight line railroads. In addition, their community is a "food desert" with no supermarkets within six miles. The nearest hospital is eight miles away. Public transportation near their community is inadequate. Recently an oil company has decided to do exploratory drilling in this community. The residents are angry and claim that the county would not issue permits to drill in the wealthy Cielito community, but their community is fair game. The residents' complaints have not influenced the county's decision to issue drilling permits. The nurses are incensed and want to do more than try to stop the drilling—they want to help make this a healthier community.

ENDNOTES

1 Institute of Medicine of the National Academies, *The Future of Nursing: Leading Change, Advancing Health* (Washington, DC: National Academies Press, 2011), 1–11.

2 Gibson Winter, *Elements for a Social Ethics* (New York: Macmillan, 1966), 215.

3 M. D. M. Fowler, "Nursing and social ethics," in *The Nursing Profession: Turning Points*, ed. N. A. Chaska (St. Louis, MO: C.V. Mosby, 1972), 24–30.

4 C. Perelman and L. Olbrechts-Tyteca, *The New Rhetoric: A Treatise on Argumentation*, trans. John Wilkinson and Purcell Weaver (Notre Dame, IN: University of Notre Dame Press, 1969), 51.

5 Ibid.

6 World Health Organization, *Closing the Gap: Policy into Practice on Social Determinants of Health* (Geneva: WHO, 2011), 2.

7 World Health Organization, *Meeting Report of the World Conference on Social Determinants of Health* in Rio de Janiero, Brazil, October19–21, 2011 (Geneva: WHO, 2012), ix.

8 M. Horkheimer, *Critical Theory* (New York: Seabury Press, 1982), 244.

9 M. Fowler, "Ethics,the profession and society," in *The Teaching of Nursing Ethics: Content and Methods*, eds. Anne Davis, Louise de Raeve, and Verena Tschudin (London: Elsevier, 2006).

10 American Nurses Association, "A Tentative Code," *American Journal of Nursing* 40, no. 9 (1940): 978.

11 ANA, *A Code for Professional Nurses* (New York: ANA, 1950).

12 American Nurses Association website, http://www.nursingworld.org/MainMenuCategories/EthicsStandards/Tools-You-Need/Code-of-Ethics-For-Nurses.html

13 ANA, *Suggested Guidelines for Handling Alleged Violations of the Code for Professional Nurses* (New York: ANA, 1964).

14 Ibid., 1.

15 ANA, *Code of Ethics for Nurses with Interpretive Statements* (Silver Spring, MD: ANA, 2001), 25.

16 ANA, *Code of Ethics for Nurses with Interpretive Statements* (Silver Spring, MD: ANA, 2015), Interpretive Statement 9.3, 35–36.

17 National League for Nursing Education, *Standard Curriculum for Schools of Nursing* (New York: NLNE, 1917).

18 California State Board of Health, Bureau of Registration of Nurses, *Schools of Nursing Requirements and Curriculum* (Sacramento, CA: State Printing Office, 1916), 7–8, 19–21, 66–67, 83–85, 105–106.

19 Marsha Fowler and Verena Tschudin, "Ethics in Nursing: An Historical Perspective," in *The Teaching of Nursing Ethics: Content and Methods*, eds. Anne Davis, Louise de Raeve, and Verena Tschudin (London: Elsevier, 2006), 13–26.

20 Marsha Fowler, "Nursing's Ethics," in *Ethical Dilemmas and Nursing Practice* (4th ed.), eds. A. Davis, M. Arosker, J. Liaschenko, and T. Drought (Norwalk, CT: Appleton & Lange, 1997), 16–33.

21 Patricia Benner, Molly Sutphen, Victoria Leonard, and Lisa Day, *Educating Nurses: A Call for Radical Transformation* (San Francisco: Jossey-Bass/Carnegie Foundation for the Advancement of Teaching, 2009), 210.

22 Esther Katz (ed.), *The Selected Papers of Margaret Sanger, Volume I: The Woman Rebel, 1900–1928* (Chicago: University of Illinois, 2002).

23 Lillian Wald, http://www.nursingworld.org/FunctionalMenuCategories/AboutANA/Honoring-

Nurses/HallofFame/19761982/waldld5595.html

24 Convention of Training School Alumnae Delegates and Representatives from the American Society of Superintendents of Training Schools for Nurses, *Proceedings of the Convention, 2–4 November 1896* (Harrisburg, PA: Harrisburg Publishing, 1896), 7.

25 "Mabel Keaton Staupers," Encyclopaedia Britanica, last modified June 5, 2014, http://www.britannica.com/EBchecked/topic/564330/Mabel-Keaton-Staupers

26 American Nurses Association, http://www.nursingworld.org/FunctionalMenuCategories/AboutANA/Honoring-Nurses/HallofFame/19962000Inductees/stauperm5584.html

27 Lynda Flanagan. *One Strong Voice?: The Story of the American Nurses' Association.* (Kansas City, MO: Lowell Press,) 1976, 166-167.

28 American Nurses Association, *A Code for Professional Nurses* (New York: ANA, 1960), 9.

29 ANA, *Code of Ethics for Nurses with Interpretive Statements* (2001), 30.

30 ANA, *Code of Ethics for Nurses with Interpretive Statements* (2015), 36–37.

31 Bernard Cohen, "Florence Nightingale," *Scientific American* 250, no. 3 (March 1984): 128–37.

32 Ibid., 15.

33 Pope, A.M., Snyder, M.A., and Mood, L.H. (eds.*) Nursing, Health, and the Environment: Report of the Committee on Enhancing Environmental Health Content in Nursing Practice.* Institute of Medicine. (Washington, DC: National Academy Press, 1995).

34 Ibid., 253.

35 Ibid., 31.

36 M. S. O'Neill, A. J. McMichael,J. Schwartz,and D. Wartenberg, "Poverty, Environment, and Health: the role of Environmental Epidemiology and Environmental Epidemiologists," *Epidemiology* 18, no. 6 (November 2007): 664.

Appendix A.
Code of Ethics for Nurses with Interpretive Statements (2015)

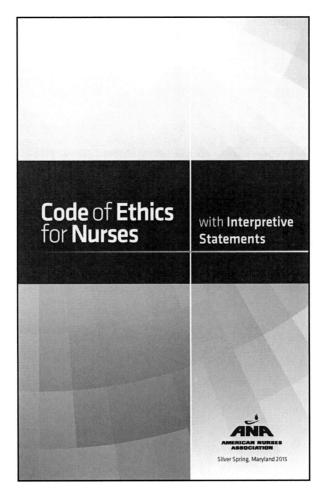

A note on correct citation of the Code: The content of the *Code of Ethics for Nurses with Interpretive Statements* ("the Code") that is here reproduced (pages 172–214) is for your convenience of reference. When citing content from the Code, cite only the page number(s) of the Code itself, not the page number(s) of Guide to the Code on which the cited content appears.

See pg. 171 for guidance on the correct citation of the Code.

Preface

The *Code of Ethics for Nurses with Interpretive Statements* (the Code*)* establishes the ethical standard for the profession and provides a guide for nurses to use in ethical analysis and decision-making. The Code is nonnegotiable in any setting. It may be revised or amended only by formal processes established by the American Nurses Association (ANA). The Code arises from the long, distinguished, and enduring moral tradition of modern nursing in the United States. It is foundational to nursing theory, practice, and praxis in its expression of the values, virtues, and obligations that shape, guide, and inform nursing as a profession.

Nursing encompasses the protection, promotion, and restoration of health and well-being; the prevention of illness and injury; and the alleviation of suffering, in the care of individuals, families, groups, communities, and populations. All of this is reflected, in part, in nursing's persisting commitment both to the welfare of the sick, injured, and vulnerable in society and to social justice. Nurses act to change those aspects of social structures that detract from health and well-being.

Individuals who become nurses, as well as the professional organizations that represent them, are expected not only to adhere to the values, moral norms, and ideals of the profession but also to embrace them as a part of what it means to be a nurse. The ethical tradition of nursing is self-reflective, enduring, and distinctive. A code of ethics for the nursing profession makes explicit the primary obligations, values, and ideals of the profession. In fact, it informs every aspect of the nurse's life.

See pg. 171 for guidance on the correct citation of the Code.

The *Code of Ethics for Nurses with Interpretive Statements* serves the following purposes:

- It is a succinct statement of the ethical values, obligations, duties, and professional ideals of nurses individually and collectively.
- It is the profession's non-negotiable ethical standard.
- It is an expression of nursing's own understanding of its commitment to society.

Statements that describe activities and attributes of nurses in this code of ethics and its interpretive statements are to be understood as normative or prescriptive statements expressing expectations of ethical behavior. The Code also expresses the ethical *ideals* of the nursing profession and is, thus, both normative and aspirational. Although this Code articulates the ethical obligations of all nurses, it does not predetermine how those obligations must be met. In some instances nurses meet those obligations individually; in other instances a nurse will support other nurses in their execution of those obligations; at other times those obligations can only and will only be met collectively. ANA's *Code of Ethics for Nurses with Interpretive Statements* addresses individual as well as collective nursing intentions and actions; it requires each nurse to demonstrate ethical competence in professional life.

Society recognizes that nurses serve those seeking health as well as those responding to illness. Nurses educate students, staff, and others in healthcare facilities. They also educate within communities, organizations, and broader populations. The term *practice* refers to the actions of the nurse in any role or setting, whether paid or as a volunteer, including direct care provider, advanced practice registered nurse, care coordinator, educator, administrator, researcher, policy developer, or other forms of nursing practice. Thus, the values and obligations expressed in this edition of the Code apply to nurses in all roles, in all forms of practice, and in all settings.

ANA's *Code of Ethics for Nurses with Interpretive Statements* is a dynamic document. As nursing and its social context change, the Code must also change. The Code consists of two components: the provisions and the accompanying interpretive statements. The provisions themselves are broad and noncontextual statements of the obligations of nurses. The interpretive statements provide additional, more specific, guidance in the application of this

See pg. 171 for guidance on the correct citation of the Code.

obligation to current nursing practice. Consequently, the interpretive statements are subject to more frequent revision than are the provisions—approximately every decade—while the provisions may endure for much longer without substantive revision.

Additional ethical guidance and details can be found in the position and policy statements of the ANA or its constituent member associations and affiliate organizations that address clinical, research, administrative, educational, public policy, or global and environmental health issues.

The origins of the *Code of Ethics for Nurses with Interpretive Statements* reach back to the late 1800s in the foundation of ANA, the early ethics literature of modern nursing, and the first nursing code of ethics, which was formally adopted by ANA in 1950. In the 65 years since the adoption of that first professional ethics code, nursing has developed as its art, science, and practice have evolved, as society itself has changed, and as awareness of the nature and determinants of global health has grown. The *Code of Ethics for Nurses with Interpretive Statements* is a reflection of the proud ethical heritage of nursing and a guide for all nurses now and into the future.

See pg. 171 for guidance on the correct citation of the Code.

Introduction

In any work that serves the whole of the profession, choices of terminology must be made that are intelligible to the whole community, are as inclusive as possible, and yet remain as concise as possible. For the profession of nursing, the first such choice is the term *patient* versus *client*. The term *patient* has ancient roots in *suffering*; for millennia the term has also connoted one who undergoes medical treatment. Yet, not all who are recipients of nursing care are either suffering or receiving medical treatment. The root of *client* implies one who listens, leans upon, or follows another. It connotes a more advisory relationship, often associated with consultation or business.

Thus, nursing serves both patients and clients. Additionally, the patients and clients can be individuals, families, communities, or populations. Recently, following a consumerist movement in the United States, some have preferred *consumer* to either *patient* or *client*. In this revision of the American Nurses Association's (ANA's) *Code of Ethics for Nurses with Interpretive Statements* (the Code), as in the past revision, ANA decided to retain the more common, recognized, and historic term *patient* as representative of the category of all who are recipients of nursing care. Thus, the term *patient* refers to clients or consumers of health care as well as to individuals or groups.

A decision was also made about the words *ethical* and *moral*. Both are neutral and categorical. That is—similar to *physical, financial,* or *historical*— they refer to a category, a type of reflection, or a behavior. They do not connote a rightness or goodness of that behavior.

Within the field of ethics, a technical distinction is made between *ethics* and *morality*. *Morality* is used to refer to what would be called personal values, character, or conduct of individuals or groups within communities and societies. *Ethics* refers to the formal study of that morality from a wide range of perspectives including semantic, logical, analytic, epistemological, and normative. Thus, ethics is a branch of philosophy or theology in which

See pg. 171 for guidance on the correct citation of the Code.

one reflects on morality. For this reason, the study of ethics is often called *moral philosophy* or *moral theology*. Fundamentally, ethics is a theoretical and reflective domain of human knowledge that addresses issues and questions about morality in human choices, actions, character, and ends.

As a field of study, ethics is often divided into metaethics, normative ethics, and applied ethics. *Metaethics* is the domain that studies the nature of ethics and moral reasoning. It would ask questions such as "Is there always an element of self-interest in moral behavior?" and "Why be good?" *Normative ethics* addresses the questions of the *ought*, the four fundamental terms of which are *right* and *wrong*, *good* and *evil*. That is, normative ethics addresses what is *right* and *wrong* in human action (what we *ought* to *do*); what is *good* and *evil* in human character (what we *ought* to *be*); and *good* or *evil* in the ends that we *ought* to seek.

Applied ethics wrestles with questions of right, wrong, good, and evil in a specific realm of human action, such as nursing, business, or law. It would ask questions such as "Is it ever morally right to deceive a research subject?" or "What is a 'good nurse' in a moral sense?" or "Are health, dignity, and well-being intrinsic or instrumental ends that nursing seeks?" All of these aspects of ethics are found in the nursing literature. However, the fundamental concern of a code of ethics for nursing is to provide normative, applied moral guidance for nurses in terms of what they ought to do, be, and seek.

Some terms used in ethics are ancient such as *virtue* and *evil*, yet they remain in common use today within the field of ethics. Other terms, such as *ethics* and *morality*, are often—even among professional ethicists—used imprecisely or interchangeably because they are commonly understood or because common linguistic use prevails. For example, one might speak of a person as lacking a "moral compass" or as having "low morals." Another example is the broader public use of the term *ethical*. Ethics is a category that refers to ethical or nonethical behavior: either a behavior is relevant to the category of ethics, or it is not. Here, the term *unethical* has no meaning, although it is commonly used in lectures and discussions—even by professional ethicists—to mean *morally blameworthy*; that is, *wrong*. The terms *should* and *must* are often substituted for the more precise normative ethical term *ought*. *Ought* indicates a moral imperative. *Must* expresses an obligation, duty, necessity, or compulsion, although not an intrinsically moral one. Likewise, *should* expresses an obligation or expediency that is not necessarily a moral imperative.

The English language continues to evolve, and the once firm and clearly understood distinctions between *may* and *can*; *will* and *shall*; and *ought*, *should*,

See pg. 171 for guidance on the correct citation of the Code.

and *must* have faded in daily language and have come to be used interchangeably in both speech or writing, except in rare instances in which the nuance is essential to an argument. To aid the reader in understanding the terms used, this revision of ANA's *Code of Ethics for Nurses with Interpretive Statements* will, for the first time, include a glossary of terms that are found within the Code.

This revision also includes another innovation: links to foundational and supplemental documents. The links to this material are available on ANA's Ethics webpage. These documents are limited to works judged by the Steering Committee as having both timely and timeless value. Nursing's ethics holds many values and obligations in common with international nursing and health communities. For example, the *Millennium Development Goals* of the United Nations, the World Medical Association's *Declaration of Helsinki* about research involving human subjects, and the International Council of Nurses' *Code of Ethics for Nurses* are documents that are both historically and contemporaneously important to U.S. nurses and nursing's ethics.

The afterword from the 2001 Code has been included and updated to reflect the 2010–2014 revision process. This Introduction, another new component of this revision, was added to provide a general orientation to the terminology and the structure of this document.

The nine provisions of the 2001 Code have been retained with some minor revisions that amplify their inclusivity of nursing's roles, settings, and concerns. Together, the nine provisions contain an intrinsic relational motif: nurse-to-patient, nurse-to-nurse, nurse-to-self, nurse-to-others, nurse-to-profession, nurse-to-society, and nursing-to-society, relations that are both national and global. The first three provisions describe the most fundamental values and commitments of the nurse; the next three address boundaries of duty and loyalty; the final three address aspects of duties beyond individual patient encounters. This revision also retains, for each provision, interpretive statements that provide more specific guidance for practice, are responsive to the contemporary context of nursing, and recognize the larger scope of nursing's concern in relation to health.

It was the intent of the Steering Committee to revise the Code in response to the complexities of modern nursing, to simplify and more clearly articulate the content, to anticipate advances in health care, and to incorporate aids that would make it richer, more accessible, and easier to use.

—Steering Committee for the Revision of the
Code of Ethics for Nurses with Interpretive Statements
September 2014

Introduction • Code of Ethics for Nurses with Interpretive Statements • **xiii**

See pg. 171 for guidance on the correct citation of the Code.

Provision 1

The nurse practices with compassion and respect for the inherent dignity, worth, and unique attributes of every person.

1.1 Respect for Human Dignity

A fundamental principle that underlies all nursing practice is respect for the inherent dignity, worth, unique attributes, and human rights of all individuals. The need for and right to health care is universal, transcending all individual differences. Nurses consider the needs and respect the values of each person in every professional relationship and setting; they provide leadership in the development and implementation of changes in public and health policies that support this duty.

1.2 Relationships with Patients

Nurses establish relationships of trust and provide nursing services according to need, setting aside any bias or prejudice. Factors such as culture, value systems, religious or spiritual beliefs, lifestyle, social support system, sexual orientation or gender expression, and primary language are to be considered when planning individual, family and population-centered care. Such considerations must promote health and wellness, address problems, and respect patients' or clients' decisions. Respect for patient decisions does not require that the nurse agree with or support all patient choices. When patient choices are risky or self-destructive, nurses have an obligation to address the behavior and to offer opportunities and resources to modify the behavior or to eradicate the risk.

1.3 The Nature of Health

Nurses respect the dignity and rights of all human beings regardless of the factors contributing to the person's health status. The worth of a person is not affected by illness, ability, socioeconomic status, functional status, or proximity to death. The nursing process is shaped by unique

Provision 1 • Code of Ethics for Nurses with Interpretive Statements • 1

See pg. 171 for guidance on the correct citation of the Code.

patient preferences, needs, values, and choices. Respect is extended to all who require and receive nursing care in the promotion of health, prevention of illness and injury, restoration of health, alleviation of pain and suffering, or provision of supportive care.

Optimal nursing care enables the patient to live with as much physical, emotional, social, and religious or spiritual well-being as possible and reflects the patient's own values. Supportive care is particularly important at the end of life in order to prevent and alleviate the cascade of symptoms and suffering that are commonly associated with dying. Support is extended to the family and to significant others and is directed toward meeting needs comprehensively across the continuum of care.

Nurses are leaders who actively participate in assuring the responsible and appropriate use of interventions in order to optimize the health and well-being of those in their care. This includes acting to minimize unwarranted, unwanted, or unnecessary medical treatment and patient suffering. Such treatment must be avoided, and conversations about advance care plans throughout multiple clinical encounters helps to make this possible. Nurses are leaders who collaborate in altering systemic structures that have a negative influence on individual and community health.

1.4 The Right to Self-Determination

Respect for human dignity requires the recognition of specific patient rights, in particular, the right to self-determination. Patients have the moral and legal right to determine what will be done with and to their own person; to be given accurate, complete, and understandable information in a manner that facilitates an informed decision; and to be assisted with weighing the benefits, burdens, and available options in their treatment, including the choice of no treatment. They also have the right to accept, refuse, or terminate treatment without deceit, undue influence, duress, coercion, or prejudice, and to be given necessary support throughout the decision-making and treatment process. Such support includes the opportunity to make decisions with family and significant others and to obtain advice from expert, knowledgeable nurses, and other health professionals.

Nurses have an obligation to be familiar with and to understand the moral and legal rights of patients. Nurses preserve, protect, and support those rights by assessing the patient's understanding of the information presented and explaining the implications of all potential decisions. When

Appendix A. Code of Ethics for Nurses with Interpretive Statements

2 • Code of Ethics for Nurses with Interpretive Statements • **Provision 1**

See pg. 171 for guidance on the correct citation of the Code.

the patient lacks capacity to make a decision, a formally designated surrogate should be consulted. The role of the surrogate is to make decisions as the patient would, based upon the patient's previously expressed wishes and known values. In the absence of an appropriate surrogate decision-maker, decisions should be made in the best interests of the patient, considering the patient's personal values to the extent that they are known.

Nurses include patients or surrogate decision-makers in discussions, provide referrals to other resources as indicated, identify options, and address problems in the decision-making process. Support of patient autonomy also includes respect for the patient's method of decision-making and recognition that different cultures have different beliefs and understandings of health, autonomy, privacy and confidentiality, and relationships, as well as varied practices of decision-making. Nurses should, for example, affirm and respect patient values and decision-making processes that are culturally hierarchical or communal.

The importance of carefully considered decisions regarding resuscitation status, withholding and withdrawing life-sustaining therapies, foregoing nutrition and hydration, palliative care, and advance directives is widely recognized. Nurses assist patients as necessary with these decisions. Nurses should promote advance care planning conversations and must be knowledgeable about the benefits and limitations of various advance directive documents. The nurse should provide interventions to relieve pain and other symptoms in the dying patient consistent with palliative care practice standards and may not act with the sole intent to end life. Nurses have invaluable experience, knowledge, and insight into effective and compassionate care at the end of life and should actively engage in related research, scholarship, education, practice, and policy development.

Individuals are interdependent members of their communities. Nurses recognize situations in which the right to self-determination may be outweighed or limited by the rights, health, and welfare of others, particularly in public health. The limitation of individual rights must always be considered a serious departure from the standard of care, justified only when there are no less-restrictive means available to preserve the rights of others, meet the demands of law, and protect the public's health.

See pg. 171 for guidance on the correct citation of the Code.

1.5 Relationships with Colleagues and Others

Respect for persons extends to all individuals with whom the nurse interacts. Nurses maintain professional, respectful, and caring relationships with colleagues and are committed to fair treatment, transparency, integrity-preserving compromise, and the best resolution of conflicts. Nurses function in many roles and settings, including direct care provider, care coordinator, administrator, educator, policy maker, researcher, and consultant.

The nurse creates an ethical environment and culture of civility and kindness, treating colleagues, coworkers, employees, students, and others with dignity and respect. This standard of conduct includes an affirmative duty to act to prevent harm. Disregard for the effects of one's actions on others, bullying, harassment, intimidation, manipulation, threats, or violence are always morally unacceptable behaviors. Nurses value the distinctive contribution of individuals or groups as they seek to achieve safe, quality patient outcomes in all settings. Additionally, they collaborate to meet the shared goals of providing compassionate, transparent, and effective health services.

Appendix A. Code of Ethics for Nurses with Interpretive Statements

4 • Code of Ethics for Nurses with Interpretive Statements • Provision 1

See pg. 171 for guidance on the correct citation of the Code.

Provision 2

The nurse's primary commitment is to the patient, whether an individual, family, group, community, or population.

2.1 Primacy of the Patient's Interests

The nurse's primary commitment is to the recipients of nursing and healthcare services—patient or client—whether individuals, families, groups, communities, or populations. Each plan of care must reflect the fundamental commitment of nursing to the uniqueness, worth, and dignity of the patient. Nurses provide patients with opportunities to participate in planning and implementing care and support that are acceptable to the patient. Honest discussions about available resources, treatment options, and capacity for self-care are essential. Addressing patient interests requires recognition of the patient's place within the family and other relationships. When the patient's wishes are in conflict with those of others, nurses help to resolve the conflict. Where conflict persists, the nurse's commitment remains to the identified patient.

2.2 Conflict of Interest for Nurses

Nurses may experience conflict arising from competing loyalties in the workplace, including conflicting expectations from patients, families, physicians, colleagues, healthcare organizations, and health plans. Nurses must examine the conflicts arising between their own personal and professional values, the values and interests of others who are also responsible for patient care and healthcare decisions, and perhaps even the values and interests of the patients themselves. Nurses address such conflicts in ways that ensure patient safety and that promote the patient's best interests while preserving the professional integrity of the nurse and supporting interprofessional collaboration.

Conflicts of interest may arise in any domain of nursing activity, including direct care, administration, education, consultation, policy development, and research. Nurses in all roles must identify and, whenever possible, avoid conflicts of interest. Nurses who bill for

Provision 2 • Code of Ethics for Nurses with Interpretive Statements • 5

See pg. 171 for guidance on the correct citation of the Code.

services and nurse executives with budgetary responsibilities must be especially aware of the potential for conflicts of interest. Healthcare financing and delivery systems may create conflict between economic self-interest and professional integrity. Bonuses, sanctions, and incentives tied to financial targets may present such conflict. Any perceived or actual conflict of interest should be disclosed to all relevant parties and, if indicated, nurses should withdraw, without prejudice, from further participation.

2.3 Collaboration

The complexity of health care requires collaborative effort that has the strong support and active participation of all health professions. Nurses should foster collaborative planning to provide safe, high-quality, patient-centered health care. Nurses are responsible for articulating, representing, and preserving the scope of nursing practice, and the unique contributions of nursing to patient care. The relationship between nursing and other health professions also needs to be clearly articulated, represented, and preserved.

Collaboration intrinsically requires mutual trust, recognition, respect, transparency, shared decision-making, and open communication among all who share concern and responsibility for health outcomes. Nurses ensure that all relevant persons, as moral agents, participate in patient care decisions. Patients do not always know what questions to ask or may be limited by a number of factors, including language or health literacy. Nurses facilitate informed decision-making by assisting patients to secure the information that they need to make choices consistent with their own values.

Collaboration within nursing is essential to address the health of patients and the public effectively. Although nurses who are engaged in nonclinical roles (e.g., educators, administrators, policy-makers, consultants, or researchers) are not primarily involved in direct patient care, they collaborate to provide high-quality care through the influence and direction of direct care providers. In this sense, nurses in all roles are interdependent and share a responsibility for outcomes in nursing care and for maintaining nursing's primary commitment to the patient.

Appendix A. *Code of Ethics for Nurses with Interpretive Statements*

6 • Code of Ethics for Nurses with Interpretive Statements • **Provision 2**

See pg. 171 for guidance on the correct citation of the Code.

2.4 Professional Boundaries

The work of nursing is inherently personal. Within their professional role, nurses recognize and maintain appropriate personal relationship boundaries. Nurse–patient and nurse–colleague relationships have as their foundation the promotion, protection, and restoration of health and the alleviation of pain and suffering. Nurse–patient relationships are therapeutic in nature but can also test the boundaries of professionalism. Accepting gifts from patients is generally not appropriate; factors to consider include the intent, the value, the nature, and the timing of the gift, as well as the patient's own cultural norms. When a gift is offered, facility policy should be followed. The intimate nature of nursing care and the involvement of nurses in important and sometimes highly stressful life events may contribute to the risk of boundary violations. Dating and sexually intimate relationships with patients are always prohibited.

Boundary violations can also occur in professional colleague relationships. In all communications and actions, nurses are responsible for maintaining professional boundaries. They should seek the assistance of peers or supervisors in managing or removing themselves from difficult situations.

Appendix A. Code of Ethics for Nurses with Interpretive Statements

See pg. 171 for guidance on the correct citation of the Code.

Provision 3

The nurse promotes, advocates for, and protects the rights, health, and safety of the patient.

3.1 Protection of the Rights of Privacy and Confidentiality

The need for health care does not justify unwanted, unnecessary, or unwarranted intrusion into a person's life. Privacy is the right to control access to, and disclosure or nondisclosure of, information pertaining to oneself and to control the circumstances, timing, and extent to which information may be disclosed. Nurses safeguard the right to privacy for individuals, families, and communities. The nurse advocates for an environment that provides sufficient physical privacy, including privacy for discussions of a personal nature. Nurses also participate in the development and maintenance of policies and practices that protect both personal and clinical information at institutional and societal levels.

Confidentiality pertains to the nondisclosure of personal information that has been communicated within the nurse–patient relationship. Central to that relationship is an element of trust and an expectation that personal information will not be divulged without consent. The nurse has a duty to maintain confidentiality of all patient information, both personal and clinical in the work setting and off duty in all venues, including social media or any other means of communication. Because of rapidly evolving communication technology and the porous nature of social media, nurses must maintain vigilance regarding postings, images, recordings, or commentary that intentionally or unintentionally breaches their obligation to maintain and protect patients' rights to privacy and confidentiality. The patient's well-being could be jeopardized, and the fundamental trust between patient and nurse could be damaged by unauthorized access to data or by the inappropriate or unwanted disclosure of identifiable information.

See pg. 171 for guidance on the correct citation of the Code.

Patient rights are the primary factors in any decisions concerning personal information, whether from or about the patient. These rights of privacy and confidentiality pertain to all information in any manner that is communicated or transmitted. Nurses are responsible for providing accurate, relevant data to members of the healthcare team and others who have a need to know. The duty to maintain confidentiality is not absolute and may be limited, as necessary, to protect the patient or other parties, or by law or regulation such as mandated reporting for safety or public health reasons.

Information used for purposes of continuity of care, education, peer review, professional practice evaluation, third-party payments, and other quality improvement or risk management mechanisms may be disclosed only under defined policies, mandates, or protocols. These written guidelines must ensure that the rights, safety, and well-being of the patient remain protected. Information disclosed should be directly relevant to a specific responsibility or a task being performed. When using electronic communications or working with electronic health records, nurses should make every effort to maintain data security.

3.2 Protection of Human Participants in Research

Stemming from the principle of respect for autonomy, respect for persons, and respect for self-determination, individuals have the right to choose whether or not to participate in research as a human subject. Participants or legal surrogates must receive sufficient and materially relevant information to make informed decisions and to understand that they have the right to decline to participate or to withdraw at any time without fear of adverse consequences or reprisal.

Information needed for informed consent includes the nature of participation; potential risks and benefits; available alternatives to taking part in the study; disclosure of incidental findings; return of research results; and an explanation of how the data will be used, managed, and protected. Those details must be communicated in a manner that is comprehensible to the patient or a legally authorized representative. Prior to initiation, all research proposals must be approved by a formally constituted and qualified institutional review board to ensure participant protection and the ethical integrity of the research.

Nurses should be aware of the special concerns raised by research involving vulnerable groups, including children, cognitively impaired persons, economically or educationally disadvantaged persons, fetuses,

See pg. 171 for guidance on the correct citation of the Code.

older adults, patients, pregnant women, prisoners, and underserved populations. The nurse who directs or engages in research activities in any capacity should be fully informed about the qualifications of the principal investigator, the rights and obligations of all those involved in the particular research study, and the ethical conduct of research in general. Nurses have a duty to question and, if necessary, to report to appropriate oversight bodies any researcher who violates participants' rights or is involved in research that is ethically questionable, as well as to advocate for participants who wish to decline to participate or to withdraw from a study before completion.

3.3 Performance Standards and Review Mechanisms

Inherent in professional nursing is a process of education and formation. That process involves the ongoing acquisition and development of the knowledge, skills, dispositions, practice experiences, commitment, relational maturity, and personal integrity essential for professional practice. Nurse educators, whether in academics or direct care settings, must ensure that basic competence and commitment to professional standards exist prior to entry into practice.

Similarly, nurse managers and executives must ensure that nurses have the knowledge, skills, and dispositions to perform professional responsibilities that require preparation beyond the basic academic programs. This is in full recognition of the relationship of nurse competencies, performance standards, review mechanisms, and educational preparation to patient safety and care outcomes. In this way, nurses—individually, collectively, and as a profession—are responsible and accountable for nursing practice and professional behavior.

3.4 Professional Responsibility in Promoting a Culture of Safety

Nurses must participate in the development, implementation, and review of and adherence to policies that promote patient health and safety, reduce errors and waste, and establish and sustain a culture of safety. When errors or near misses occur, nurses must follow institutional guidelines in reporting such events to the appropriate authority and must ensure responsible disclosure of errors to patients. Nurses must establish processes to investigate causes of errors or near misses and to address system factors that may have been contributory. While ensuring that nurses are held accountable for individual practice, errors should be corrected or remediated, and

Appendix A. Code of Ethics for Nurses with Interpretive Statements

See pg. 171 for guidance on the correct citation of the Code.

disciplinary action taken only if warranted. When error occurs, whether it is one's own or that of a coworker, nurses may neither participate in, nor condone through silence, any attempts to conceal the error.

Following the appropriate intra-institutional sequence of reporting to authority is critical to maintaining a safe patient care environment. Nurses must use the chain of authority when a problem or issue has grown beyond their problem-solving capacity or their scope of responsibility or authority. Issue reporting in a timely manner promotes a safe environment. Communication should start at the level closest to the event and should proceed to a responsive level as the situation warrants.

3.5 Protection of Patient Health and Safety by Acting on Questionable Practice

Nurses must be alert to and must take appropriate action in all instances of incompetent, unethical, illegal, or impaired practice or actions that place the rights or best interests of the patient in jeopardy. To function effectively, nurses must be knowledgeable about ANA's *Code of Ethics for Nurses with Interpretive Statements*; standards of practice for the profession; relevant federal, state, and local laws and regulations; and the employing organization's policies and procedures.

When nurses become aware of inappropriate or questionable practice, the concern must be expressed to the person involved, focusing on the patient's best interests as well as on the integrity of nursing practice. When practices in the healthcare delivery system or organization threaten the welfare of the patient, nurses should express their concern to the responsible manager or administrator or, if indicated, to an appropriate higher authority within the institution or agency or to an appropriate external authority.

When incompetent, unethical, illegal, or impaired practice is not corrected and continues to jeopardize patient well-being and safety, nurses must report the problem to appropriate external authorities such as practice committees of professional organizations, licensing boards, and regulatory or quality assurance agencies. Some situations are sufficiently egregious as to warrant the notification and involvement of all such groups and/or law enforcement.

Nurses should use established processes for reporting and handling questionable practices. All nurses have a responsibility to assist whistleblowers who identify potentially questionable practices that are factually supported in order to reduce the risk of reprisal against the

See pg. 171 for guidance on the correct citation of the Code.

reporting nurse. State nurses' associations should be prepared to provide their members with advice and support in the development and evaluation of such processes and reporting procedures. Factual documentation and accurate reporting are essential for all such actions. When a nurse chooses to engage in the act of responsible reporting about situations that are perceived as unethical, incompetent, illegal, or impaired, the professional organization has a responsibility to protect the practice of nurses who choose to report their concerns through formal channels. Reporting questionable practice, even when done appropriately, may present substantial risk to the nurse; however, such risk does not eliminate the obligation to address threats to patient safety.

3.6 Patient Protection and Impaired Practice

Nurses must protect the patient, the public, and the profession from potential harm when practice appears to be impaired. The nurse's duty is to take action to protect patients and to ensure that the impaired individual receives assistance. This process begins with consulting supervisory personnel, followed by approaching the individual in a clear and supportive manner and by helping the individual access appropriate resources. The nurse should extend compassion and caring to colleagues throughout the processes of identification, remediation, and recovery. Care must also be taken in identifying any impairment in one's own practice and in seeking immediate assistance.

Nurses must follow policies of the employing organization, guidelines outlined by the profession, and relevant laws to assist colleagues whose job performance may be adversely affected by mental or physical illness, fatigue, substance abuse, or personal circumstances. In instances of impaired practice, nurses within all professional relationships must advocate for appropriate assistance, treatment, and access to fair institutional and legal processes. Advocacy includes supporting the return to practice of individuals who have sought assistance and, after recovery, are ready to resume professional duties.

If impaired practice poses a threat or danger to patients, self, or others, regardless of whether the individual has sought help, a nurse must report the practice to persons authorized to address the problem. Nurses who report those whose job performance creates risk should be protected from retaliation or other negative consequences. If workplace policies for the protection of impaired nurses do not exist or are inappropriate—that is, they deny the nurse who is reported access to due legal process or they demand resignation—nurses may obtain guidance from professional associations, state peer assistance programs, employee assistance programs, or similar resources.

Provision 3 • Code of Ethics for Nurses with Interpretive Statements • **13**

See pg. 171 for guidance on the correct citation of the Code.

Provision 4

The nurse has authority, accountability, and responsibility for nursing practice; makes decisions; and takes action consistent with the obligation to promote health and to provide optimal care.

4.1 Authority, Accountability, and Responsibility

Nurses bear primary responsibility for the nursing care that their patients and clients receive and are accountable for their own practice. Nursing practice includes independent direct nursing care activities; care as ordered by an authorized healthcare provider; care coordination; evaluation of interventions; delegation of nursing interventions; and other responsibilities such as teaching, research, and administration. In every role, nurses have vested authority, and are accountable and responsible for the quality of their practice. Additionally, nurses must always comply with and adhere to state nurse practice acts, regulations, standards of care, and ANA's *Code of Ethics for Nurses with Interpretive Statements*.

Given the context of increased complexity, development of evidence, and changing patterns in healthcare delivery, the scope of nursing practice continues to evolve. Nurses must exercise judgment in accepting responsibilities, seeking consultation, and assigning activities to others who provide nursing care. Where advanced practice registered nurses (APRNs) have prescriptive authority, these are not acts of delegation. Both the APRN issuing the order and the nurse accepting the order are responsible for the judgments made and are accountable for the actions taken.

4.2 Accountability for Nursing Judgments, Decisions, and Actions

To be accountable, nurses follow a code of ethical conduct that includes moral principles such as fidelity, loyalty, veracity, beneficence, and respect for the dignity, worth, and self-determination of patients, as well as adhering to the scope and standards of nursing practice. Nurses in all roles are accountable for decisions made and actions taken in the course

See pg. 171 for guidance on the correct citation of the Code.

of nursing practice. Systems and technologies that assist in clinical practice are adjunct to, not replacements for, the nurse's knowledge and skill. Therefore, nurses are accountable for their practice even in instances of system or technology failure.

4.3 Responsibility for Nursing Judgments, Decisions, and Actions

Nurses are always accountable for their judgments, decisions, and actions; however, in some circumstances, responsibility may be borne by both the nurse and the institution. Nurses accept or reject specific role demands and assignments based on their education, knowledge, competence, and experience, as well as their assessment of the level of risk for patient safety. Nurses in administration, education, policy, and research also have obligations to the recipients of nursing care. Although their relationships with patients are less direct, in assuming the responsibilities of a particular role, nurses not in direct care share responsibility for the care provided by those whom they supervise and teach. Nurses must not engage in practices prohibited by law or delegate activities to others that are prohibited by their state nurse practice acts or those practice acts of other healthcare providers.

Nurses have a responsibility to define, implement, and maintain standards of professional practice. Nurses must plan, establish, implement, and evaluate review mechanisms to safeguard patients, nurses, colleagues, and the environment. These safeguards include peer review processes, staffing plans, credentialing processes, and quality improvement and research initiatives. Nurses must bring forward difficult issues related to patient care and/or institutional constraints upon ethical practice for discussion and review. The nurse acts to promote inclusion of appropriate individuals in all ethical deliberation. Nurse executives are responsible for ensuring that nurses have access to and inclusion on organizational committees and in decision-making processes that affect the ethics, quality, and safety of patient care. Nurses who participate in those committees and decision-making processes are obligated to actively engage in, and contribute to, the dialogue and decisions made.

Nurses are responsible for assessing their own competence. When the needs of the patient are beyond the qualifications or competencies of the nurse, that nurse must seek consultation and collaboration from qualified nurses, other health professionals, or other appropriate resources. Educational resources should be provided by agencies or organizations and used by nurses to maintain and advance competence. Nurse educators

See pg. 171 for guidance on the correct citation of the Code.

in any setting should collaborate with their students to assess learning needs, to develop learning outcomes, to provide appropriate learning resources, and to evaluate teaching effectiveness.

4.4 Assignment and Delegation of Nursing Activities or Tasks

Nurses are accountable and responsible for the assignment or delegation of nursing activities. Such assignment or delegation must be consistent with state practice acts, organizational policy, and nursing standards of practice.

Nurses must make reasonable effort to assess individual competence when delegating selected nursing activities. This assessment includes the evaluation of the knowledge, skill, and experience of the individual to whom the care is assigned or delegated; the complexity of the tasks; and the nursing care needs of the patient.

Nurses are responsible for monitoring the activities and evaluating the quality and outcomes of the care provided by other healthcare workers to whom they have assigned or delegated tasks. Nurses may not delegate responsibilities such as assessment and evaluation; they may delegate selected interventions according to state nurse practice acts. Nurses must not knowingly assign or delegate to any member of the nursing team a task for which that person is not prepared or qualified. Employer policies or directives do not relieve the nurse of responsibility for making assignment or delegation decisions.

Nurses in management and administration have a particular responsibility to provide a safe environment that supports and facilitates appropriate assignment and delegation. This environment includes orientation and skill development; licensure, certification, continuing education, and competency verification; adequate and flexible staffing; and policies that protect both the patient and the nurse from inappropriate assignment or delegation of nursing responsibilities, activities, or tasks. Nurses in management or administration should facilitate open communication with healthcare personnel allowing them, without fear of reprisal, to express concerns or even to refuse an assignment for which they do not possess the requisite skill.

Nurses functioning in educator or preceptor roles share responsibility and accountability for the care provided by students when they make clinical assignments. It is imperative that the knowledge and skill of the nurse or nursing student be sufficient to provide the assigned nursing care under appropriate supervision.

Provision 4 • Code of Ethics for Nurses with Interpretive Statements • **17**

See pg. 171 for guidance on the correct citation of the Code.

Provision 5

The nurse owes the same duties to self as to others, including the responsibility to promote health and safety, preserve wholeness of character and integrity, maintain competence, and continue personal and professional growth.

5.1 Duties to Self and Others

Moral respect accords moral worth and dignity to all human beings regardless of their personal attributes or life situation. Such respect extends to oneself as well: the same duties that we owe to others we owe to ourselves. Self-regarding duties primarily concern oneself and include promotion of health and safety, preservation of wholeness of character and integrity, maintenance of competence, and continuation of personal and professional growth.

5.2 Promotion of Personal Health, Safety, and Well-Being

As professionals who assess, intervene, evaluate, protect, promote, advocate, educate, and conduct research for the health and safety of others and society, nurses have a duty to take the same care for their own health and safety. Nurses should model the same health maintenance and health promotion measures that they teach and research, obtain health care when needed, and avoid taking unnecessary risks to health or safety in the course of their professional and personal activities. Fatigue and compassion fatigue affect a nurse's professional performance and personal life. To mitigate these effects, nurses should eat a healthy diet, exercise, get sufficient rest, maintain family and personal relationships, engage in adequate leisure and recreational activities, and attend to spiritual or religious needs. These activities and satisfying work must be held in balance to promote and maintain their own health and well-being. Nurses in all roles should seek this balance, and it is the responsibility of nurse leaders to foster this balance within their organizations.

Appendix A. Code of Ethics for Nurses with Interpretive Statements

See pg. 171 for guidance on the correct citation of the Code.

5.3 Preservation of Wholeness of Character

Nurses have both personal and professional identities that are integrated and that embrace the values of the profession, merging them with personal values. Authentic expression of one's own moral point of view is a duty to self. Sound ethical decision-making requires the respectful and open exchange of views among all those with relevant interests. Nurses must work to foster a community of moral discourse. As moral agents, nurses are an important part of that community and have a responsibility to express moral perspectives, especially when such perspectives are integral to the situation, whether or not those perspectives are shared by others and whether or not they might prevail.

Wholeness of character pertains to all professional relationships with patients or clients. When nurses are asked for a personal opinion, they are generally free to express an informed personal opinion as long as this maintains appropriate professional and moral boundaries and preserves the voluntariness or free will of the patient. Nurses must be aware of the potential for undue influence attached to their professional role. Nurses assist others to clarify values in reaching informed decisions, always avoiding coercion, manipulation, and unintended influence. When nurses care for those whose health condition, attributes, lifestyle, or situations are stigmatized, or encounter a conflict with their own personal beliefs, nurses must render compassionate, respectful and competent care.

5.4 Preservation of Integrity

Personal integrity is an aspect of wholeness of character that requires reflection and discernment; its maintenance is a self-regarding duty. Nurses may face threats to their integrity in any healthcare environment. Such threats may include requests or requirements to deceive patients, to withhold information, to falsify records, or to misrepresent research aims. Verbal and other forms of abuse by patients, family members, or coworkers are also threats; nurses must be treated with respect and need never tolerate abuse.

In some settings, expectations that nurses will make decisions or take actions that are inconsistent with nursing ideals and values, or that are in direct violation of this *Code of Ethics for Nurses with Interpretive Statements*, may occur. Nurses have a right and a duty to act according to their personal and professional values and to accept compromise only if

See pg. 171 for guidance on the correct citation of the Code.

reaching a compromise preserves the nurse's moral integrity and does not jeopardize the dignity or well-being of the nurse or others. Compromises that preserve integrity can be difficult to achieve but are more likely to be accomplished where there is an open forum for moral discourse and a safe environment of mutual respect.

When nurses are placed in circumstances that exceed moral limits or that violate moral standards in any nursing practice setting, they must express to the appropriate authority their conscientious objection to participating in these situations. When a particular decision or action is morally objectionable to the nurse, whether intrinsically so or because it may jeopardize a specific patient, family, community, or population, or when it may jeopardize nursing practice, the nurse is justified in refusing to participate on moral grounds. Conscience-based refusals to participate exclude personal preference, prejudice, bias, convenience, or arbitrariness.

Acts of conscientious objection may be acts of moral courage and may not insulate nurses from formal or informal consequences. Nurses who decide not to participate on the grounds of conscientious objection must communicate this decision in a timely and appropriate manner. Such refusal should be made known as soon as possible, in advance and in time for alternate arrangements to be made for patient care. Nurse executives should ensure the availabilty of policies that address conscientious objection. Nurses are obliged to provide for patient safety, to avoid patient abandonment, and to withdraw only when assured that nursing care is available to the patient.

When the integrity of nurses is compromised by patterns of institutional behavior or professional practice, thereby eroding the ethical environment and resulting in moral distress, nurses have an obligation to express their concern or conscientious objection individually or collectively to the appropriate authority or committee. Nurse administrators must respond to concerns and work to resolve them in a way that preserves the integrity of the nurses. They must seek to change enduring activities or expectations in the practice setting that are morally objectionable.

Appendix A. Code of Ethics for Nurses with Interpretive Statements

Provision 5 • Code of Ethics for Nurses with Interpretive Statements • **21**

See pg. 171 for guidance on the correct citation of the Code.

5.5 Maintenance of Competence and Continuation of Professional Growth

Competence is a self-regarding duty. It affects not only the quality of care rendered but also one's self-respect, self-esteem, and the meaningfulness of work. Nurses must maintain competence and strive for excellence in their nursing practice, whatever the role or setting. Nurses are responsible for developing criteria for evaluation of practice and for using those criteria in both peer and self-assessments. To achieve the highest standards, nurses must routinely evaluate their own performance and participate in substantive peer review.

Professional growth requires a commitment to lifelong learning. Such learning includes continuing education and self-study, networking with professional colleagues, self-study, professional reading, achieving specialty certification, and seeking advanced degrees. Nurses must continue to learn about new concepts, issues, concerns, controversies, and healthcare ethics relevant to the current and evolving scope and standards of nursing practice.

5.6 Continuation of Personal Growth

Nursing care addresses the whole person as an integrated being; nurses should also apply this principle to themselves. Professional and personal growth reciprocate and interact. Activities that broaden nurses' understanding of the world and of themselves affect their understanding of patients; those that increase and broaden nurses' understanding of nursing's science and art, values, ethics, and policies also affect nurses' self-understanding. Nurses are encouraged to read broadly, continue life-long learning, engage in personal study, seek financial security, participate in a wide range of social advocacy and civic activities, and pursue leisure and recreational activities.

See pg. 171 for guidance on the correct citation of the Code.

Provision 6

The nurse, through individual and collective effort, establishes, maintains, and improves the ethical environment of the work setting and conditions of employment that are conducive to safe, quality health care.

6.1 The Environment and Moral Virtue

Virtues are universal, learned, and habituated attributes of moral character that predispose persons to meet their moral obligations; that is, *to do* what is right. There is a presumption and expectation that we will commonly see virtues such as integrity, respect, moderation, and industry in all those whom we encounter. Virtues are what we are *to be* and make for a morally "good person." Certain particular attributes of moral character might not be expected of everyone but are expected of nurses. These include knowledge, skill, wisdom, patience, compassion, honesty, altruism, and courage. These attributes describe what the nurse is to be as a morally "good nurse." Additionally, virtues are necessary for the affirmation and promotion of the values of human dignity, well-being, respect, health, independence, and other ends that nursing seeks.

For virtues to develop and be operative, they must be supported by a moral milieu that enables them to flourish. Nurses must create, maintain, and contribute to morally good environments that enable nurses to be virtuous. Such a moral milieu fosters mutual caring, communication, dignity, generosity, kindness, moral equality, prudence, respect, and transparency. These virtues apply to all nurses, colleagues, patients, or others.

6.2 The Environment and Ethical Obligation

Virtues focus on what is *good* and *bad* in regard to whom we are *to be* as moral persons; obligations focus on what is *right and wrong* or what we are *to do* as moral agents. Obligations are often specified in terms of principles such as beneficence or doing good; nonmaleficence or doing no harm; justice or treating people fairly; reparations, or making amends for harm; fidelity; and respect for persons. Nurses, in all roles, must

See pg. 171 for guidance on the correct citation of the Code.

create a culture of excellence and maintain practice environments that support nurses and others in the fulfillment of their ethical obligations.

Environmental factors contribute to working conditions and include but are not limited to: clear policies and procedures that set out professional ethical expectations for nurses; uniform knowledge of the Code and associated ethical position statements. Peer pressure can also shape moral expectations within a work group. Many factors contribute to a practice environment that can either present barriers or foster ethical practice and professional fulfillment. These include compensation systems, disciplinary procedures, ethics committees and consulting services, grievance mechanisms that prevent reprisal, health and safety initiatives, organizational processes and structures, performance standards, policies addressing discrimination and incivility position descriptions, and more. Environments constructed for the equitable, fair, and just treatment of all reflect the values of the profession and nurture excellent nursing practice.

6.3 Responsibility for the Healthcare Environment

Nurses are responsible for contributing to a moral environment that demands respectful interactions among colleagues, mutual peer support, and open identification of difficult issues, which includes ongoing professional development of staff in ethical problem solving. Nurse executives have a particular responsibility to assure that employees are treated fairly and justly, and that nurses are involved in decisions related to their practice and working conditions. Unsafe or inappropriate activities or practices must not be condoned or allowed to persist. Organizational changes are difficult to achieve and require persistent, often collective efforts over time. Participation in collective and inter-professional efforts for workplace advocacy to address conditions of employment is appropriate. Agreements reached through such actions must be consistent with the nursing profession's standards of practice and the *Code of Ethics for Nurses with Interpretive Statements.*

Nurses should address concerns about the healthcare environment through appropriate channels and/or regulatory or accrediting bodies. After repeated efforts to bring about change, nurses have a duty to resign from healthcare facilities, agencies, or institutions where there are sustained patterns of violation of patient's rights, where nurses are required to compromise standards of practice or personal integrity, or where the administration is unresponsive to nurses' expressions of concern. Following

See pg. 171 for guidance on the correct citation of the Code.

resignation, reasonable efforts to address violations should continue. The needs of patients may never be used to obligate nurses to remain in persistently morally unacceptable work environments. By remaining in such an environment, even if from financial necessity, nurses risk becoming complicit in ethically unacceptable practices and may suffer adverse personal and professional consequences.

The workplace must be a morally good environment to ensure ongoing safe, quality patient care and professional satisfaction for nurses and to minimize and address moral distress, strain, and dissonance. Through professional organizations, nurses can help to secure the just economic and general welfare of nurses, safe practice environments, and a balance of interests. These organizations advocate for nurses by supporting legislation; publishing position statements; maintaining standards of practice; and monitoring social, professional, and healthcare changes.

Appendix A. Code of Ethics for Nurses with Interpretive Statements

Provision 6 • Code of Ethics for Nurses with Interpretive Statements • **25**

See pg. 171 for guidance on the correct citation of the Code.

Provision 7

The nurse, in all roles and settings, advances the profession through research and scholarly inquiry, professional standards development, and the generation of both nursing and health policy.

7.1 Contributions through Research and Scholarly Inquiry

All nurses must participate in the advancement of the profession through knowledge development, evaluation, dissemination, and application to practice. Knowledge development relies chiefly, though not exclusively, upon research and scholarly inquiry. Nurses engage in scholarly inquiry in order to expand the body of knowledge that forms and advances the theory and practice of the discipline in all its spheres. Nurse researchers test existing and generate new nursing knowledge. Nursing knowledge draws from and contributes to corresponding sciences and humanities.

Nurse researchers may involve human participants in their research, as individuals, families, groups, communities, or populations. In such cases, nursing research conforms to national and international ethical standards for the conduct of research employing human participants. Community consultation can help to ensure enhanced protection, enhanced benefits, legitimacy, and shared responsibility for members of communities during all phases of the research process. Additionally, when research is conducted with the use of animals, all appropriate ethical standards are observed.

Nurses take care to ensure that research is soundly constructed, significant, worthwhile, and in conformity with ethical standards including review by an Institutional Review Board prior to initiation. Dissemination of research findings, regardless of results, is an essential part of respect for the participants. Knowledge development also occurs through the process of scholarly inquiry, clinical and educational innovation, and interprofessional collaboration. Dissemination of findings is fundamental to ongoing disciplinary discourse and knowledge development.

See pg. 171 for guidance on the correct citation of the Code.

Nurses remain committed to patients/participants throughout the continuum of care and during their participation in research. Whether the nurse is data collector, investigator, member of an institutional review board, or care provider, the patients' rights and autonomy must be honored and respected. Patients'/participants' welfare may never be sacrificed for research ends.

Nurse executives and administrators should develop the structure and foster the processes that create an organizational climate and infrastructure conducive to scholarly inquiry. In addition to teaching research methods, nurse educators should teach the moral standards that guide the profession in the conduct and dissemination of its research. Research utilization and evidence informed practice are expected of all nurses.

7.2 Contributions through Developing, Maintaining, and Implementing Professional Practice Standards

Practice standards must be developed by nurses and grounded in nursing's ethical commitments and developing body of knowledge. These standards must also reflect nursing's responsibility to society. Nursing identifies its own scope of practice as informed, specified, or directed by state and federal law and regulation, by relevant societal values, and by ANA's *Code of Ethics for Nurses with Interpretive Statements* and other foundational documents.

Nurse executives establish, maintain, and promote conditions of employment that enable nurses to practice according to accepted standards. Professional autonomy and self-regulation are necessary for implementing nursing standards and guidelines and for assuring quality care.

Nurse educators promote and maintain optimal standards of education and practice in every setting where learning activities occur. Academic educators must also seek to ensure that all their graduates possess the knowledge, skills, and moral dispositions that are essential to nursing.

7.3 Contributions through Nursing and Health Policy Development

Nurses must lead, serve, and mentor on institutional or agency policy committees within the practice setting. They must also participate as advocates or as elected or appointed representatives in civic activities related to health care through local, regional, state, national, or global initiatives.

See pg. 171 for guidance on the correct citation of the Code.

Nurse educators have a particular responsibility to foster and develop students' commitment to the full scope of practice, to professional and civic values, and to informed perspectives on nursing and healthcare policy. Nurse executives and administrators must foster institutional or agency policies that reinforce a work environment committed to promoting evidence informed practice and to supporting nurses' ethical integrity and professionalism. Nurse researchers and scholars must contribute to the body of knowledge by translating science; supporting evidence informed nursing practice; and advancing effective, ethical healthcare policies, environments, and a balance of patient–nurse interests.

Provision 7 • Code of Ethics for Nurses with Interpretive Statements • **29**

See pg. 171 for guidance on the correct citation of the Code.

Provision 8

The nurse collaborates with other health professionals and the public to protect human rights, promote health diplomacy, and reduce health disparities.

8.1 Health Is a Universal Right

The nursing profession holds that health is a universal human right. Therefore, the need for nursing is universal. As the World Health Organization states: "…the highest attainable standard of health is a fundamental right of every human being." This right has economic, political, social, and cultural dimensions. It includes: access to health care, emergency care, and trauma care; basic sanitation; education concerning the prevention, treatment, and control of prevailing health problems; food security; immunizations; injury prevention; prevention and control of locally endemic diseases and vectors; public education concerning health promotion and maintenance; potable water; and reproductive health care. This affirmation of health as a fundamental, universal human right is held in common with the United Nations, the International Council of Nurses, and many human rights treaties.

8.2 Collaboration for Health, Human Rights, and Health Diplomacy

All nurses commit to advancing health, welfare, and safety. This nursing commitment reflects the intent to achieve and sustain health as a means to the common good so that individuals and communities worldwide can develop to their fullest potential and live with dignity. Ethics, human rights, and nursing converge as a formidable instrument for social justice and health diplomacy that can be amplified by collaboration with other health professionals. Nurses understand that the lived experiences of inequality, poverty, and social marginalization contribute to the deterioration of health globally.

Nurses must address the context of health, including social determinants of health such as poverty, access to clean water and clean air, sanitation, human rights violations, hunger, nutritionally sound food, education, safe

Appendix A. Code of Ethics for Nurses with Interpretive Statements

See pg. 171 for guidance on the correct citation of the Code.

medications, and healthcare disparities. Nurses must lead collaborative partnerships to develop effective public health legislation, policies, projects, and programs that promote and restore health, prevent illness, and alleviate suffering.

Such partnerships must raise health diplomacy to parity with other international concerns such as commerce, treaties, and warfare. Human rights must be diligently protected and promoted and may be interfered with only when necessary and in ways that are proportionate and in accord with international standards. Examples might include communicable disease reporting, helmet laws, immunization requirements, mandatory reporting of abuse, quarantine, and smoking bans.

8.3 Obligation to Advance Health and Human Rights and Reduce Disparities

Advances in technology, genetics, and environmental science require robust responses from nurses working together with other health professionals for creative solutions and innovative approaches that are ethical, respectful of human rights, and equitable in reducing health disparities. Nurses collaborate with others to change unjust structures and processes that affect both individuals and communities. Structural, social, and institutional inequalities and disparities exacerbate the incidence and burden of illness, trauma, suffering, and premature death.

Through community organizations and groups, nurses educate the public; facilitate informed choice; identify conditions and circumstances that contribute to illness, injury, and disease; foster healthy life styles; and participate in institutional and legislative efforts to protect and promote health. Nurses collaborate to address barriers to health—poverty homelessness, unsafe living conditions, abuse and violence, and lack of access—by engaging in open discussion, education, public debate, and legislative action. Nurses must recognize that health care is provided to culturally diverse populations in this country and across the globe. Nurses should collaborate to create a moral milieu that is sensitive to diverse cultural values and practices.

See pg. 171 for guidance on the correct citation of the Code.

8.4 Collaboration for Human Rights in Complex, Extreme, or Extraordinary Practice Settings

Nurses must be mindful of competing moral claims—that is, conflicting values or obligations—and must bring attention to human rights violations in all settings and contexts. Of grave concern to nurses are genocide, the global feminization of poverty, abuse, rape as an instrument of war, hate crimes, human trafficking, the oppression or exploitation of migrant workers, and all such human rights violations. The nursing profession must respond when these violations are encountered. Human rights may be jeopardized in extraordinary contexts related to fields of battle, pandemics, political turmoil, regional conflicts, environmental catastrophes or disasters where nurses must necessarily practice in extreme settings, under altered standards of care. Nurses must always stress human rights protection with particular attention to preserving the human rights of vulnerable groups such as the poor, the homeless, the elderly, the mentally ill, prisoners, refugees, women, children, and socially stigmatized groups.

All actions and omissions risk unintended consequences with implications for human rights. Thus, nurses must engage in discernment, carefully assessing their intentions, reflectively weighing all possible options and rationales, and formulating clear moral justifications for their actions. Only in extreme emergencies and under exceptional conditions, whether due to forces of nature or to human action, may nurses subordinate human rights concerns to other considerations. This subordination may occur when there is both an increase in the number of ill, injured, or at-risk patients and a decrease in access to customary resources and healthcare personnel.

A utilitarian framework usually guides decisions and actions with special emphasis on transparency, protection of the public, proportional restriction of individual liberty, and fair stewardship of resources. Conforming to international emergency management standards and collaborating with public health officials and members of the healthcare team are essential throughout the event.

Appendix A. Code of Ethics for Nurses with Interpretive Statements

See pg. 171 for guidance on the correct citation of the Code.

Provision 9

The profession of nursing, collectively through its professional organizations, must articulate nursing values, maintain the integrity of the profession, and integrate principles of social justice into nursing and health policy.

9.1 Articulation and Assertion of Values

Individual nurses are represented by their professional associations and organizations. These groups give united voice to the profession. It is the responsibility of a profession collectively to communicate, affirm, and promote shared values both within the profession and to the public. It is essential that the profession engage in discourse that supports ongoing self-reflection, critical self-analysis, and evaluation. The language that is chosen evokes the shared meaning of nursing, as well as its values and ideals, as it interprets and explains the place and role of nursing in society. The profession's organizations communicate to the public the values that nursing considers central to the promotion or restoration of health, the prevention of illness and injury, and the alleviation of pain and suffering. Through its professional organizations, the nursing profession must reaffirm and strengthen nursing values and ideals so that when those values are challenged, adherence is steadfast and unwavering. Acting in solidarity, the ability of the profession to influence social justice and global health is formidable.

9.2 Integrity of the Profession

The values and ethics of the profession should be affirmed in all professional and organizational relationships whether local, inter-organizational, or international. Nursing must continually emphasize the values of respect, fairness, and caring within the national and global nursing communities in order to promote health in all sectors of the population. A fundamental responsibility is to promote awareness of and adherence to the codes of ethics for nurses (the American Nurses Association and the International Council of Nurses and others). Balanced policies and practices regarding access to nursing education, workforce sustainability, and nurse migration and utilization are requisite to

See pg. 171 for guidance on the correct citation of the Code.

achieving these ends. Together, nurses must bring about the improvement of all facets of nursing, fostering and assisting in the education of professional nurses in developing regions across the globe.

The nursing profession engages in ongoing formal and informal dialogue with society. The covenant between the profession and society is made explicit through the *Code of Ethics for Nurses with Interpretive Statements*, foundational documents, and other published standards of nursing specialty practice; continued development and dissemination of nursing scholarship; rigorous educational requirements for entry into practice, advanced practice, and continued practice including certification and licensure; and commitment to evidence informed practice.

9.3 Integrating Social Justice

It is the shared responsibility of professional nursing organizations to speak for nurses collectively in shaping health care and to promulgate change for the improvement of health and health care locally, nationally, and internationally. Nurses must be vigilant and take action to influence leaders, legislators, governmental agencies, non-governmental organizations, and international bodies in all related health affairs to address the social determinants of health. All nurses, through organizations and accrediting bodies involved in nurse formation, education, and development, must firmly anchor students in nursing's professional responsibility to address unjust systems and structures, modeling the profession's commitment to social justice and health through content, clinical and field experiences, and critical thought.

9.4 Social Justice in Nursing and Health Policy

The nursing profession must actively participate in solidarity with the global nursing community and health organizations to represent the collective voice of U.S. nurses around the globe. Professional nursing organizations must actively engage in the political process, particularly in addressing legislative and regulatory concerns that most affect—positively and negatively—the public's health and the profession of nursing. Nurses must promote open and honest communication that enables nurses to work in concert, share in scholarship, and advance a nursing agenda for health. Global health, as well as the common good, are ideals that can be realized when all nurses unite their efforts and energies.

Appendix A. Code of Ethics for Nurses with Interpretive Statements

See pg. 171 for guidance on the correct citation of the Code.

Social justice extends beyond human health and well-being to the health and well-being of the natural world. Human life and health are profoundly affected by the state of the natural world that surrounds us. Consistent with Florence Nightingale's historic concerns for environmental influences on health, and with the metaparadigm of nursing, the profession's advocacy for social justice extends to eco-justice. Environmental degradation, aridification, earth resources exploitation, ecosystem destruction, waste, and other environmental assaults disproportionately affect the health of the poor and ultimately affect the health of all humanity. Nursing must also advocate for policies, programs, and practices within the healthcare environment that maintain, sustain, and repair the natural world. As nursing seeks to promote and restore health, prevent illness and injury, and alleviate pain and suffering, it does so within the holistic context of healing the world.

Provision 9 • Code of Ethics for Nurses with Interpretive Statements • **37**

See pg. 171 for guidance on the correct citation of the Code.

Afterword

The development of the *Code of Ethics for Nurses with Interpretive Statements* (Code) is a benchmark both for the American Nurses Association (ANA) and for the profession of nursing as a whole.

In its articles of incorporation, ANA set forth the objectives of the Association as follows:

> The object of the Association shall be: to establish and maintain a code of ethics, to the end that the standard of nursing education be elevated; the usefulness, honor, and interests of the nursing profession be promoted; public opinion in regard to duties, responsibilities, and requirements of nurses be enlightened; emulation and concert of action in the profession be stimulated; professional loyalty be fostered, and friendly intercourse between nurses be facilitated. (Alumnae, 1896)

> The first object, then, was the creation and maintenance of a code of ethics for nurses.... The ANA is recognized nationally and internationally as the spokes-organization for nursing in the United States, and as the basis for the US membership in the International Council of Nurses based in Geneva, Switzerland. (Fowler, 2006)

Therefore, the *Code of Ethics for Nurses with Interpretive Statements* serves all U.S. nurses in all settings and in all roles. The Code is also incorporated into the nurse practice acts of a number of states, according it actual regulatory force in those states.

See pg. 171 for guidance on the correct citation of the Code.

The evolution of the Code dates from Articles of Incorporation of 1896; from 1893, when the "Nightingale Pledge" was written and administered at commencement; and from 1926 and 1940, when tentative codes were suggested but not formally ratified. In 1950, the ANA House of Delegates formally adopted *A Code for Professional Nurses*. It was not accompanied by interpretive statements although the *American Journal of Nursing* subsequently published a series of articles that served this function. There were several subsequent revisions of the Code, approximately every decade, some more substantive than others. The 2001 revision was the first time in 25 years that both the provisions of the Code and the interpretive statements were thoroughly revised.

This 2015 revision is the result of changes made by the Code of Ethics Steering Committee and was informed by 7,800 responses from 2,780 nurses during an online survey of the 2001 Code for public comment. The draft of the revised Code was posted for public comment; more than 1,500 comments from almost 1,000 nurses were received. This 2015 revision of the Code reflects comments from hundreds of nurses across the United States and abroad, multiple drafts, review by the ANA Ethics Advisory Board, and approval by the ANA Board of Directors.

The ethical tradition manifested in every iteration of the Code is self-reflective, enduring, and distinctive. That is, the Code steadfastly supports nurses across all settings and in all roles. The Code is particularly useful at the beginning of the 21st century because it reiterates the fundamental values and commitments of the nurse (Provisions 1–3), identifies the boundaries of duty and loyalty (Provisions 4–6), and describes the duties of the nurse that extend beyond individual patient encounters (Provisions 7–9).

It also addresses the variety of relationships that nurses encounter in the course of their professional duties. The achievement of a true global awareness about the human condition; the sociopolitical, economic, interdependent, environmental context of all humanity; and the universal need for health care are the most important moral challenges of the 21st century. This Code summons nurses to actively meet these challenges.

ANA's *Code of Ethics for Nurses with Interpretive Statements* is the promise that nurses are doing their best to provide care for their patients and their communities and are supporting each other in the process so that all nurses can fulfill their ethical and professional obligations. This Code is an important tool that can be used now as leverage to a better future for nurses, patients, and health care.

Index

American Recovery and Reinvestment Act (2009), 45
American Society of Superintendents of Training Schools for Nurse, 60
analysis, in nursing process, xxi
Angelou, Maya, 153
Anthony, Susan, 153
anukampa, 1–2
Aristotle, 4
Asians, 138
assessment, in nursing process, xxi
attentiveness, 30
attributed dignity, 8
Auckland University, 120
authority of the nurse, 62–63
autonomy and autonomous decision-making (patient), 15, 17–18
  diminished capacity for, 104
  loss of, 30
  refusal of treatment, 133
  See also respect for autonomy
autonomy of nurses and nursing practice, 62, 63, 68, 70, 105
Avodah, 125

B
Barton, Clara Harlowe, 160
Beauchamp, Tom, xxii, xxiii–xxiv, xxvi,15, 29, 48, 77
bedside principles, xxiv
Beecher, Henry, 119
Belmont Report, xxii, 15, 17, 29, 47, 48
beneficence, xxiii, 15, 29, 47, 66, 104
Bethune, Mary McLeod, 162
Bickerdyke, Mary Ann, 160
bioethical principles, 15, 29, 104
  See also beneficence; justice; nonmalfience; respect for autonomy
biomedical ethics, 29
  See also bioethical principles; *Principles of Biomedical Ethics*

Bioterrorism and Other Public Health Emergencies: Altered Standards of Care in Mass Casualty Events, 141
birth control, 45, 67
Book of Job, 3
Bread for the World, 125
bribes, 35
Buddha, 2
Buddhism, 2–3
bullying in the workplace, 18, 100
Bureau of Registration of Nurses (California), 159

C
California State Board of Health, 159
California State Legislature, 63
California State Nurses Association (CSNA), 96
Callahan, Daniel, xxvii
carcinoma in situ, 120–121
care-giving, xxv, 29–30, 32
care-receiving, xxv, 30,
caring, xxiv–xxv, 29–30, 32–33, 53–54
Carnegie Report, 160
Centers for Disease Control and Prevention (CDC), 138
character, wholeness of, 81
Charter for Compassion, 6–7
children, consent of, 49
Childress, James, xxii, xxiii–xxiv, xxvi, 15, 29, 48, 77
Ciclovia, 125
citizens, 14
civic engagement, 14
civil rights, 133
civil rights movement 12, 164
Civil War (US), 151
clients. *See* patients
clinical equipoise, 117–118
Closing the Gap: From Evidence to Action, 124

decision-making, *See* ethical decision-making; nursing judgements, decisions, and actions
delegation of responsibility, 61–62, 68–70
Department of Health and Human Services (DHHS), 45, 47, 121, 122, 139, 141
detainees, 144
diagnosis, in nursing process, xxi
dignity
  attributed, 8
  inflorescent, 8
  intrinsic, 8
  of the nurse, 73, 107
  of the patient, 20, 75
  of persons, 1, 78
    See also human dignity; Provision 1; Provision 5
discrimination, 12, 156–157
  unjust, 12, 156
disparities. *See* health disparities
diversion program, 53
Dix, Dorothea Lynde, 160
domestic violence, 43, 102
duties
  rights and, 133
  to self and others, 78–79, 104–105
  self-regarding, 79
duty-based ethics, 76
Düwell, Marcus, 9

E

Ebola crisis, 14, 80
Economic Security Program, 96
economics, 136
Educating Nurses: A Call for Radical Transformation, (Carnegie Report), 117, 160
egalitarianism, 157
electronic medical records (EMR), 44

environment. *See* healthcare environment
environmental health, 164–165
epideictic discourse, 153–154
equipoise principle, 117–118
ethic of care, 28, 29–30
  phases and moral elements of, xxiv–xxv
ethical decision-making, xxii– xxvii, 28, 157
  controversies in, xxvi
  Jonsen's four boxes, xxii–xxiii
  models, xxii–xxv
  nursing process and, xx
  principles and, 15, 77
  suggested questions, xxvii
ethical obligation(s), 65, 104–105
  access to health care and, 133–134
  guidelines for meeting, 64
  virtues and, 29
ethical principlism, xxiii–xxiv, xxvi, 27, 29
ethics
  of care, xxiv–xxv
  duty-based, 76
  law and, 66–67
  normative, 102
  obligation-based, 76
  virtue-based (virtue ethics), xxiv, 75–76
eudaimon, 5
evaluation, in nursing process, xxii
evidence-based practice, 123–124
evidence-informed practice, 123–125
excellences, 103
Expert Panel on Global Nursing and Health, 137
expertise of nurses, expectation of. See Provision 4
extraordinary circumstances/ settings, 143–144
extreme conditions, 142–143

obligation to advance, 137–140
Universal Declaration of Human Rights (1948), 7, 44, 132, 144
Human Rights Guidelines for Nurses in Clinical and Other Research, 46, 114
human subjects in research, rights of, 46–49
humanities, scholarly inquiry as research in, 116–117

I
identity, 78
Imago Dei, 8
immigrants, 14, 134
impaired practice, 53–54
impairment, 53
implementation, in nursing process, xxii
inflorescent dignity, 8
informed consent, 16–18
  informedness and, 16
  legal surrogates and, 18
  voluntariness in, 16, 17
  vulnerable groups and, 144
informedness, 16
Institute for Scientific Information, 117
Institute of Medicine (IOM), 152, 165
  Future of Nursing report, 100–101
Institutional Animal Care and Use Committee (IACUC), 118
institutional review boards (IRBs), 107, 118
instrumental goods, 103
integrity, 78
  preservation of, 86–88
  professional, 53
International Care Ethics (ICE) Observatory, 28
International Council of Nurses (ICN), 144

International Monetary Fund (IMF), 136
Interpretation of the Statements of the Code for Professional Nurses, 113
interpretive statements, xix
  development of, viii
  See also each Provision
intimate labor, 31
intrinsic dignity, 8
intrinsic goods, 103

J
Jameton, Andrew, 78–79
Johnstone, Megan-Jane, 87
Joint Statement on Delegation, 69
Jonsen's four boxes (evaluation of moral dilemmas), xxii–xxiii
judgement. *See* nursing judgements, decisions, and actions; substituted judgment
justice, xxiii, 47–48, 104, 124

K
kampana, 2
Kant, Immanuel, 8, 15, 29, 78
Kantian formalism, 102
karoti, 2
karuna, 1–2
karuóá, 2
Kennedy, John, 153
kindness, 3
King, Martin Luther, Jr., 138, 153
kióáti, 2
kiriyati, 2
knowledge development, 114–115, 117, 121
Kohlberg, Lawrence, 26
Kramer, Marlene, 99

L
Laennec, René, 64
lateral violence, 18
law, ethics and, 66–67

Le Guin, Ursula, 154
legal liability, 65
liability, 59
licensure exam, 60
loyalty, 25–26, 108

M

MacArthur, Douglas, 153
Macklin, Ruth, 9
Magnet Recognition Program, 106
mass casualty events, 140–142
meaning and value structures,
    155–156
medical indications, xxii–xxiii
medical profession, 130
medical research, protection of
    human participants in, 46–49
medicine, 130
Medicine and the Reign of
    Technology, 64
men in the nursing profession, 74
Milgram obedience experiment, 120
Millennium Development Goals
    (MDGs), 132
mobbing (bullying) in workplace, 18
*Model Guidelines: A Nondisciplinary
    Alternative Program for Chemical-
    ly Impaired Nurses*, 54
moral
    development, 27
    dilemmas, xxii–xxiii, 99, 102
    disposition, 50
    distress, xxiii, 25, 99, 101–102
    ethic of care, moral elements of,
        xvii
    principles, 20, 66
    self-respect, 73
    suasion, 66
    uncertainty, 87, 99, 102
    virtue, 102–103
*Moral Boundaries: A Political
    Argument for an Ethics of Care*
    (Tronto), 29

moral mileu of nursing. *See*
    Provision 6
mortality rates, 138–139

N

National Commission for the
    Protection of Human Subjects
    in Biomedical and Behavioral
    Research, 47, 101
National Council of State Boards of
    Nursing (NCSBN), 54, 69
National Database of Nursing Quality
    Indicators (NDNQI), 123
National Foundation on the Arts and
    Humanities Act (1965), 116
National League for Nursing, 60
National League for Nursing
    Accrediting Commission, 101
National League for Nursing
    Education (NLNE), 60, 159
National Women's Hospital (Auck-
    land, New Zealand), 120
natural disasters, 140
Nazi medical atrocities, 16
neglect, 108
New Mexico Board of Nursing,
    53–54
Newton-Smith, W.H., 115–116
Nightingale, Florence, 42, 70, 164
Nightingale Pledge, 26, 41–42,
    76, 129
non-Hispanic blacks, 138
non-Hispanic whites, 138
nonmaleficence, 104, xxiii
norms
    of obligation, 102
    of value, 102–103
no-strike policy, 96–97
Notes on Nursing (1869), 70
Nuremberg Code, 16, 118–119
*Nurse in Research: ANA Guidelines on
    Ethical Values, The* 114
Nurse Practice Act, 63

self-rule, 15–16

Silence Kills: Seven Crucial Conversations for Healthcare, 106, 108

Siracusa Principles, 142–143

Slee, Margaret Higgins Sanger, 160

"slow code", 88

social determinants of health, xvii, 132, 139, 154,156, 159–160

social ethics, 31, 74, 152–153
  professional associations and, 151–166

social justice
  functions of , xvii
  in health policy, 160–166
  integration of, 159–160
  in nursing, 160–166
  professional organizations and, 157
  See also Provision 9

social structures
  health and human rights and unjust, 137
  nursing ethics and, 155–156

Special Olympics, 125

specialing (private duty nursing), 151–152

staffing, 70, 86, 87

Stand on Guard for Thee, 142

Standard Curriculum for Schools of Nursing, 159

standards of nursing practice, 50, 122

Standards of Nursing Practice, 61

Standards of Professional Nursing Practice (ANA), 122

state nursing associations (SNAs), 96, 157

Staupers, Mabel Keaton, 161–162

structural adjustment programmes (SAPs), 136

substance abuse, 53, 139

substituted judgment, 17

A Suggested Code (1926), 41, 73, 81, 88, 95, 129–130

Suggested Guidelines for Handling Violations of the Code for Professional Nurses, 66, 158

suicide, 138–139

Sulmasy, Daniel, 8

supererogation, 80

surrogate, 17, 48–49

syphilis, 119

T

tabula rasa, 103

Tanakh, 3

Task Force for the Revision of Code, 115

Tearoom Trade Experiment, 119–120

technical policy discourse, 107

television programs, 124

telos/teloi, 103

The Tentative Code (1940), 7, 42, 76, 79, 88–89, 96, 130, 156

Tompkins, Sally, 160

town councils, 124

Trained Nurse and Hospital Review (1889 article on nursing ethics), 79

tuberculosis, 162

Tubman, Araminta, 160

Tuskegee Institute, 119

U

United Nations, 132
  Basic Principles for the Treatment of Prisoners, 144
  Siracusa Principles, 142–143
  social determinants of health and, 154

United Nations Conference on Trade and Development (UNCTAD), 136

Universal Declaration of Human Rights (1948), 7, 44, 132, 144

universal ethical principles.
See ethical principlism
universal right(s)
health as, 131–132
University of Toronto Joint Centre for
Bioethics, 142
unjust discrimination, 12, 56
utilitarianism, 102

V

vaccination program, 138
Vaccines for Children program, 138
values
articulation and assertion of, 155
norms of, 102–103
nursing values, 83, 87, 151
structures, 155–156
van der Cingel, M., 5
vegetative state, 36
vices, 103
violence
domestic, 43, 102
exposure to, 139
health disparities and, 137
lateral (bullying), 18, 100
patient, 80
sexual and gender-based, 140
workplace, 100
virtue ethics, xxiv, 75–76
virtue(s), xxvi, 75, 102–103
compassion as virtue, 2–5
justice and, 30, 48
Visuddhimagga (Path of Purification),
2
voluntariness, 16
voluntary consent of subjects in
research, 118
volunteer service, 125

vulnerable individuals and groups,
84, 119, 120, 165
in care relationships, equality
and, 30
informed consent and, 144
justice and, 48

W

Wald, Lillian, 60, 161
war, 140
well-being, promotion of, 79–90
whistleblowing, 49–50
Whitman, Walt, 160
wholeness of character, 81
Willowbrook State School, 119
Woman Rebel, The, 161
World Bank, 136
World Health Organization (WHO),
118, 131, 135–136, 152
World Medical Association (WMA),
16, 119
World War II, 118–119, 151, 152,
162
Worth of the nurse, patient, person.
See dignity; human dignity; Pro-
vision 1; Provision 5